Advanced Rhythmic Concepts for Improvisation

A Path to Fluency in Odd Meters and Polyrhythms for All Instruments

Dave Allen

I0808769

Online Audio

To access the online audio recording go to:
WWW.MELBAY.COM/30923MEB

© 2022 by Mel Bay Publications, Inc. All Rights Reserved.
WWW.MELBAY.COM

Contents

1. INTRODUCTION

It is common for students of jazz to spend enormous amounts of time studying and practicing harmony. Chord progressions, arpeggios, scales, and lines usually take up a large part of any jazz curriculum. These things are undoubtedly important and must be worked at vigorously, but it is important to keep in mind that this accumulated harmonic information is relatively useless if it is played without a strong time feel. A few simple inside notes placed beautifully within a swing feel (or any other groove), have more value than hundreds of notes that may be correct and very clever, but do not connect well with the rhythm section or with the underlying pulse. These crucial elements of development as an improviser are sometimes neglected, or they are expected to come about naturally without conscious effort and attention.

The demands and expectations of improvising musicians has never been greater than they are today. Players are expected to have an expansive rhythmic vocabulary, and the bar is set very high. Rhythm is the more abstract, more difficult to codify, element of improvisation. Developing a strong time feel, cultivating a personal approach to phrasing, playing fluently within complex rhythmic situations, phrasing over the bar line, being relaxed while playing faster tempos, these concepts are not talked about as much because they are more difficult to put down on paper and make into a method.

The goal of this book is to provide practical exercises, primarily as play-along tracks for the developing to advanced improviser interested in expanding their rhythmic vocabulary. My view is that any musician's time feel and understanding of the modern jazz language should be developed through direct improvisation and performance experience. The examples within this book are meant to be used for individual practice, ensembles, improvisation classes, and as a springboard for compositional ideas. The material here can be arranged for any instrumentation, and my hope is that musicians will expand on these ideas and use them like seeds. I will briefly discuss some fundamentals, but the focus of the book will be on how to become more fluent when improvising in odd-meters, as well as applying irregular rhythmic patterns in improvisation, arranging and composition.

These exercises and examples were either composed for this book or taken from my own compositions. I have tried to avoid repetition of material which is already easily accessible through other books and websites. My focus will be on bass lines, claves, and comping patterns. Each example can be thought of as a section of a tune. I have also included chapters on applying rhythmic patterns to standard forms, and a brief look at polyrhythms.

This book offers 52 backing tracks with a rhythm section made up of guitar, bass, and drums. I am grateful to Mark Ferber (drums) and Shane Aaserud (bass) for their hard work and creativity. The rest of the tracks include only guitar, or guitar with percussion, some of which can also be used as backing tracks, which is indicated by the abbreviation, BT.

"That something is difficult must be one more reason for us to do it." – Rainer Maria Rilke

2. FUNDAMENTALS

Before going on to some of the more complicated rhythmic patterns here, the student should be confident that their basic time feel is as strong as possible. This means being able to play flowing and consistent quarter notes, eighth notes, and triplets in 4/4 and 3/4. It is also very important to have developed a basic sense of rhythmic structure and form, such as being able to feel the passage of 4 or 8 bars sections, as well as longer forms, without losing your place. Some students may be ready to move on immediately, if they have no difficulty with the exercises.

Though it may not be a requirement for every musician to swing, the players who develop a strong swing feel are more likely to have a larger and deeper time feel in any style of music they might pursue. This book assumes that the student is working on, or has already worked extensively on their swing feel and basic pulse, and is ready to explore more complex material. It can't be overstated that any student of jazz improvisation should spend a significant amount of time listening to the great masters of rhythm. There is no substitute for time spent listening as this is the primary way that we get to know the fundamentals of music as well as being a great source of inspiration.

Time feel is important in any style of music. As jazz musicians, or better yet, as modern improvising musicians, improving our sense of time and our control of our time feel, and expanding our rhythmic vocabulary, will enrich everything and anything that we might play. This takes a lot of practice and years of playing in situations that push each player to experiment, progress and grow. Just as we have a natural speaking or singing voice, and maybe a personal melodic or harmonic vocabulary, we can also discover our true rhythmic voice. It is a process of discovering what YOUR time feel sounds like. Paying close attention to it and becoming more sensitive to the nuances of time will help you on this journey. Ultimately, we want to be able to express ourselves in a flexible way that is free from the bar line or structure, while at the same time, being firmly anchored to the fundamentals of the groove.

Time Feel

Basic steps to learning a groove:

Subdividing the beats in a measure by twos, threes and fours

Subdividing each beat by eighths or triplets or sixteenths

Adding rhythmic layering (polyrhythms, groupings, and accents)

Breakdown of a time feel:

Be firmly anchored in the pulse.

Know where the downbeat is at all times without having to state it.

Feeling and internalizing the subdivisions

Pay attention to the placement of each note and its relationship to the pulse.

Holding the tempo (not rushing or dragging)

Consistency of feel

Metronome Exercise

Start these exercises by using just one scale or mode that you are very familiar with. You can also play completely free of any harmonic restrictions, so as to focus entirely on rhythm.

Exercise 1: Choose a medium-slow tempo to start. Set the metronome so it clicks on beats 2 and 4. Start out playing quarter notes only. Ground yourself into the beat. Try to make the quarter notes as large and as relaxed as you can, the way a bass player would. The 8th notes should swing. Pay close attention to the relationship between the 8th notes and the 8th-note triplets.

Play the following sequence:

Play only quarter notes.

Play only quarter-note triplets.

Play only 8th notes.

Play only 8th-note triplets.

Play only upbeats (the second 8th note of each beat, which will feel like the third note of each 8th-note triplet).

- Try not to break the flow once you have started. Keep a steady stream of notes or alternate between measures of notes and measures of rests.
- Focus your attention on the consistency of the time feel and flow. Experiment with your placement of the notes. Does it feel rushed, ahead of the beat, or behind it? Is it laid-back and swinging, or is it dragging and becoming disconnected from the pulse?
- The next step is to mix the various rhythms together. You can start with alternating two, four, or eight bars of each one. For example: 2 bars of quarters/2 bars of quarter note triplets/2 bars of 8ths/2 bars of 8th-note triplets.
- Then reverse that sequence so you arrive back at the quarter note. Check whether you are able to transition between each rhythm immediately, without there being an awkward moment of adjustment.
- Now add some harmonic motion to see if you can stay consistent rhythmically while playing chord changes. Try this same set of exercises on a blues form. If that feels strong enough, move on to standards of various difficulties.
- Once you are playing within a progression, this exercise becomes both a rhythmic and a harmonic workout. Whatever the harmonic or formal difficulty, the priority will still be on a consistent, relaxed flow of notes. If that proves too difficult, either simplify the chords, or decrease the tempo. Find the tempo where you can keep the line relaxed and flowing while also playing the chord changes. Then very slowly increase the tempo. These exercises can also be tried using a straight-8th groove such as a bossa.

Time Strengthening Exercises

Exercise 2: Set the metronome so that only beat 1 is heard and then play or sing the melody of a standard to coincide with it. Now do the same thing with the metronome set to click only on beat 2, then only on beat 3, and finally - only on beat 4. Keep your place by feeling the downbeat at all times. Next, you can try improvising through the changes of the tune with the metronome set to mark each of the 4 beats, one at a time. If you are unsure whether or not you are accurately staying aligned with the metronome, record yourself while doing this exercise and listen back to it while counting. For a greater challenge, you can also set the metronome to give you the downbeat every 2 bars, or every 4 bars. Now you have to keep your place with very little to guide you. The stronger our sense of time, the better off we will be when playing with other musicians.

Exercise 3: Play one chorus of a standard with the metronome set on beats 2 and 4, then play one chorus without the metronome. Turn the metronome on again to check to see if you were able to maintain the original tempo.

Exercise 4: Set the metronome to 30 bpm or slower. Each click will represent one beat. Start by playing one note along with the click until you are firmly grounded. This in itself is a test of our concentration and can be a good way to begin any practice session.

Now play through the sequence below, repeating each measure/group as many times as you need to until the notes lie evenly within the beat. Using a set scale or melody, like the ones below, allows us to play the right number of notes without needing to count. This is especially useful when we go above 8. At first, you may want to try just 1 through 8 before going on to 9 through 16.

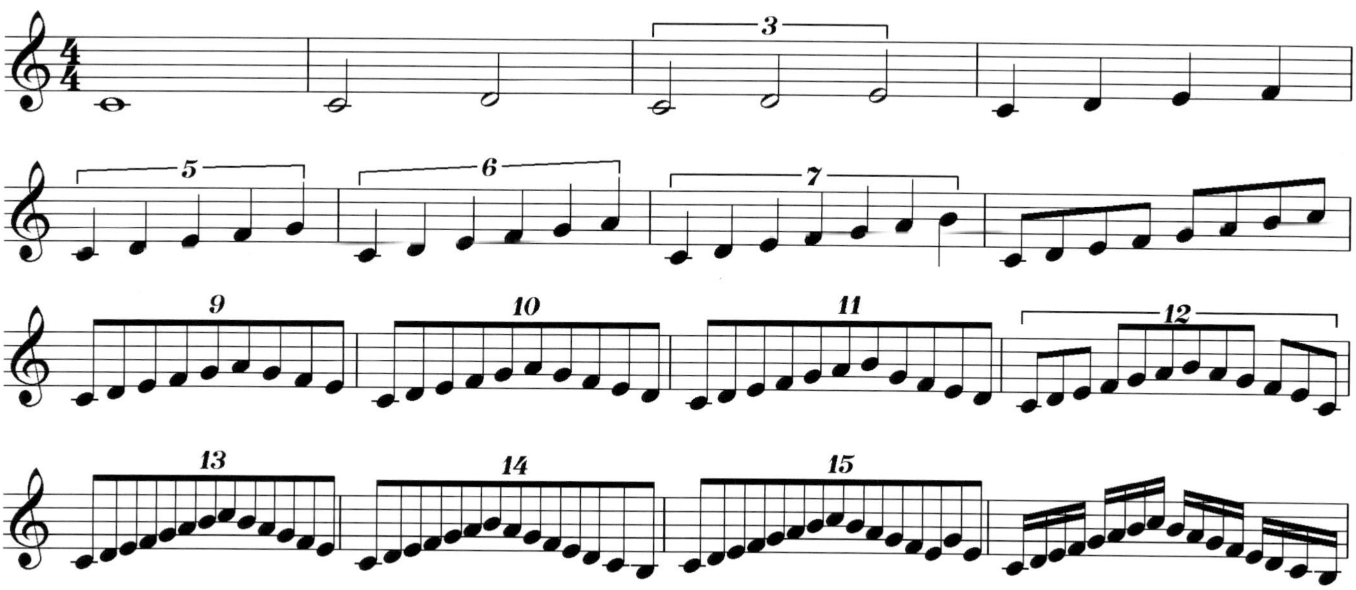

3. TRIPLET PATTERNS AND GROUPINGS

Triplet Exercise 1

Clap each rhythm with the metronome on the quarter note. Then try tapping the quarter with one hand while tapping the triplet rhythms with the other hand.

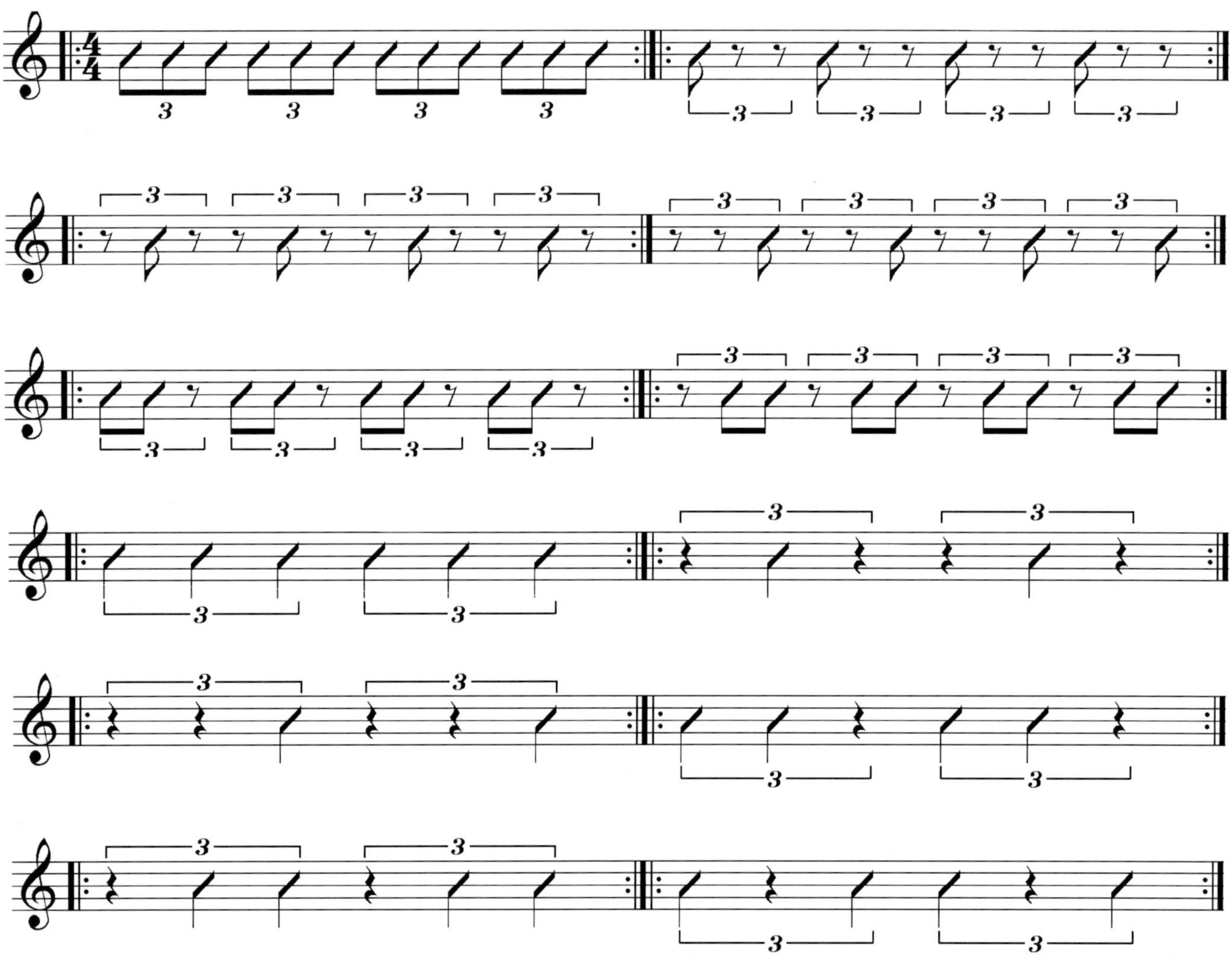

Triplet Groupings

Using harmonic and melodic patterns is helpful when learning to feel various note groupings. The following exercises will use intervals and arpeggios as a means of creating groupings and accents within triplets. These harmonic patterns should already be easy for you to play on your instrument before you attempt to use them in this way. If you are having any trouble playing the arpeggio sequence in time, stop and practice out of time before trying to apply them to these exercises.

It is helpful to begin these exercises by playing continuous triplets, making sure the flow is consistent before starting the accents. If at any time you feel yourself drifting away from the metronome or pulse, go back to the quarter note to anchor yourself. Then begin the triplets without accents before attempting the grouping.

Example 1: Twos (using 3rds)

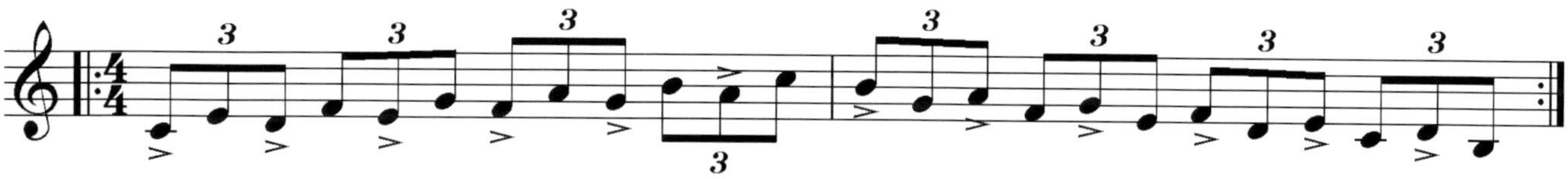

Example 2: Fours (Using 7th chords)

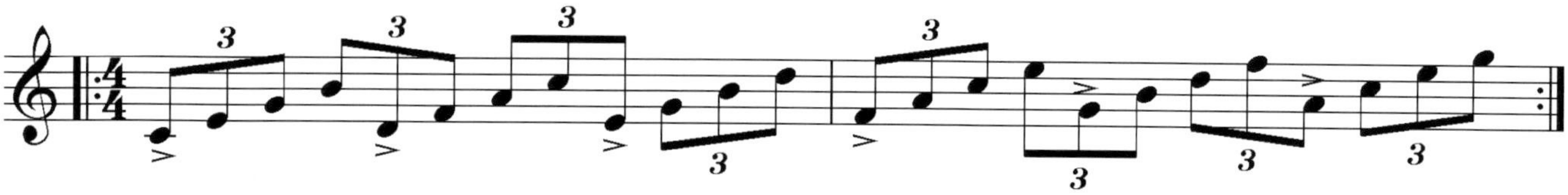

Example 3

Use the same notes as Example 2 but with the metronome on beats 2 and 4. Notice how the pattern feels different this way.

Example 4

This line has a hypnotic effect. Though it is still the same grouping of 4, it can be more difficult tohang on to.

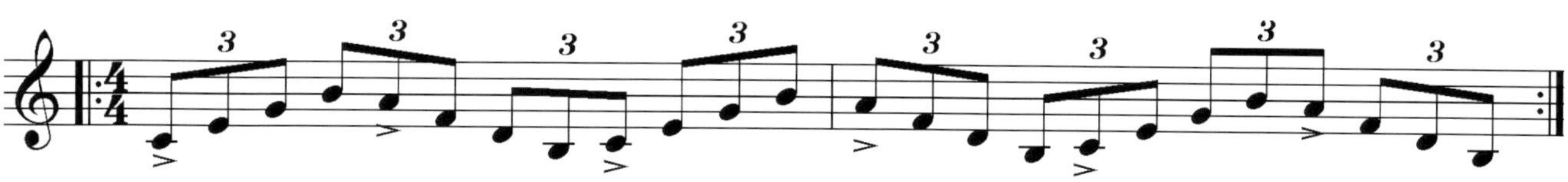

Quarter Note Triplets

Example 5: Twos

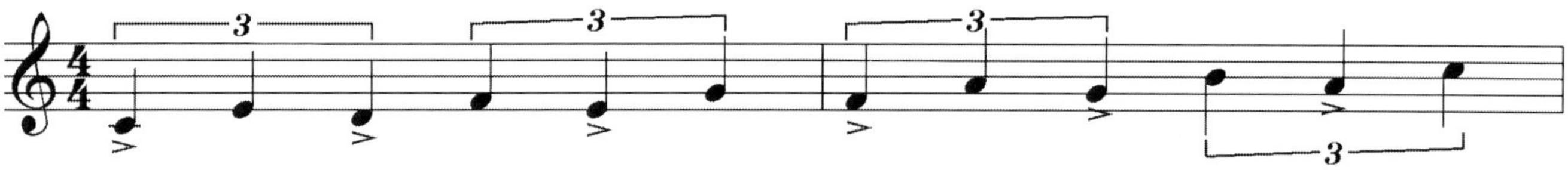

Example 6: Fours

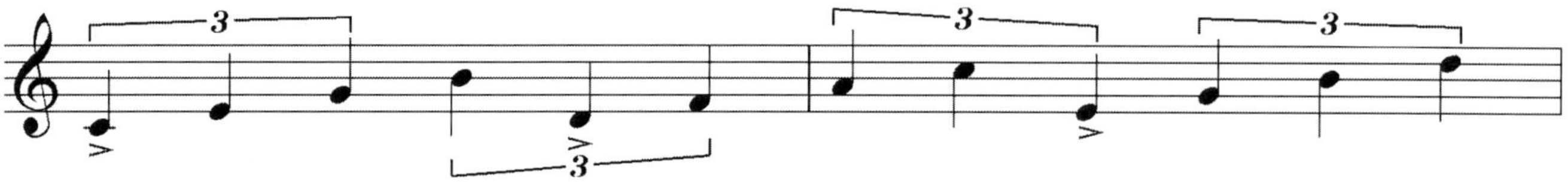

Example 7

Adding the 9th to each chord we create groups of 5. This pattern turns around every five bars, but this can also be used in 2 or 4-bar phrases.

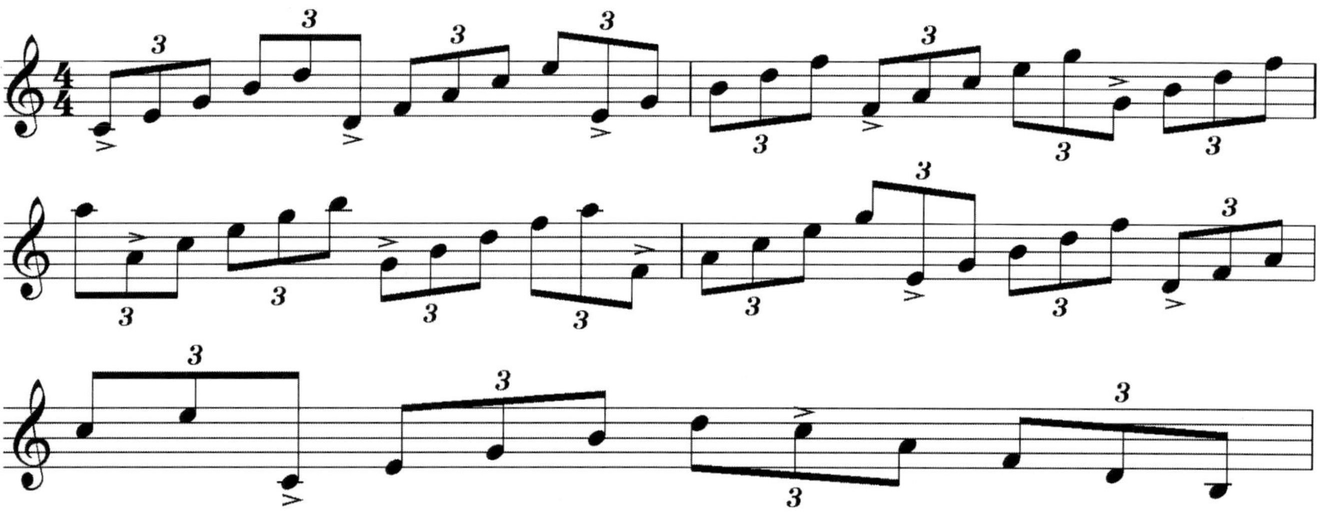

Example 8

More groupings of 5 notes (from smaller groupings of 3 and 2)

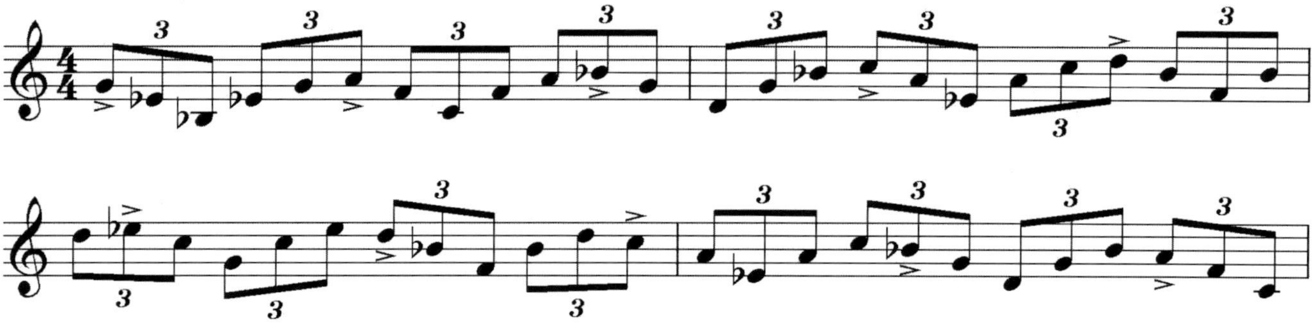

Triplet Exercise 2: Three over two

Try the following exercises with both hands tapping. Use a metronome if needed. It can also be played on guitar, piano or any chord-capable instrument. Once you feel somewhat comfortable with the rhythms, tap or play them while counting the numbers out loud. There are more polyrhythmic exercises like this in chapter 15.

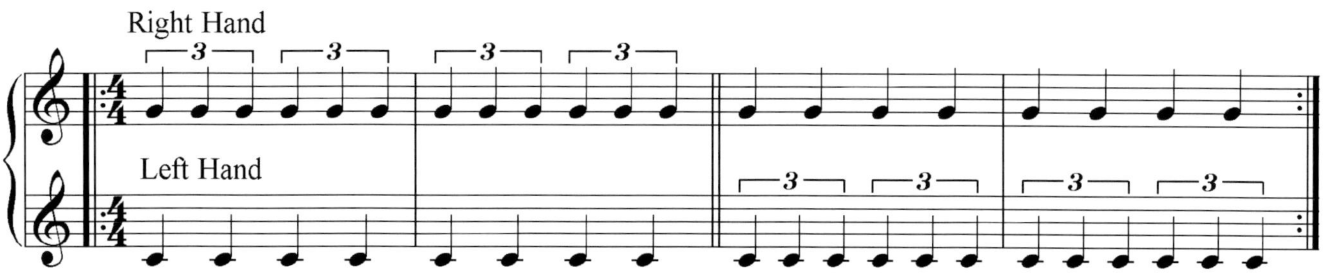

Twos

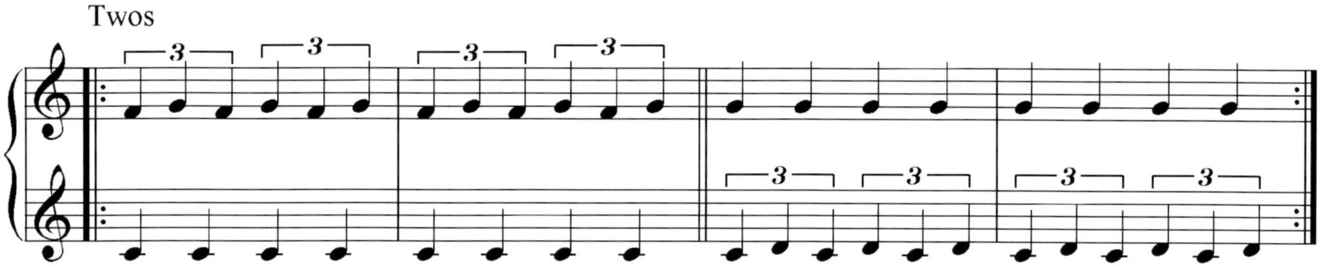

Fours

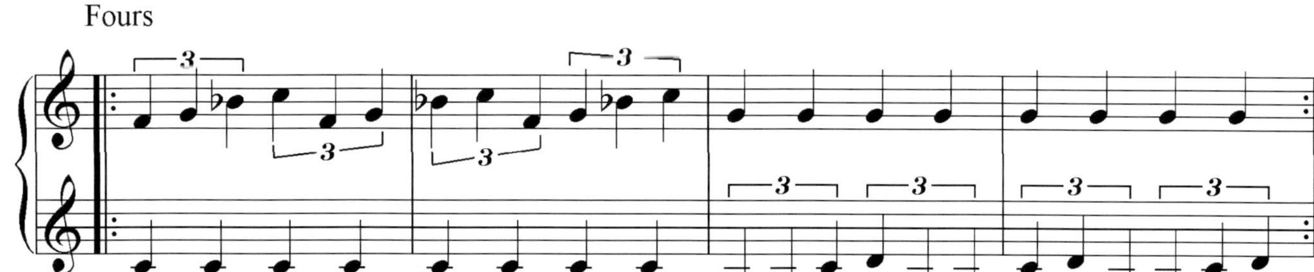

Fives

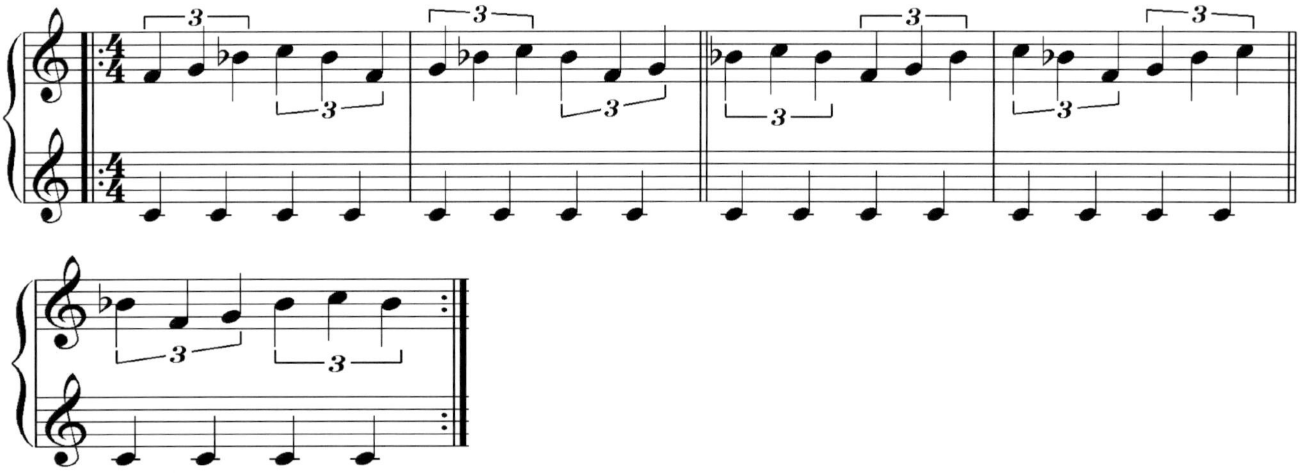

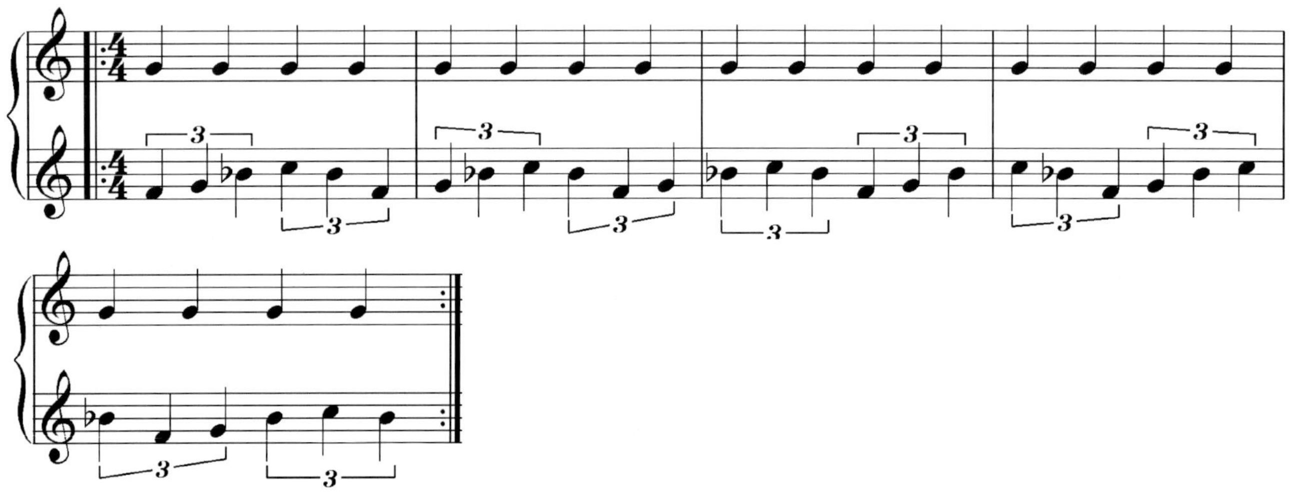

More Eighth-Note Triplet Patterns

This example presents a pattern of triplet eighth notes followed by an 8th rest. The pattern moves by one 8th note every two measures. Each two-measure phrase can be practiced by itself before playing through all of them. Make sure to stay grounded in the quarter-note pulse while playing.

Example 9

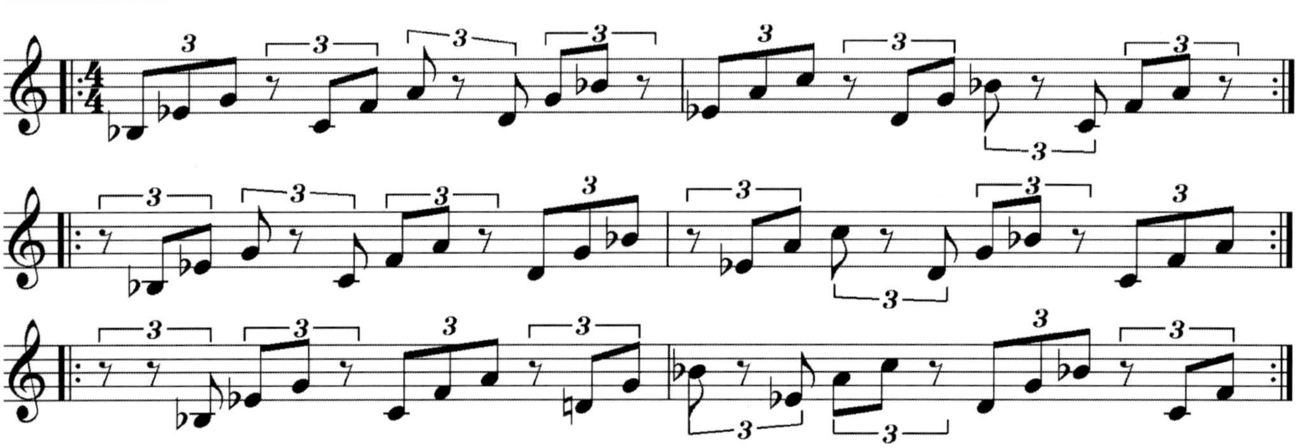

Example 10

This example also shifts by an 8th note every two measures.

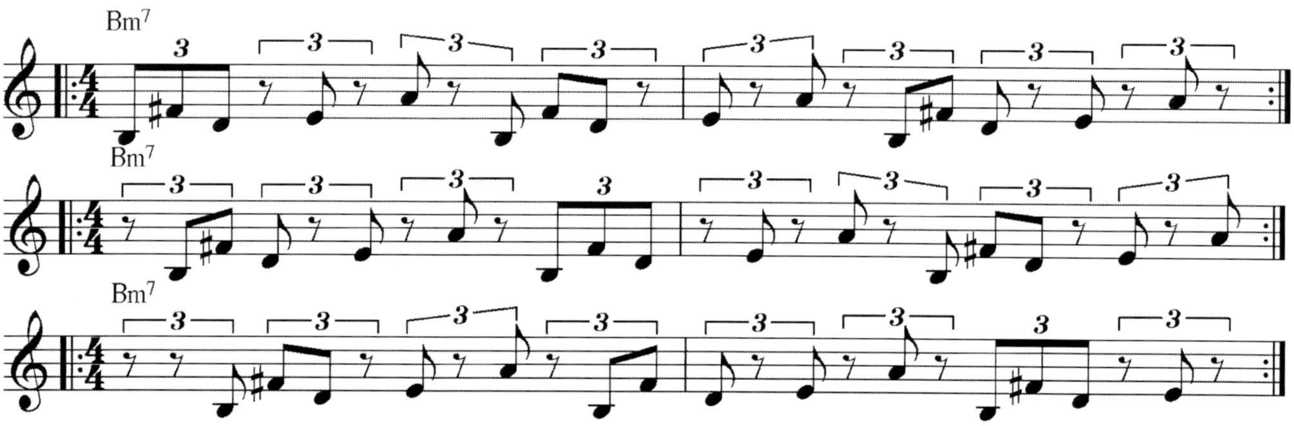

Example 11 (BT)

In this example we take the first two bars of Example 10 and use them as a bass line for improvisation.

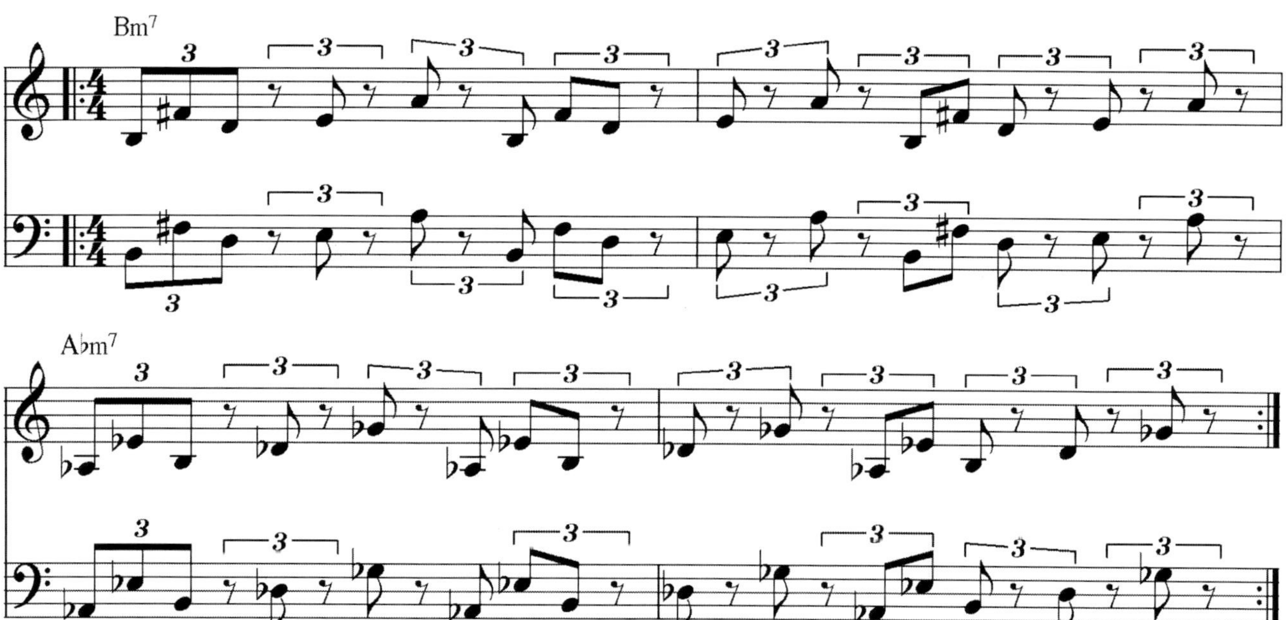

Rhythmic Counterpoint

Example 12

Here is the same bass line with a melody placed where the rests are so that every note of the triplet subdivision is represented.

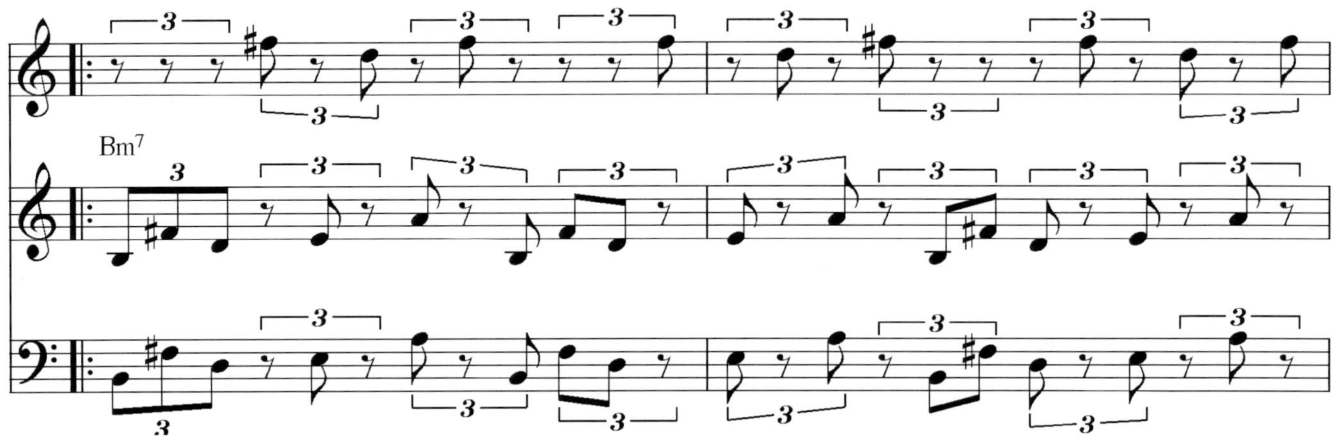

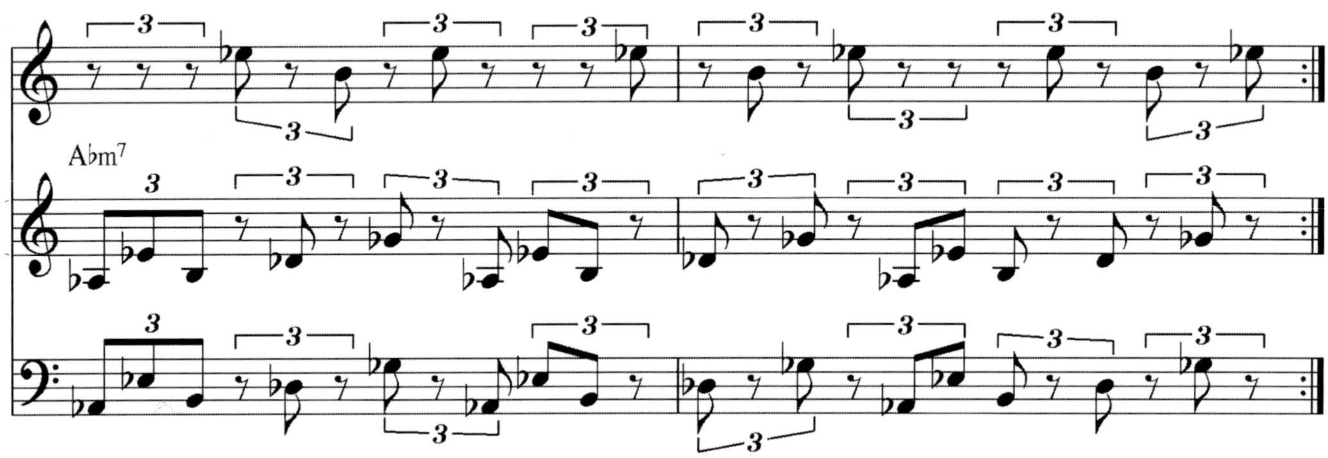

Example 13 (BT)

Here, the chords are placed where the bass line has rests.

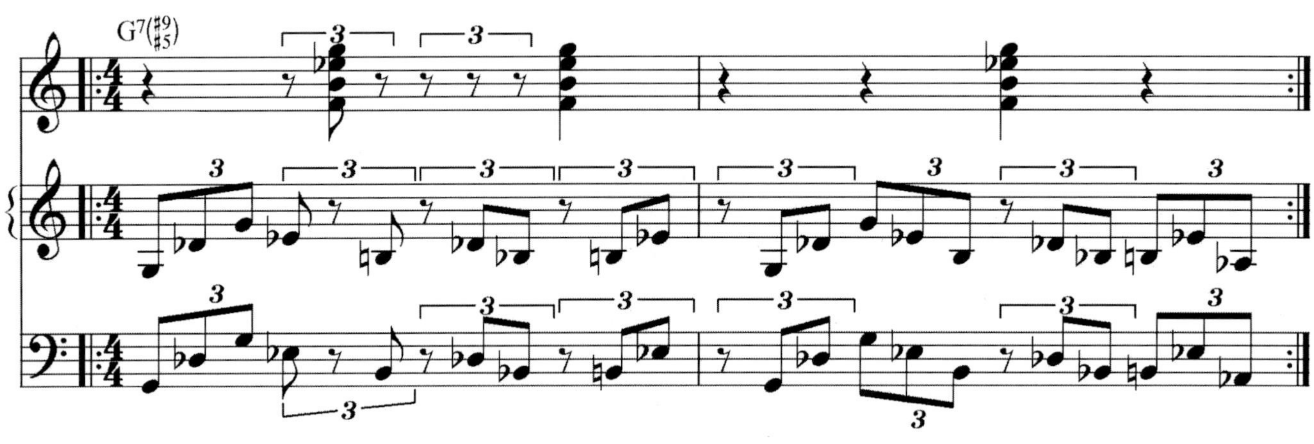

Layering triplets can create a rich rhythmic tapestry. Here are the first two lines from my piece, "African Song".

Example 14: "African Song"

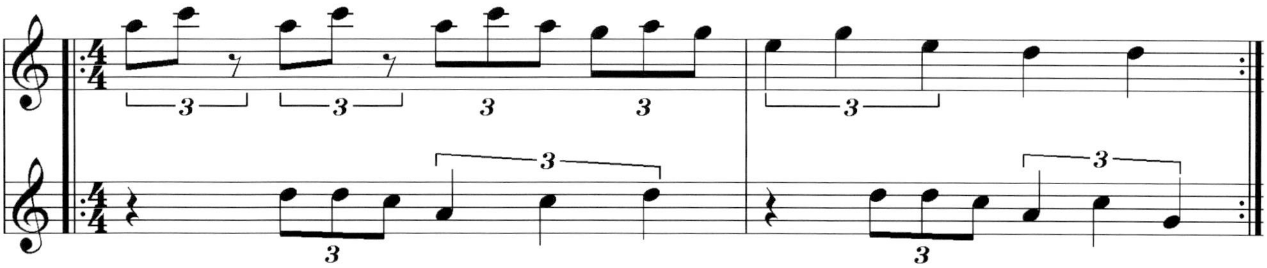

Example 15: "African Song"

Here are two additional lines.

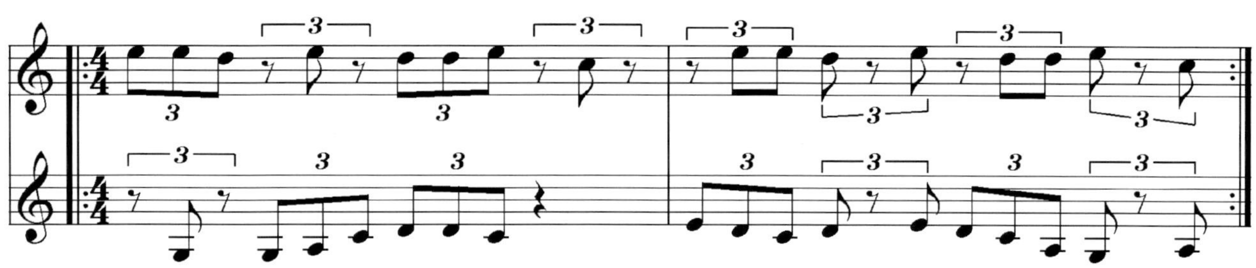

Now combine all four lines. These parts should be tried one at a time at first. Then you can either record the parts or play them with other musicians. The parts are interchangeable. The bottom line works well as a bass line and can be played an octave lower. Experiment with playing any two parts simultaneously. Try improvising over these layers.

Example 16: "African Song" four-part

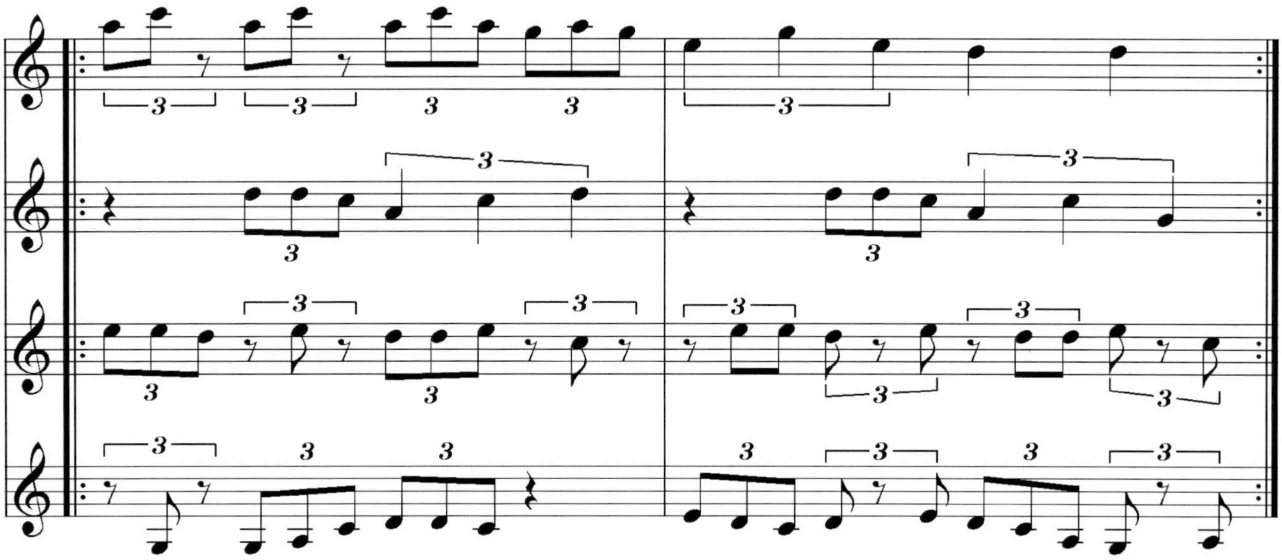

More Triplet Grooves

Example 17 (BT)

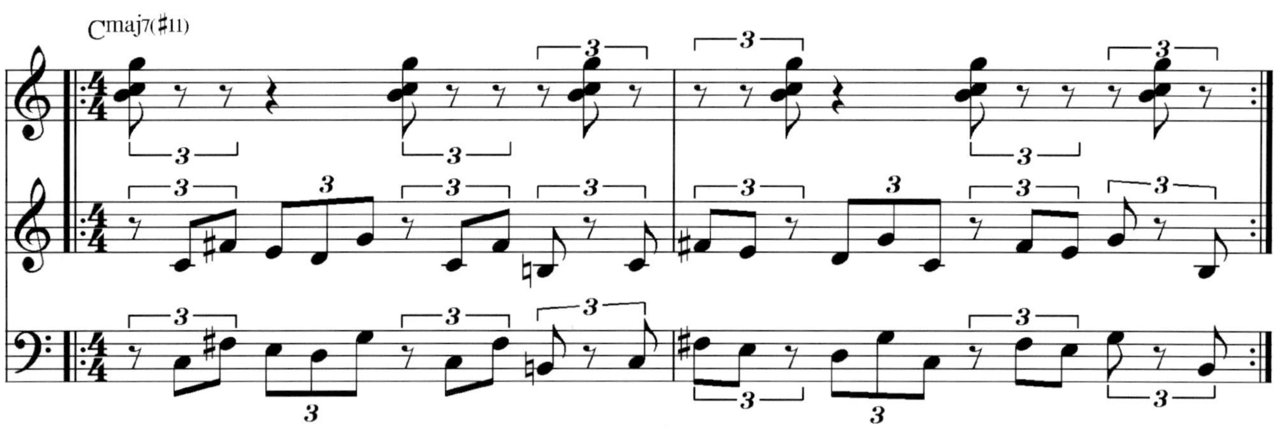

Example 18

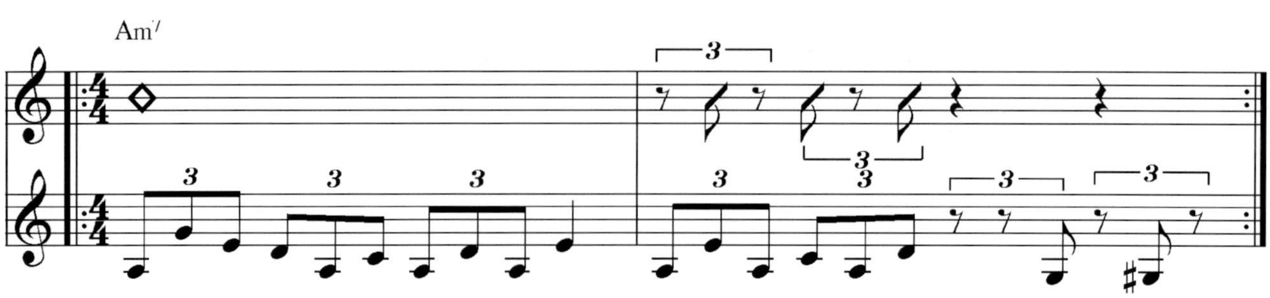

Example 19 (BT)

In this example, I have taken the pattern that was the low A note in Example 18 and used it for chord placement. Then I created a bass line that is placed where the rests are in the upper rhythm.

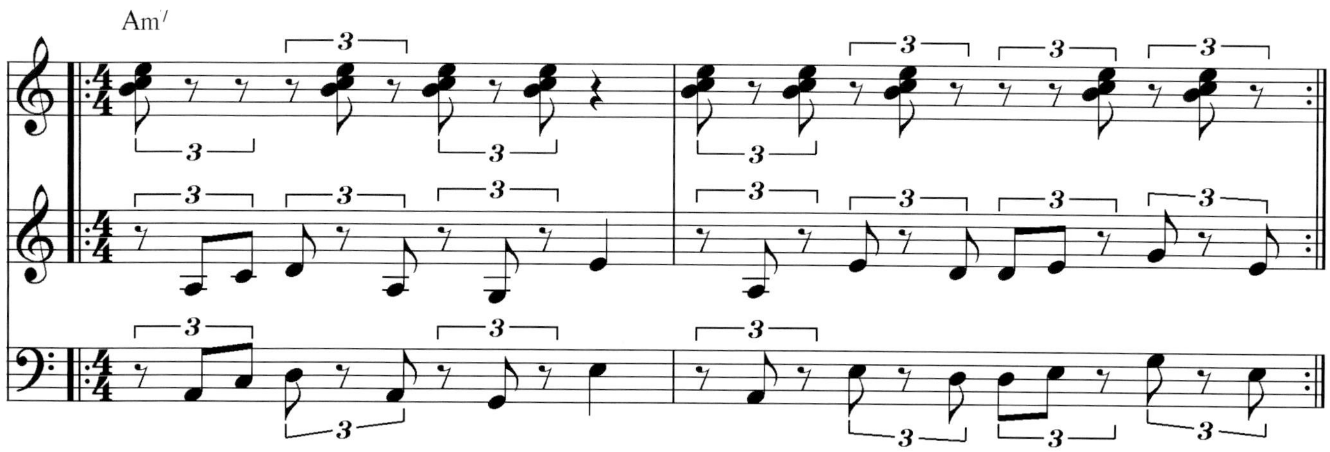

Example 20: Triplet Groove (BT)

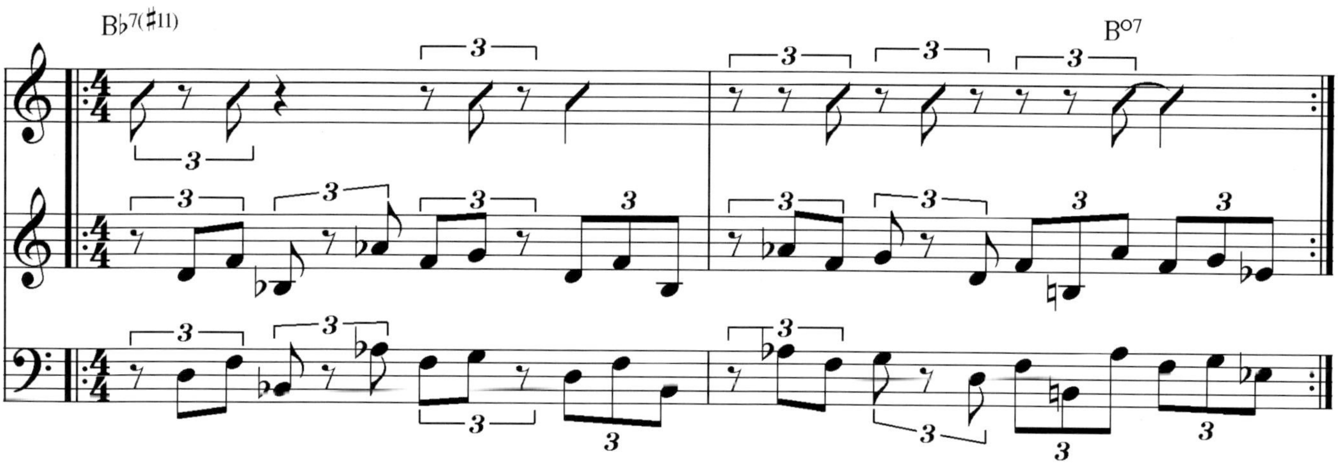

4. APPLYING RHYTHMIC PATTERNS TO STANDARD FORMS IN 4/4

Exercise: Clap these rhythm patterns with the metronome set on the quarter note, then try it with the metronome on beats 2 and 4. In order to make the pattern fit into 8 bars, there is a dotted quarter at the end of the cycle of 8 or 16 beats

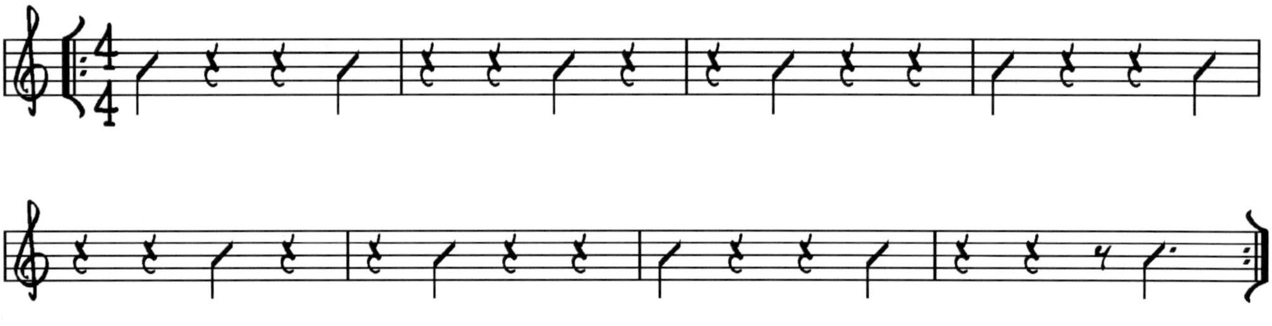

Here's the same pattern, now in a 16-measure form.

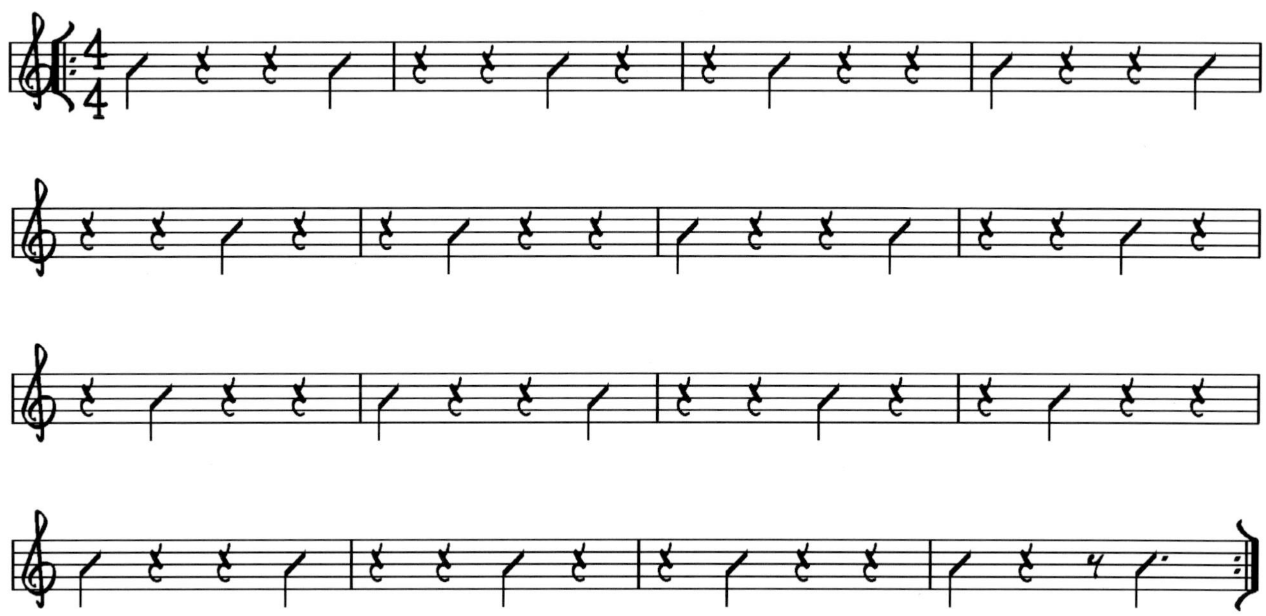

Now we will apply this 3-beat dotted half pattern to the blues form. Depending on the chord progression, we may have to make some adjustments to the placement of the chords to conform to this rhythmic pattern. Some chords will be anticipated, and some delayed. There are times when a chord needs to be played twice, or a passing chord can be placed in those spots to keep the harmonic movement flowing. Keep in mind that you do not want to feel this pattern as if it is in 3/4. Feel the threes in their relationship to the 4/4 as they pass across the measures. Concentrate on feeling the 4/4 blues form just as you would if there was no 3-beat pattern.

Example 21: Dotted Half Blues with rhythm section

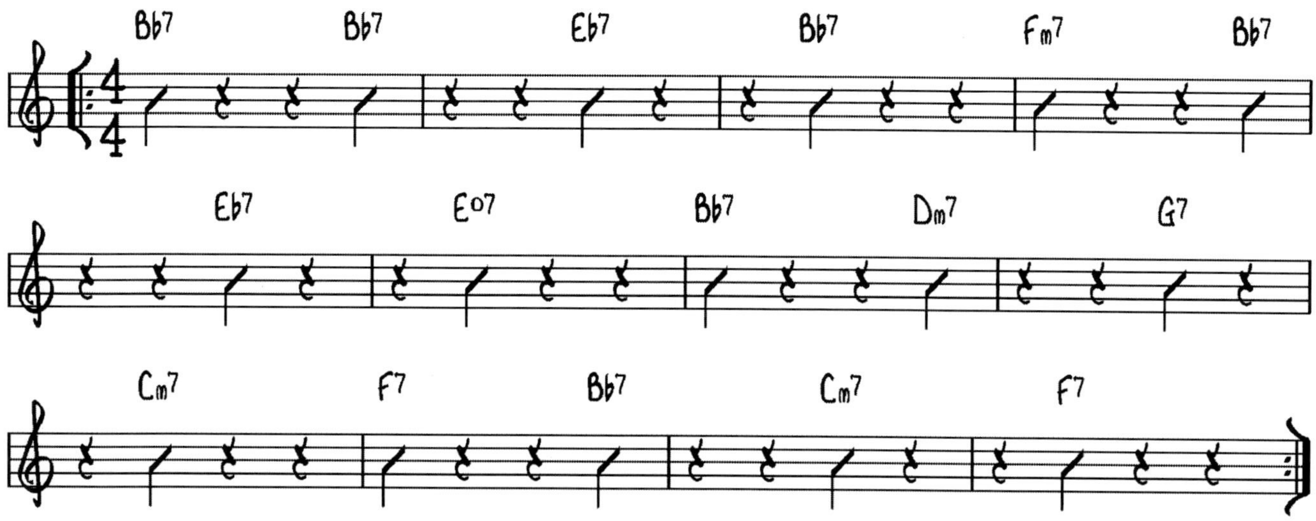

Here is the A section of "Just One Thing" using the 3-beat dotted half note pattern. When playing this chart with a group, you have the choice of using the rhythm only for chord placement, or everyone in the group can play the hits. These examples work best when using a medium to medium up swing feel. I have added a few passing chords for harmonic motion.

Example 22: "Just One Thing" with rhythm section

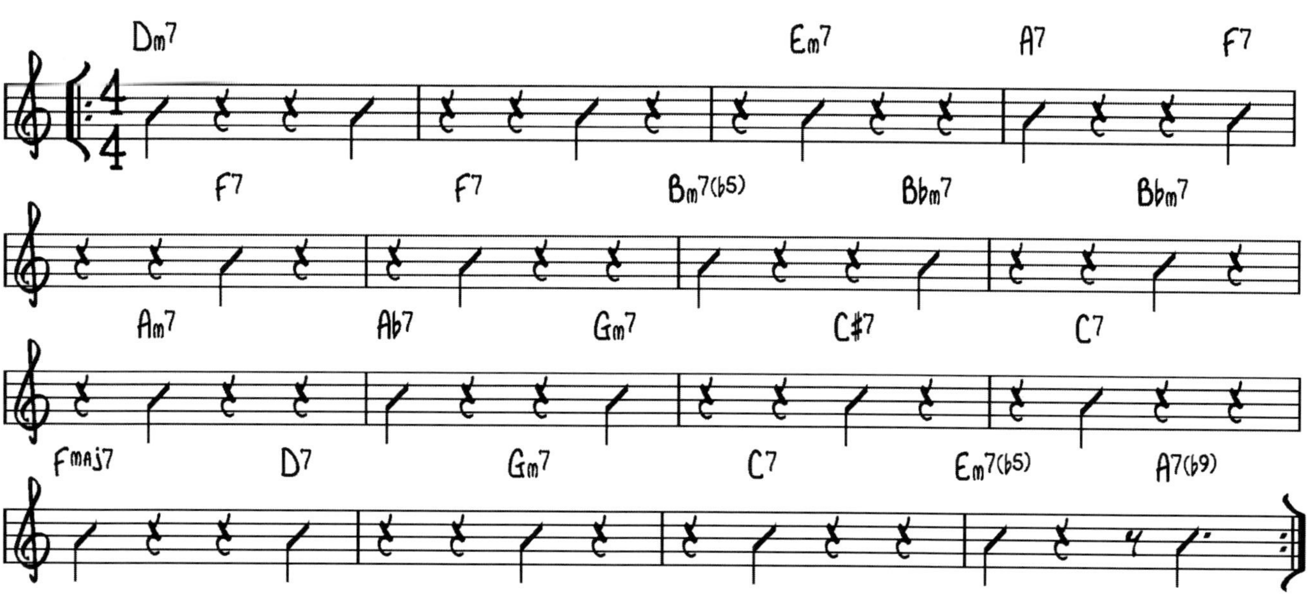

Now we will use the dotted quarter note. Here we have more choices for where to realign the rhythmic pattern within the form. An effective method is to play 4 or 8-bar patterns with an extra quarter note onthe last beat of each cycle. Clap the following rhythms with the metronome clicking on the quarter note, and then try it with the metronome on only beats 2 and 4.

4-bar dotted quarter pattern

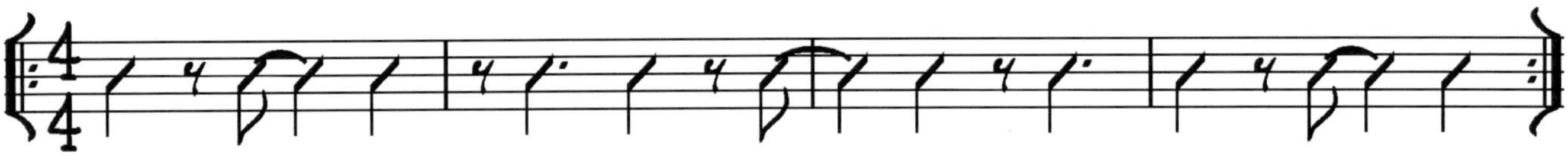

8-bar dotted quarter pattern

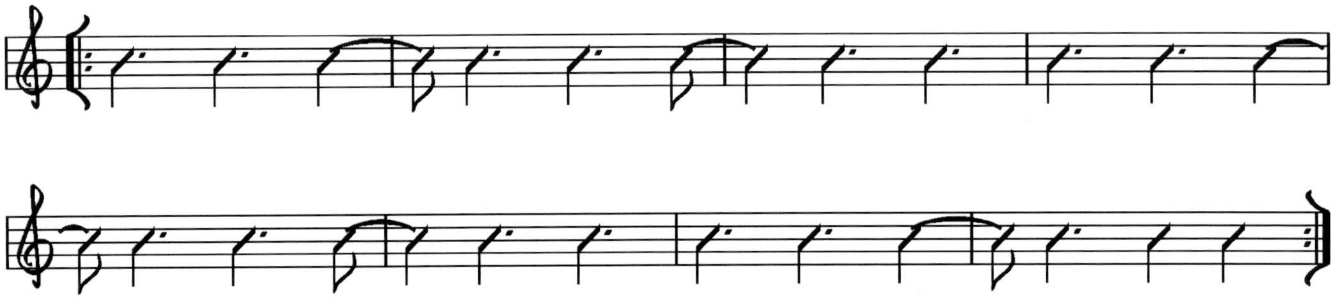

Example 23: "Dotted Quarter Blues" with rhythm section

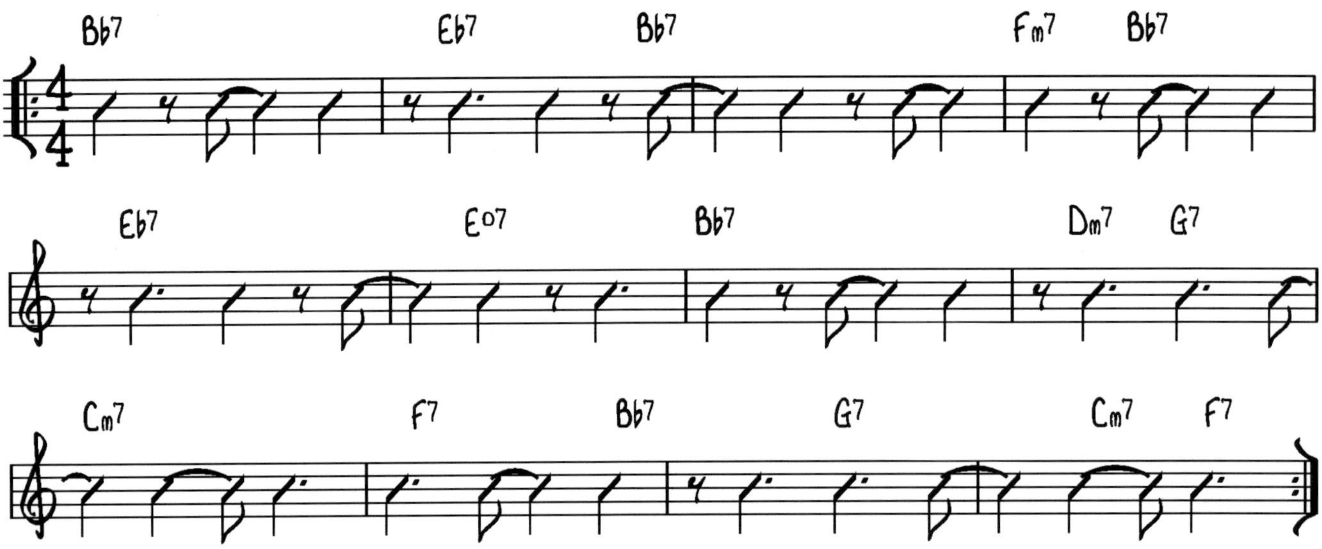

This page has been left blank to avoid an awkward page turn.

Here is the four-measure pattern applied to the A section of "No or Yes"

Example 24 "No or Yes" with rhythm section

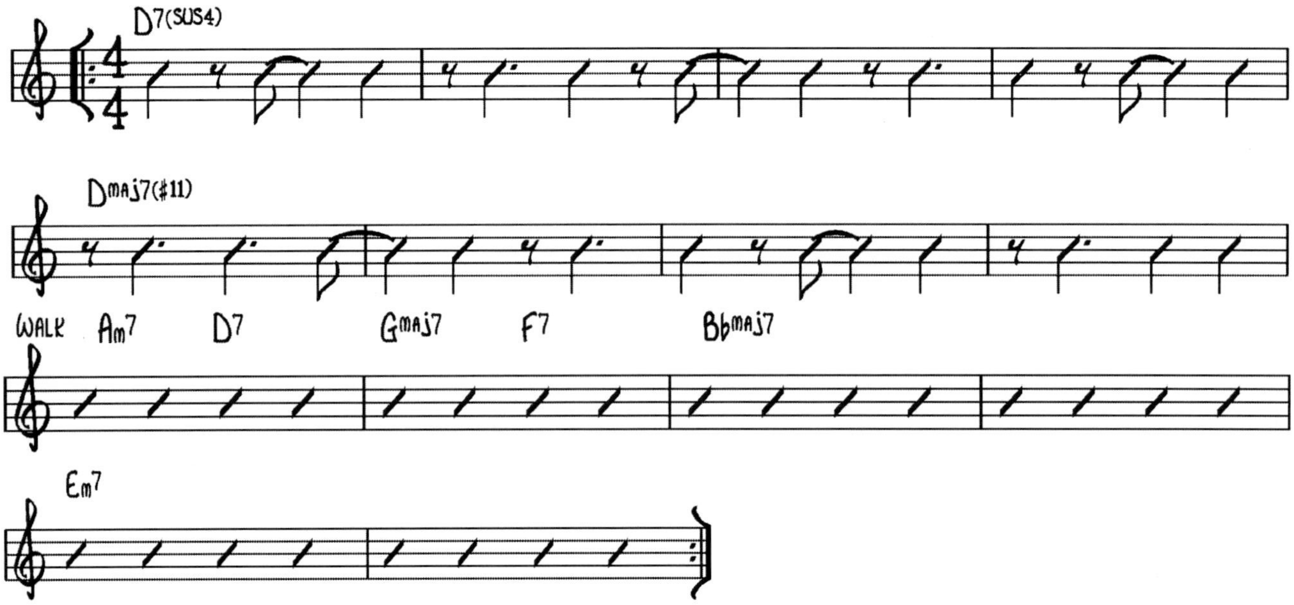

Example 25: "No or Yes" Full form with rhythm section

The complete form of "No or Yes", using the 8-bar dotted quarter pattern in the A section, and the 16-bar dotted half pattern in the B section.

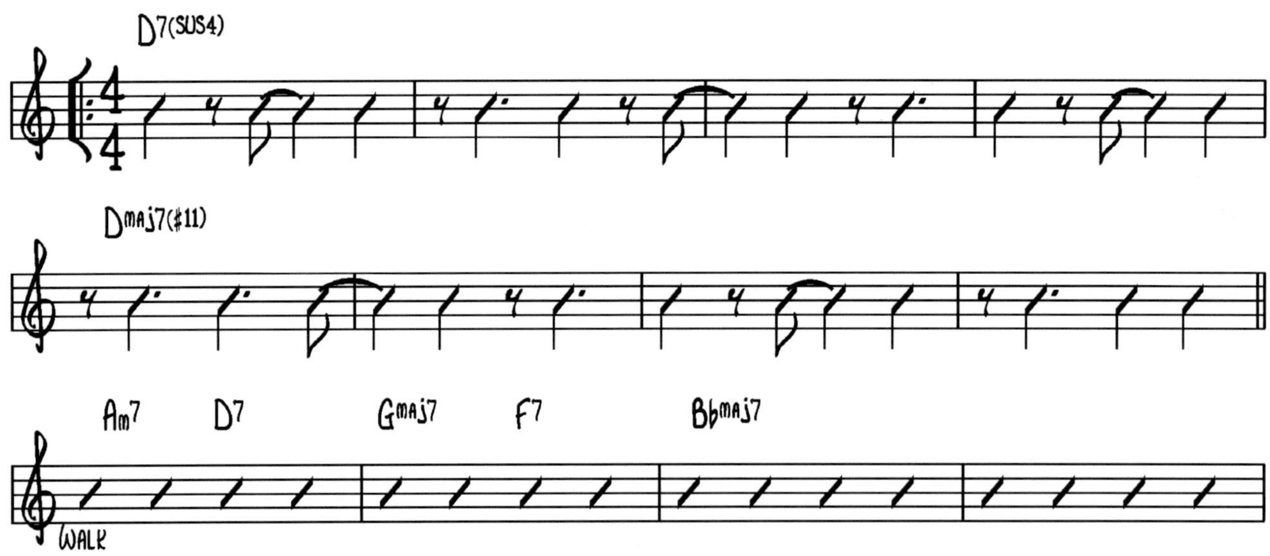

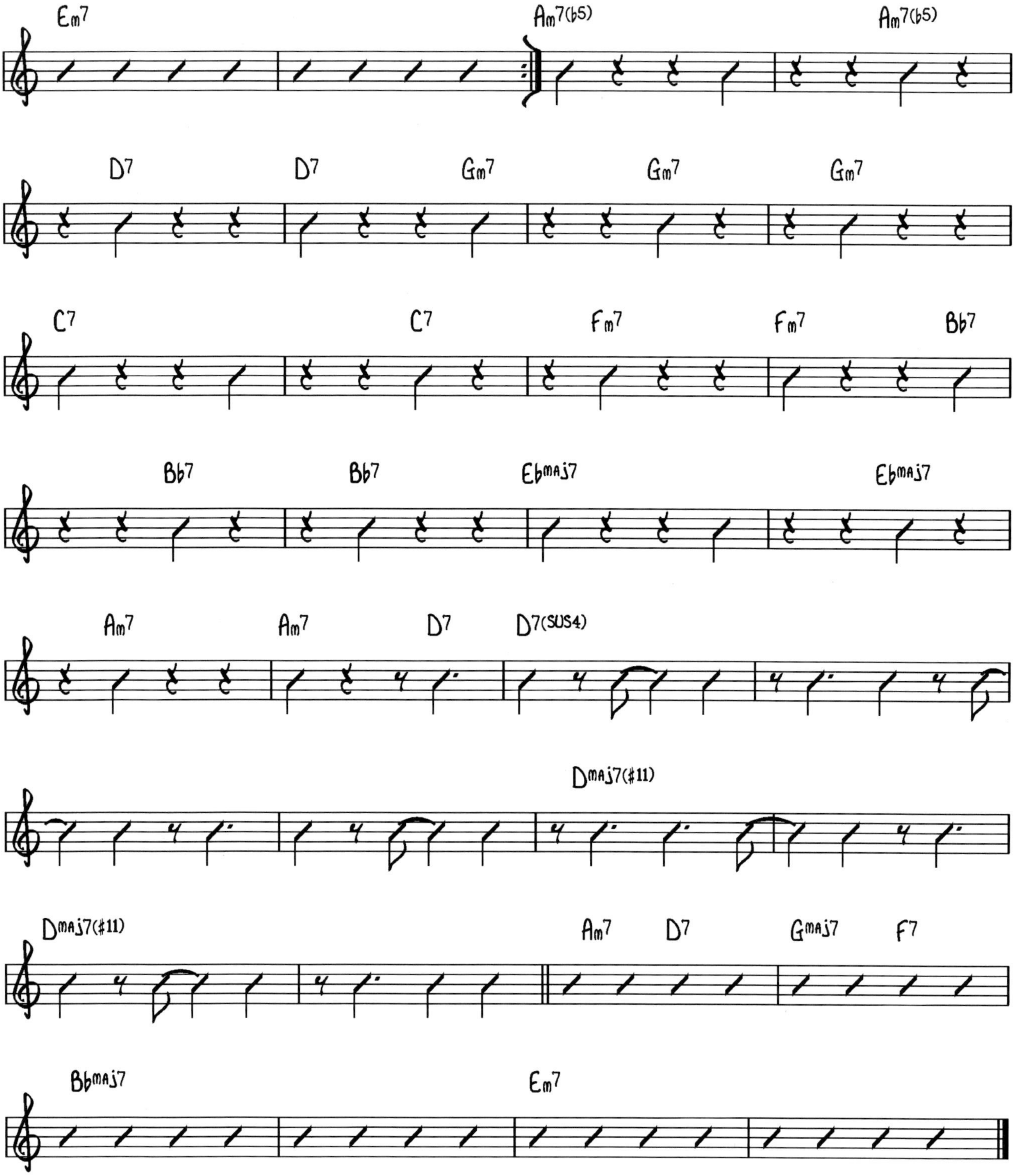
Em7
Am7(b5)
Am7(b5)
D7
D7
Gm7
Gm7
Gm7
C7
C7
Fm7
Fm7
Bb7
Bb7
Bb7
Ebmaj7
Ebmaj7
Am7
Am7
D7
D7(SUS4)
Dmaj7(#11)
Dmaj7(#11)
Am7
D7
Gmaj7
F7
Bbmaj7
Em7

Metronome Exercise:

Set your metronome to mark the dotted half-note 3-beat pattern (as in Example 21). Make sure you keep track of where the actual downbeat is and that you are feeling the pattern in its relationship to 4/4. Now play or sing the melody or chords of a simple standard while making sure that you stay aligned with the metronome. At first, it can be easy to drift into 3/4 accidentally. Once you feel more confident about where you are in the measure, you'll be able to improvise just like you would with the metronome set on beats 2 and 4.

Changing the meter of a standard and adding a few rhythmic twists can give you a new perspective on something familiar. Here is "G.S." in 3/4. I have used half notes over the bar line to give some sections the feeling of 4/4. Play the melody and chords exactly where they are placed and then improvise.

Example 26: "G.S." with rhythm section

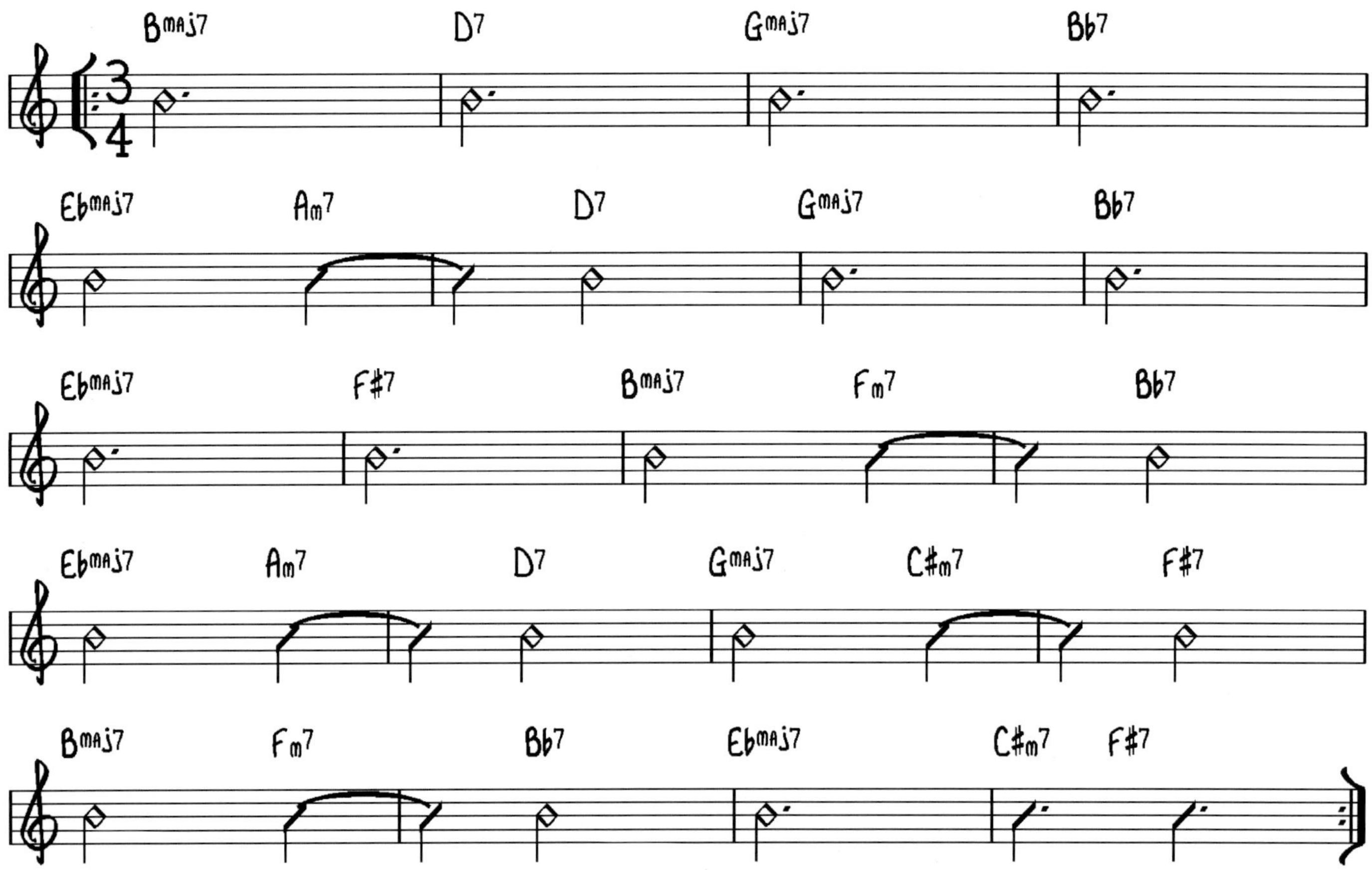

5. USING GROUPINGS AND RHYTHMIC LAYERING IN 4/4

One way to create rhythmic tension in 4/4 is to experiment with different rhythmic groupings and layers. The following pattern is made up of groups of five 8th notes. The central underlying pulse is the half note. Try tapping the half notes with your foot while clapping the bass rhythm.

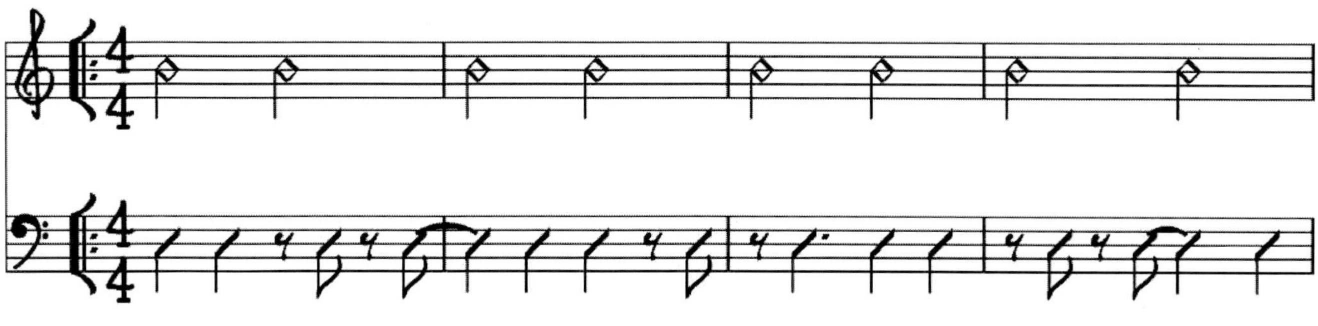

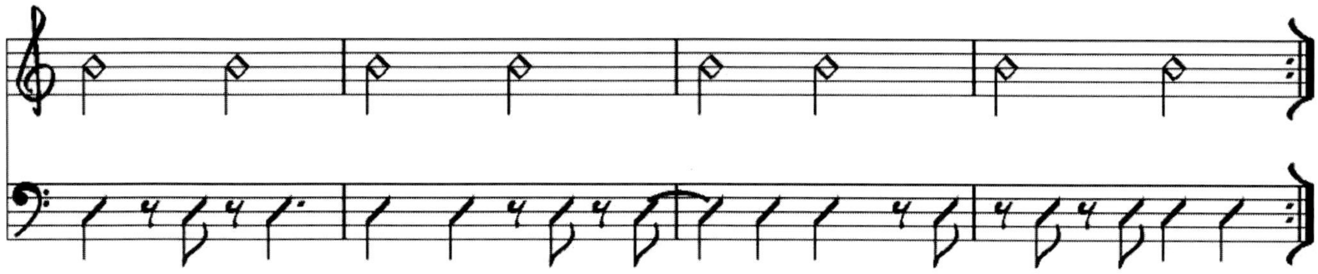

You can see that the pattern repeats every 5 bars. I have changed the last bar to create a rhythmic turnaround which makes an 8-bar section.

The bass line of my composition "Pulsion" uses this rhythmic pattern. The full composition is included in the appendix. The piece (or groove) should be felt in 4/4 (or in 2) and not in 5. It is important to hear the bass line's relationship to the half note. Otherwise, the groove may not be phrased correctly.

Example 27: "Pulsion" with bass and drums (BT for bass clef see Example 28)

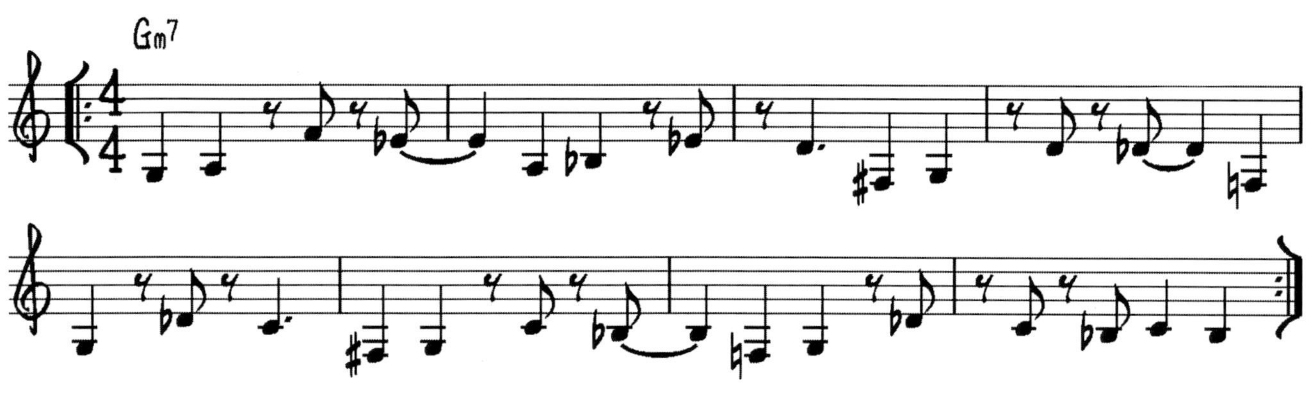

Here is a different pattern using groups of six 8th notes starting on the upbeat of the third beat. Clap the rhythm against a quarter note pulse. The rhythm is evenly spaced and always begins on upbeats except for the second half of the last measure.

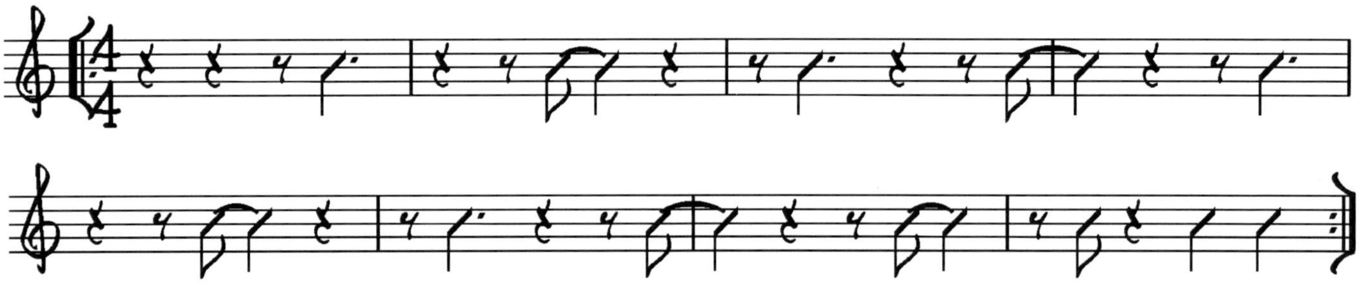

Now we'll put these two patterns together. Try to clap or play the upper chordal rhythm along with a recording of the bass line (Example 27).

Example 28: "Pulsion" A section with rhythm section and guitar

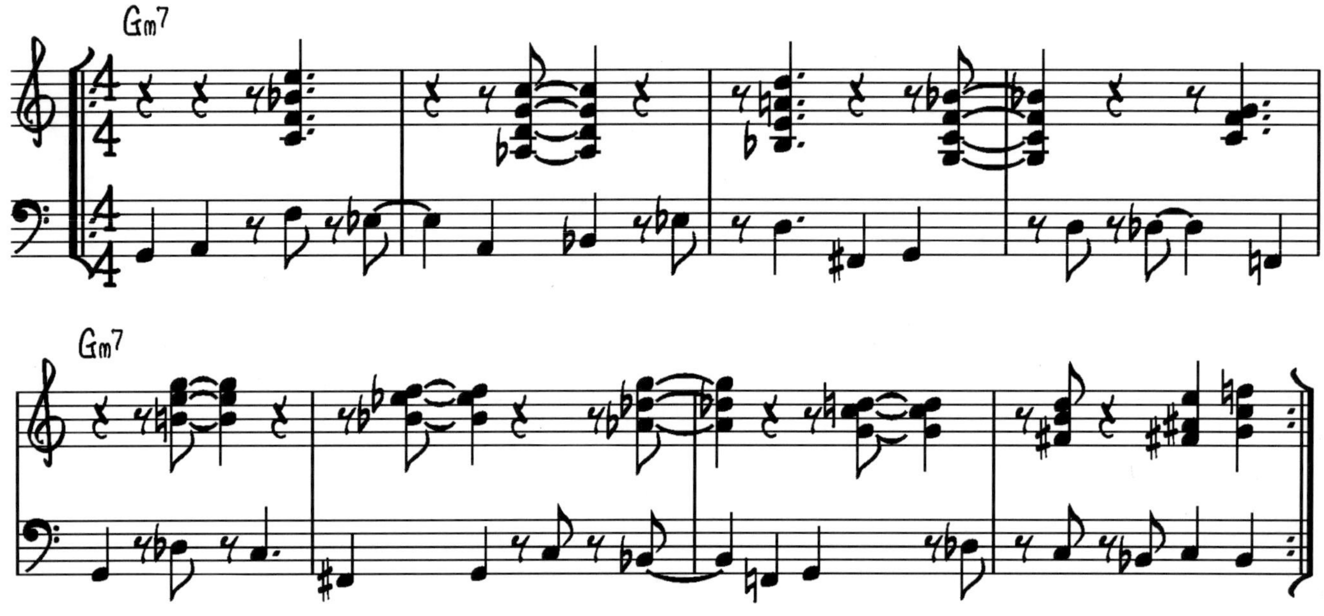

As you will see in the full score on page 90, there is also an additional melody placed on top of these two layers. This section is also used for solos. Record them in a loop or use the backing track. The harmony is G minor with flexible chromatic motion. It is essential to feel the half-note pulse underneath the layers as you play. With practice, you can phrase lines the same as if you were playing a regular 4/4 groove.

In the B section of "Pulsion," I use the same pattern of 8th notes grouped in fives, but now in a 4-bar cycle. The chords occur every three beats.

Example 29: "Pulsion" B section with bass and drums

Example 29A: "Pulsion" B section with rhythm section plus guitar

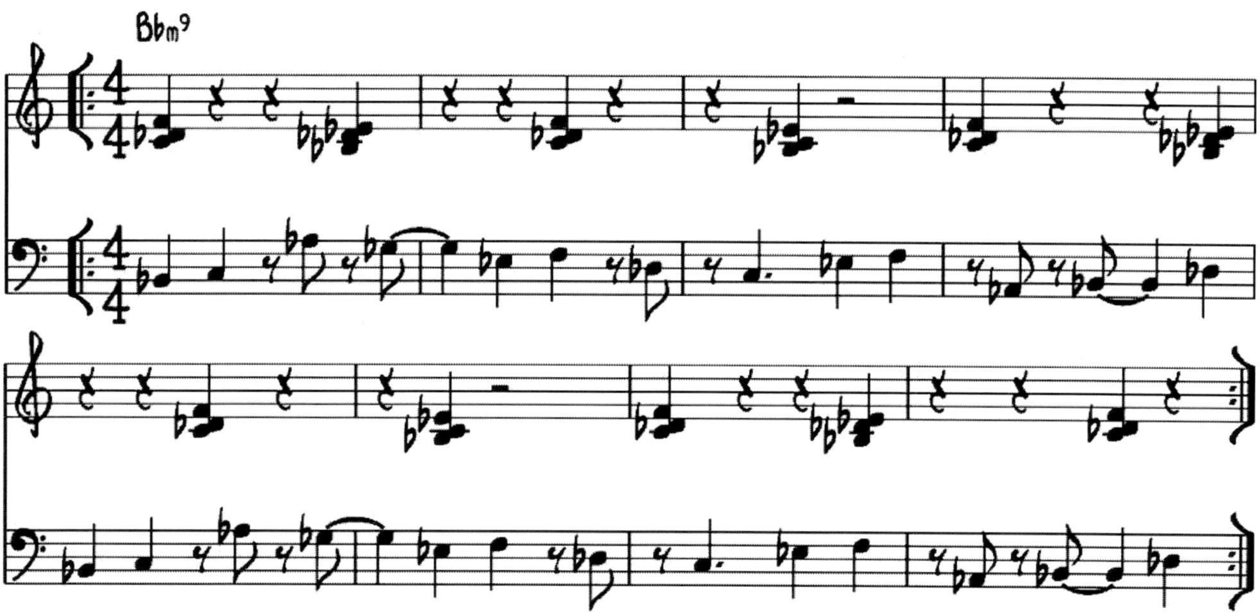

This excerpt from my composition "Thread" is also in 4/4, but the placement of bass notes and chords can imply other rhythms.

Example 30: "Thread"

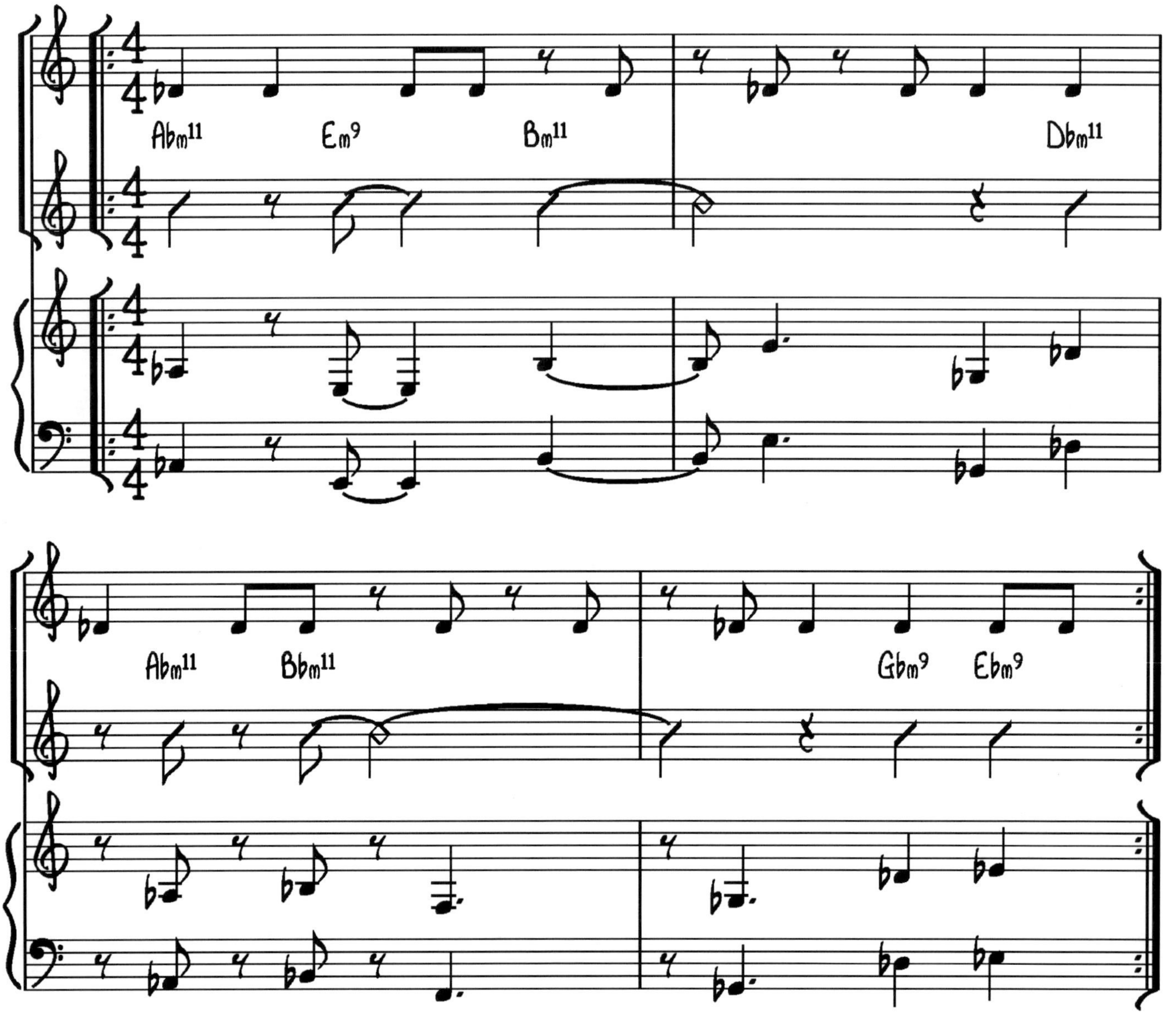

6. ODD METERS

Any meter or rhythmic pattern can be broken down into twos and threes or felt as a series of long and short pulses. There are the numbers, the math of rhythm, and then there is the feeling of the rhythm. It can be possible to feel the shape of a groove without having a mathematical understanding of it. It is extremely interesting (and beyond the scope of this book) how the body can feel and "understand" a groove or rhythm without there being any actual numbers involved. When we here a song in 4/4 we usually do not count to it. Our goal is to come to feel and understand more complex rhythmic structures in the same way, by spending time with them.

If you are new to odd meters you might listen to the audio tracks first without counting. But then we do need to break the rhythm down and get to know it's duration and contour. Keep in mind that 5/4 is not 4/4 plus an extra beat. 5/4 has a feeling of its own, as do all of the meters. Whatever the groove is, we want it to feel circular and continuous, just like when we play 4/4. We don't want to start over at each downbeat. Odd meters should not sound "odd" (the term irregular-meter is probably a better name for it.)

In the following examples you will find bass line patterns, along with some comping patterns and layers, to aid in getting to know the shape and feeling of each meter. I have made most of the examples harmonically simple so that the focus is on rhythm. Any of these bass lines, chord patterns, and melodies can be altered to be more harmonically challenging.

For each example you can start by clapping each individual rhythm while keeping the quarter or 8th-note pulse with a metronome. Some examples could be played with two hands, either tapping or at the piano. Pianists can try the exercises with two hands and guitarists and other string instruments can play some of the exercises using two or more strings. Try the upper and lower parts individually before attempting them simultaneously.

About the Odd Meter Studies:

- These examples are not meant to be sight-reading material. Each example should be played repeatedly until you can feel the groove without counting. Use the backing tracks to get to know each groove. You may want to improvise over a groove for 10 to 20 minutes a day to truly learn it.

- Some of the examples can be joined together, and the student is encouraged to experiment with these patterns as they go. I have tried to vary the keys. If joining together two or more examples the lines can be transposed accordingly.

- Most examples use a straight 8th note feel unless otherwise noted.

7. FIVES

The most common breakdown of 5/4 and 5/8 is to divide the measure into 3 and 2. It can be felt as long-long-short-short. Start with a quarter note pulse on the metronome and clap these rhythms while counting.

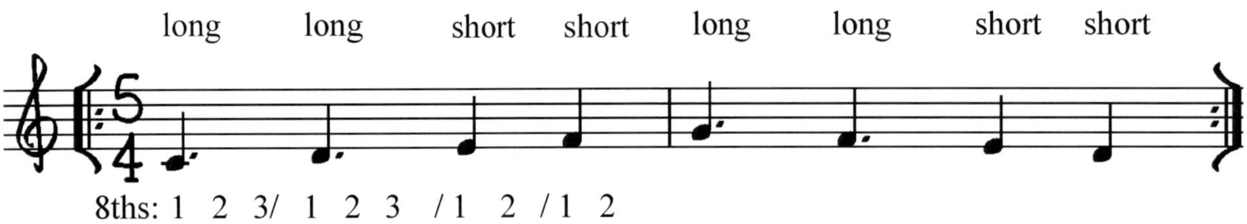

Now try improvising over the same dotted/normal quarter-note rhythm used as a bass line.

Example 31: 5/4 with rhythm section

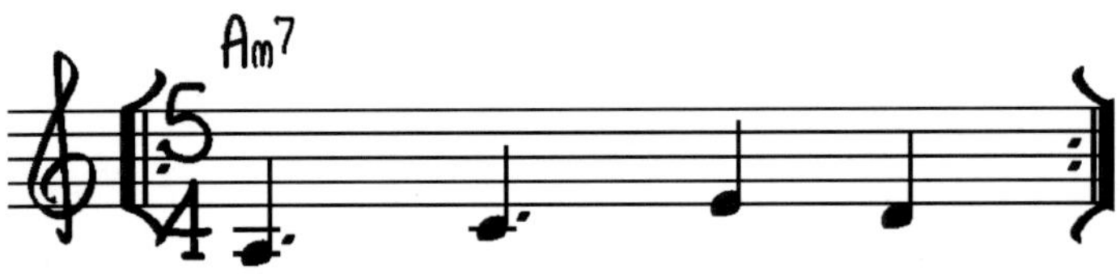

Below is the same 3 and 2 division with a common counter rhythm layered on top of it. Try tapping them out using both hands simultaneously. The resulting pattern can be helpful for internalizing the feeling of five.

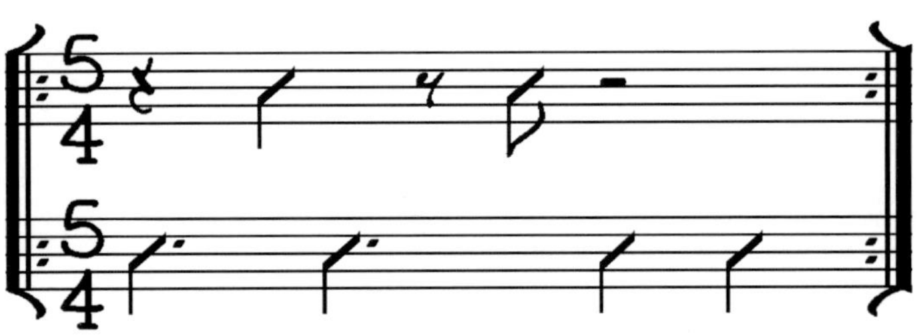

Turn that pattern around and we have 2 and 3.

Example 32: 5/4 retrograde clave (BT)

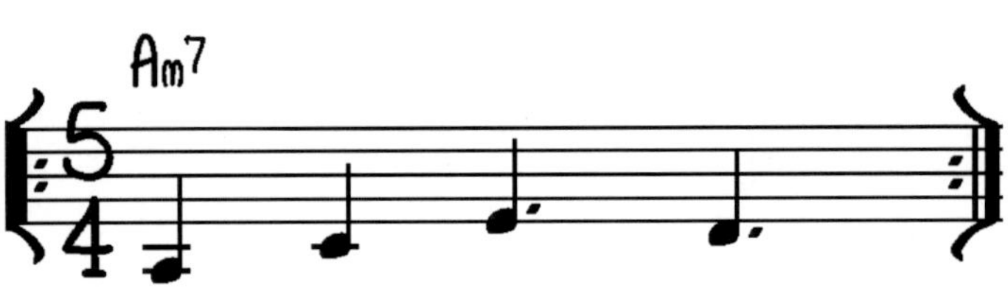

If we combine the 3 and 2 clave with the 2 and 3, we have an interesting layered rhythm:

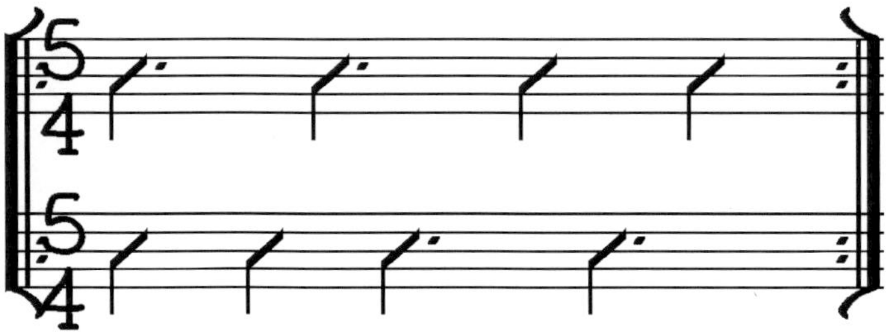

Now try these rhythms over the 3 and 2 clave. They can be clapped or played as a chord or a melody. In these two examples the rhythm of the first bar is displaced by an 8th note in the second bar. For the recorded track, each measure is played twice as indicated. Remove the repeats and you have a two-measure pattern.

Example 33

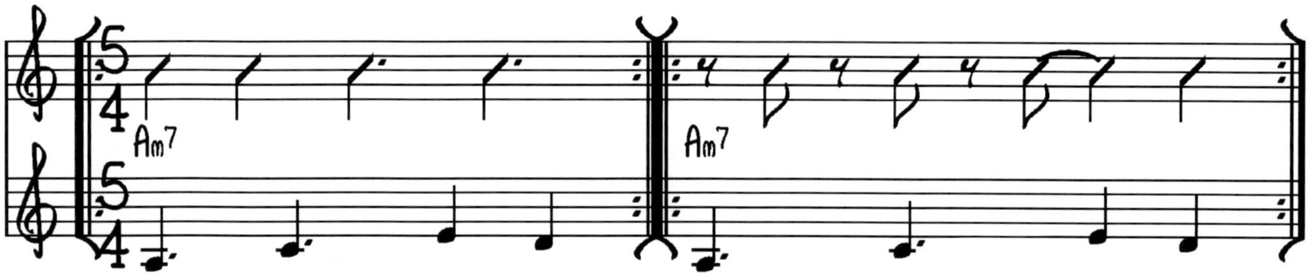

Example 34

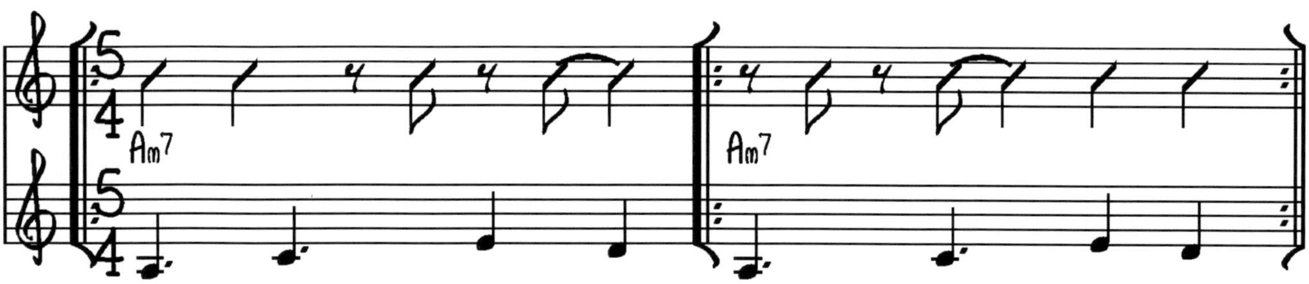

More 5/4 Grooves

Example 35: Two-chord 5/4 vamp (BT)

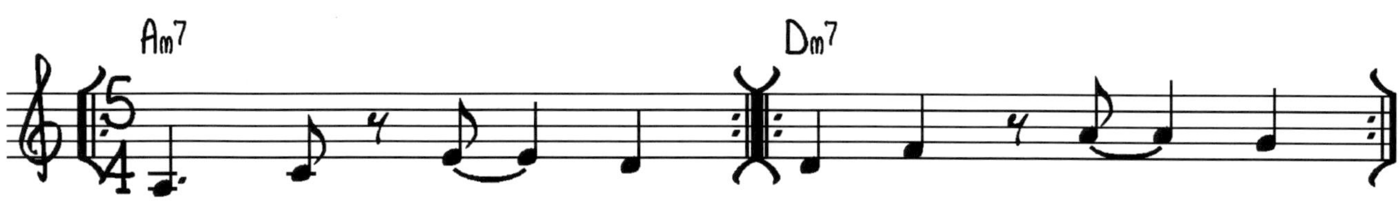

The following example shows how we can create a counter rhythm that results in a complex, layered groove. Play separately before combining them.

Example 36: 5/4 with counter rhythms

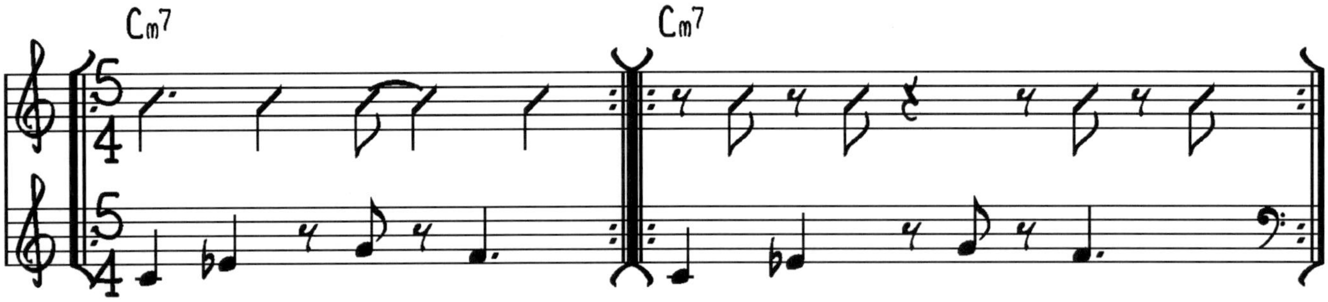

The following example is a bass line from my composition "Momentum" and can be a guide to feeling five in a more flexible way.

Example 37: "Momentum" with rhythm section

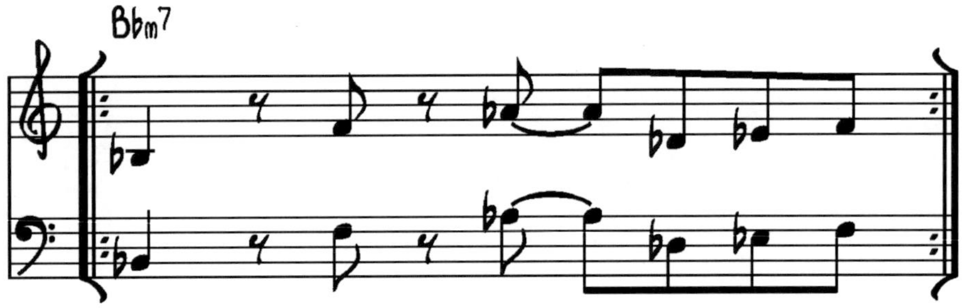

Examples 38 to 42 use the same bass line as an anchor for different comping patterns. Each pattern is played several times, then the track continues so that you can try the pattern with bass and drums.

Example 38 with rhythm section

This example alternates between the common clave and the retrograde clave.

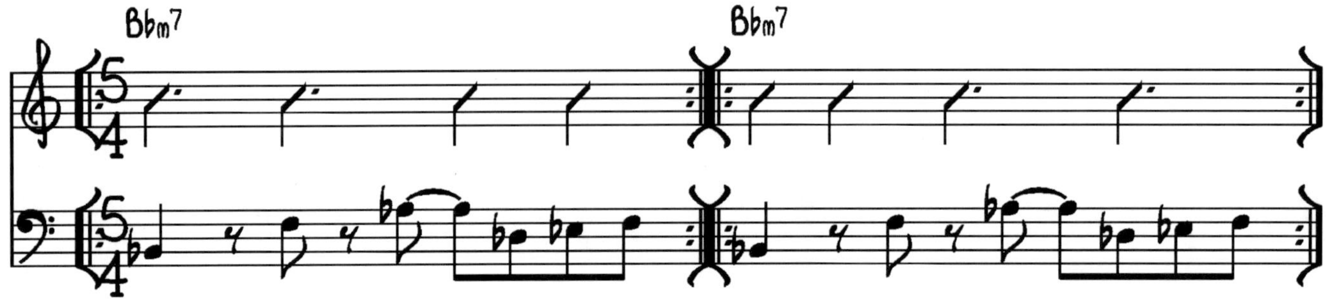

Example 39 with rhythm section

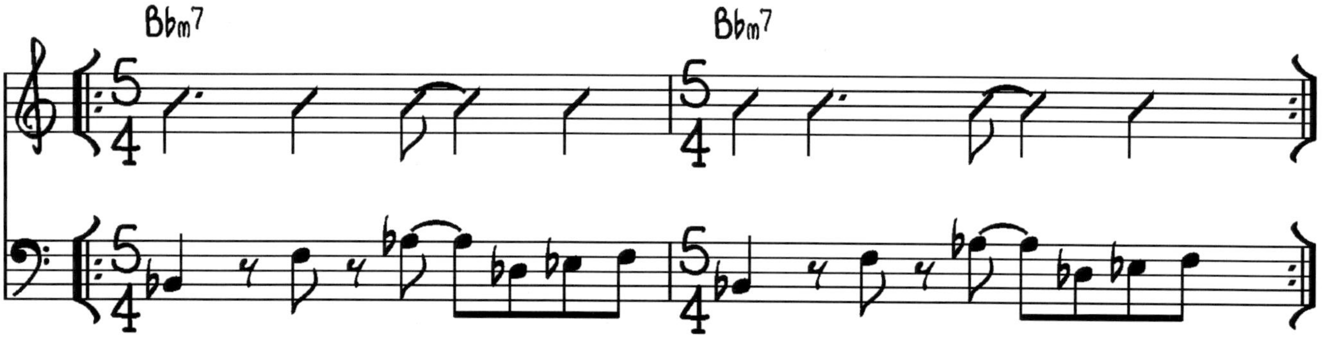

Example 40 with rhythm section

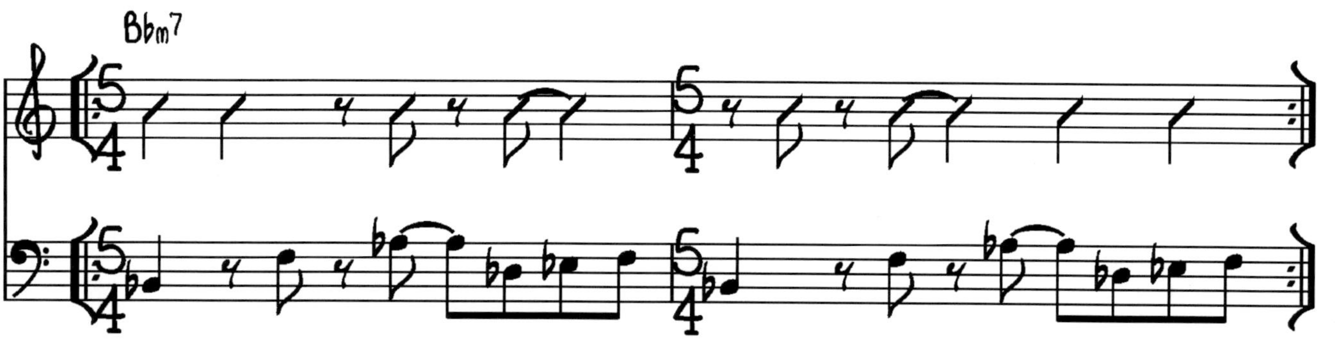

This dotted-quarter pattern completes its cycle every three measures (to the double-bar line). If we want it to be an even four measures, we can create a rhythmic turnaround by adding quarter notes on the 4th and 5th beats of the fourth measure as shown here.

Example 41: Dotted-quarter pattern with rhythm section

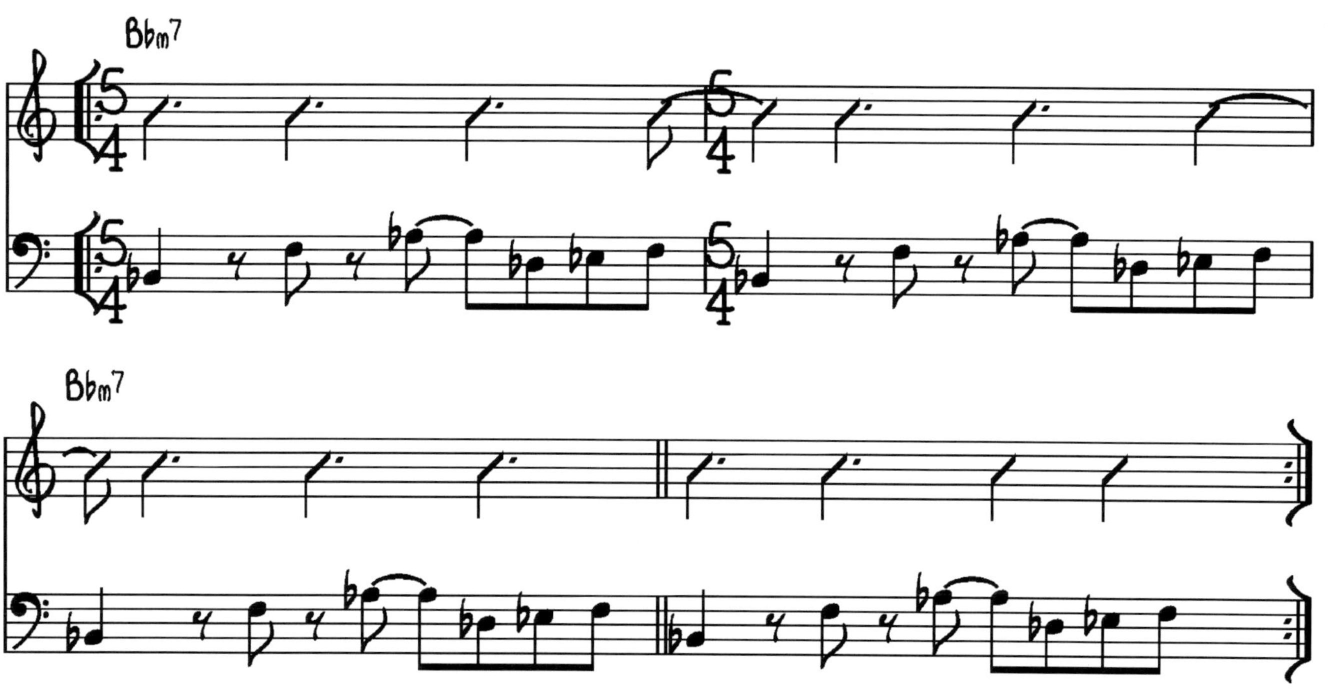

We can also break up the dotted-quarter duration into two 8th notes and an 8th rest. This rhythm can be used as a melody, a comping line, or as the chordal rhythm. I have also added a third layer using a three-beat cycle where chords can be placed. The result is groupings of 3 quarters against grouping of 3 eighths.

Example 42: Three layers in 5/4 with rhythm section

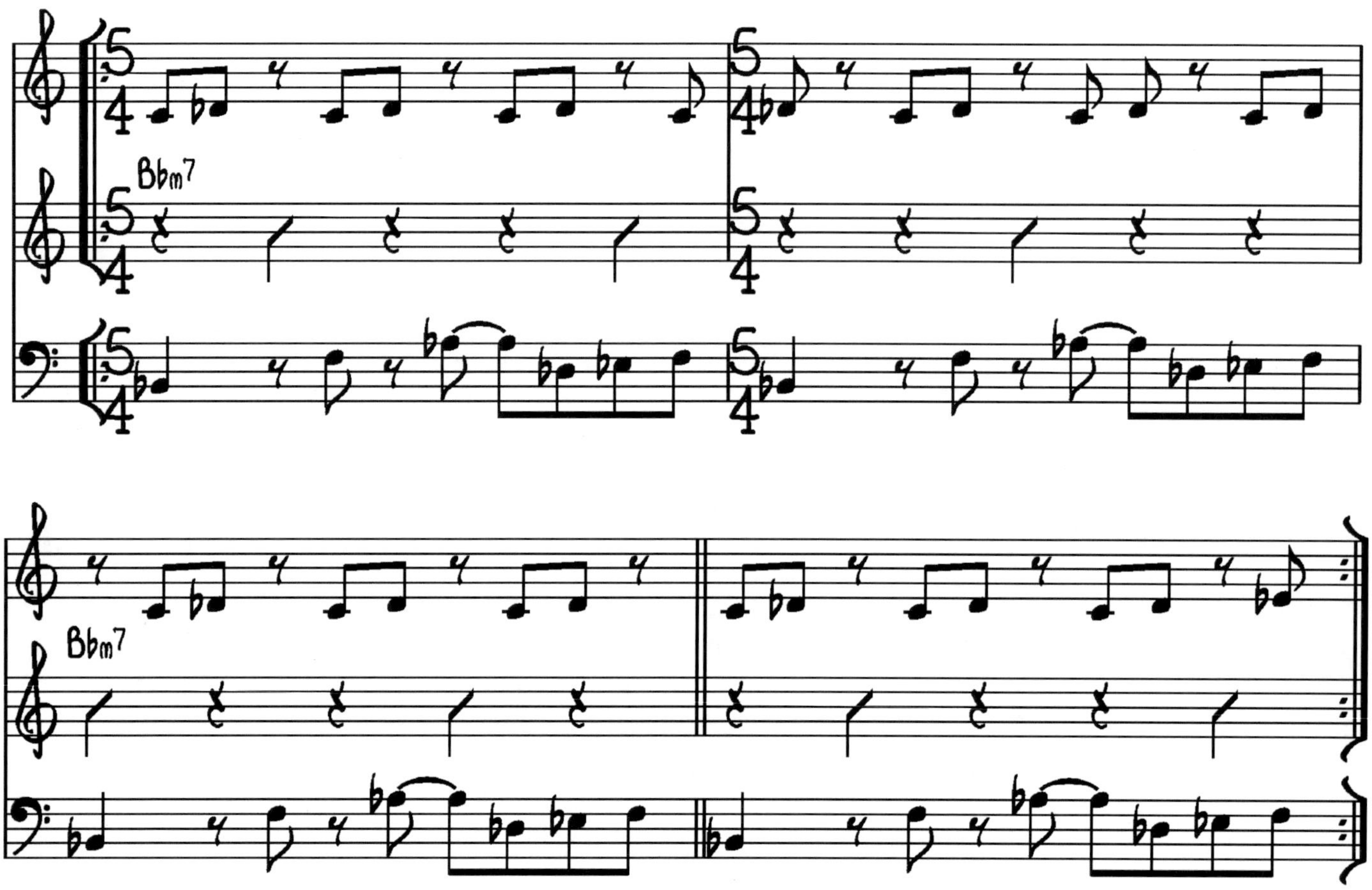

Example 43: "5/4 Blues" with rhythm section (BT, bass and drums only)

Example 44: "5/4 Blues" with rhythm section and guitar

Swing feel

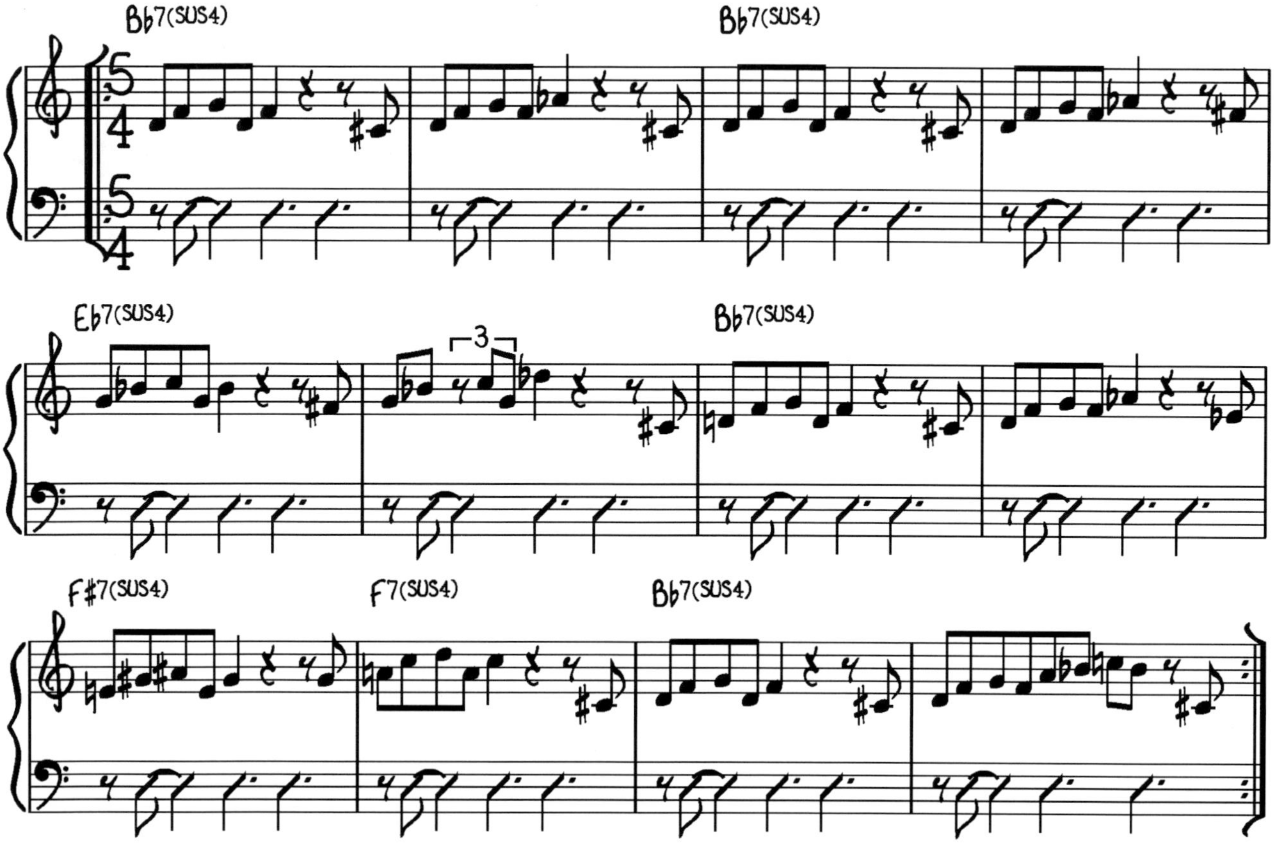

Example 45: Four variations with rhythm section

Here are 4 more rhythmic variations used as bass lines. Each measure can serve as a groove in itself. Play each measure individually before going on to play along with the four-measure backing track.

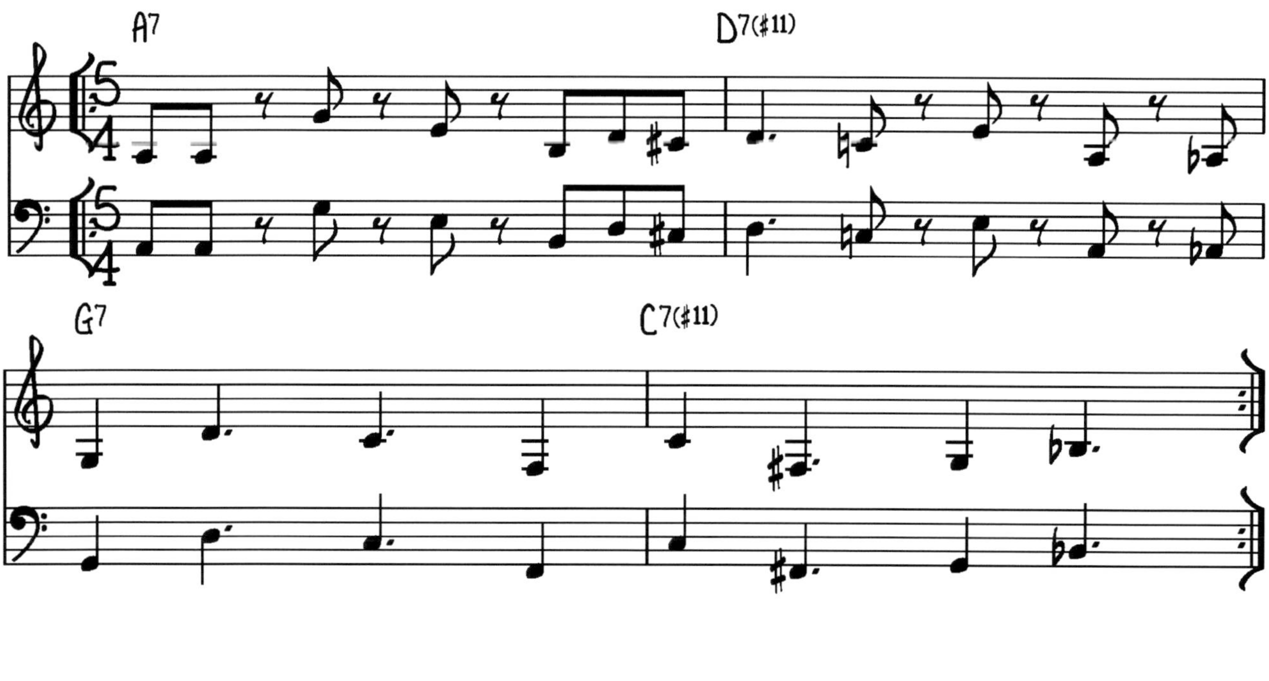

Adding Chord Progressions:

Example 46 (BT)

Now try the 3 and 2 division with a ii-V-I-vi chord progression which moves in half steps.

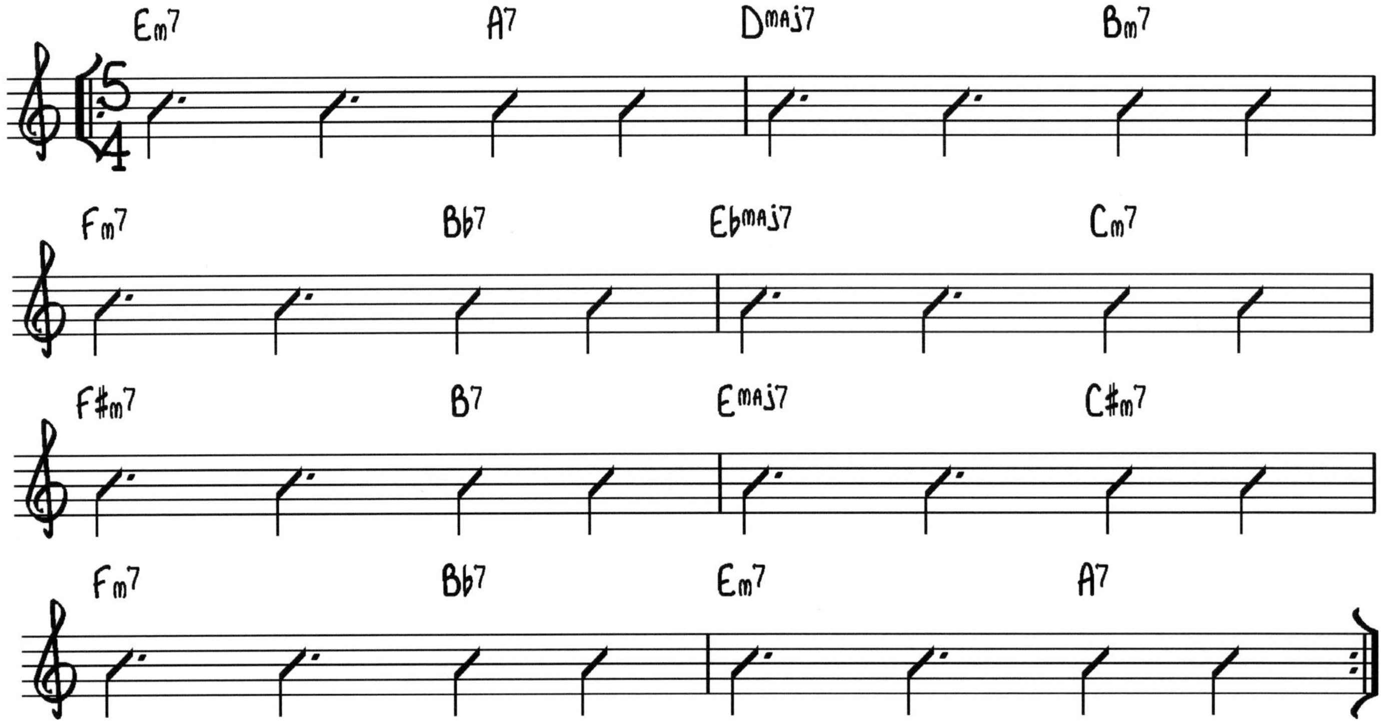

Example 46A (BT)

The retrograde clave of 3 and 2 using the same progression.

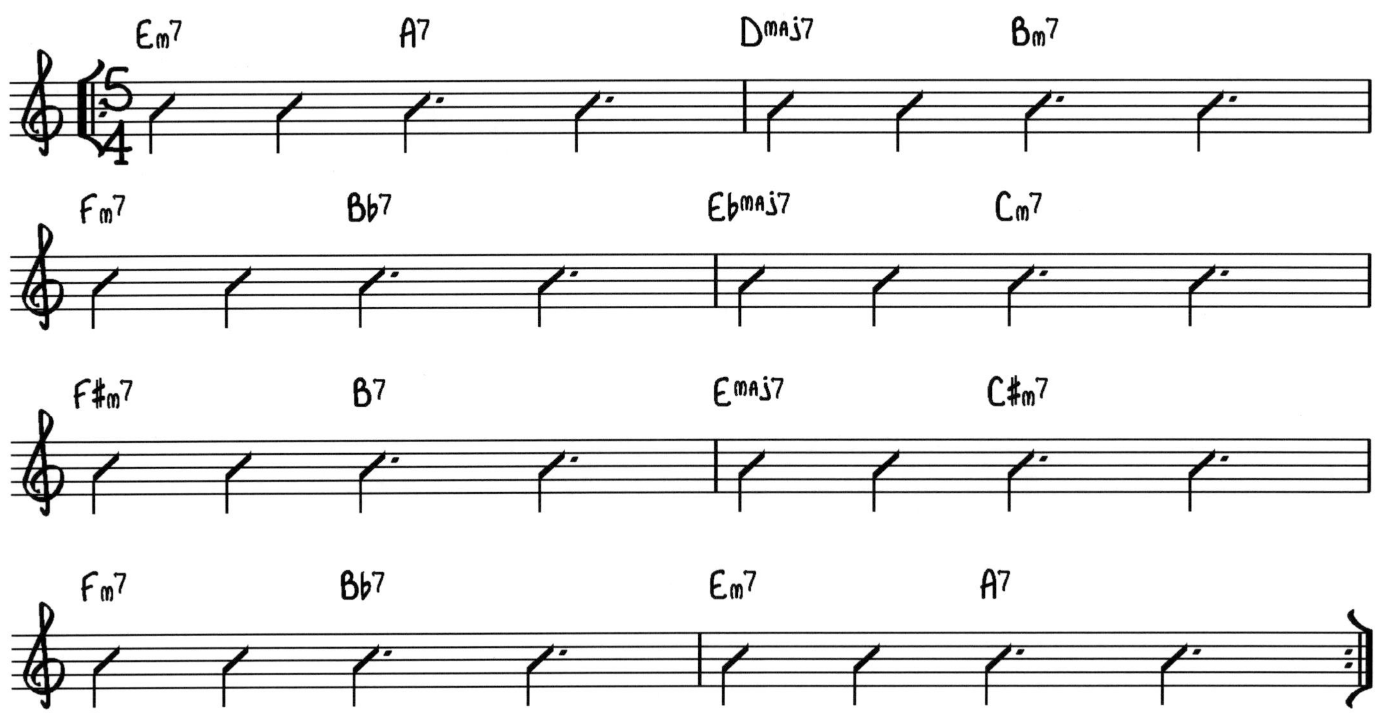

Example 47: "Available Light" with rhythm section

This next example can be felt as a slow five. The recording begins with 2 measures of chords before the rhythm section enters.

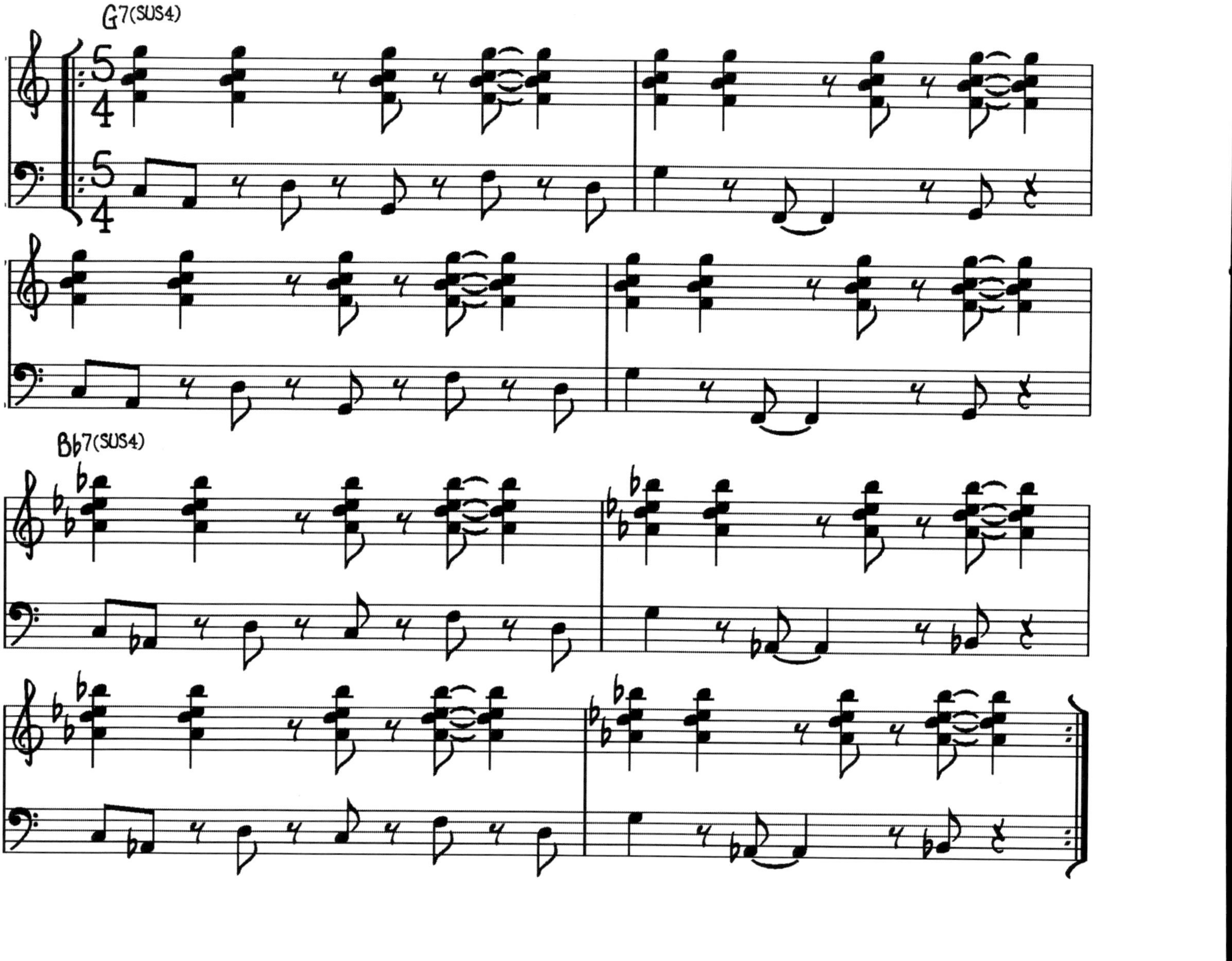

8. SEVENS

Many musicians might agree that 7/4 is the easiest odd meter to learn. The most common division is 4 and 3. It lends itself well to standards because the chord changes can easily be divided into bars of 4/4 and 3/4.

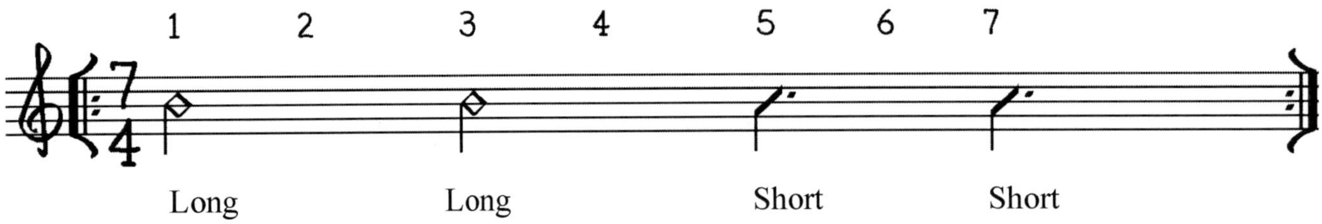

Now we will break up the measure into various patterns of quarters and dotted quarters. Clap these variations along with a metronome or the clave.

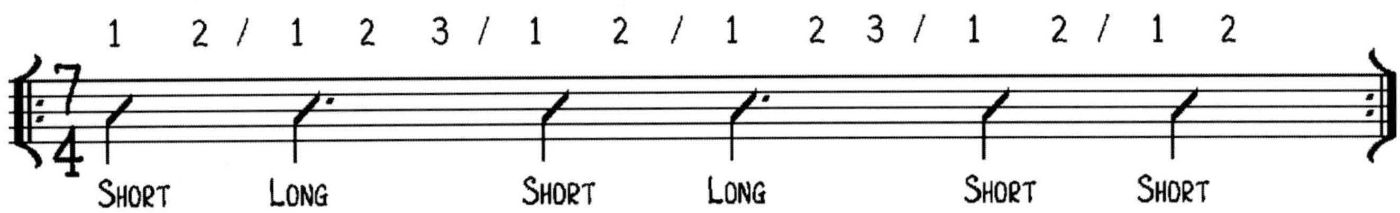

More variations; these will be explored further in Examples 48 – 50:

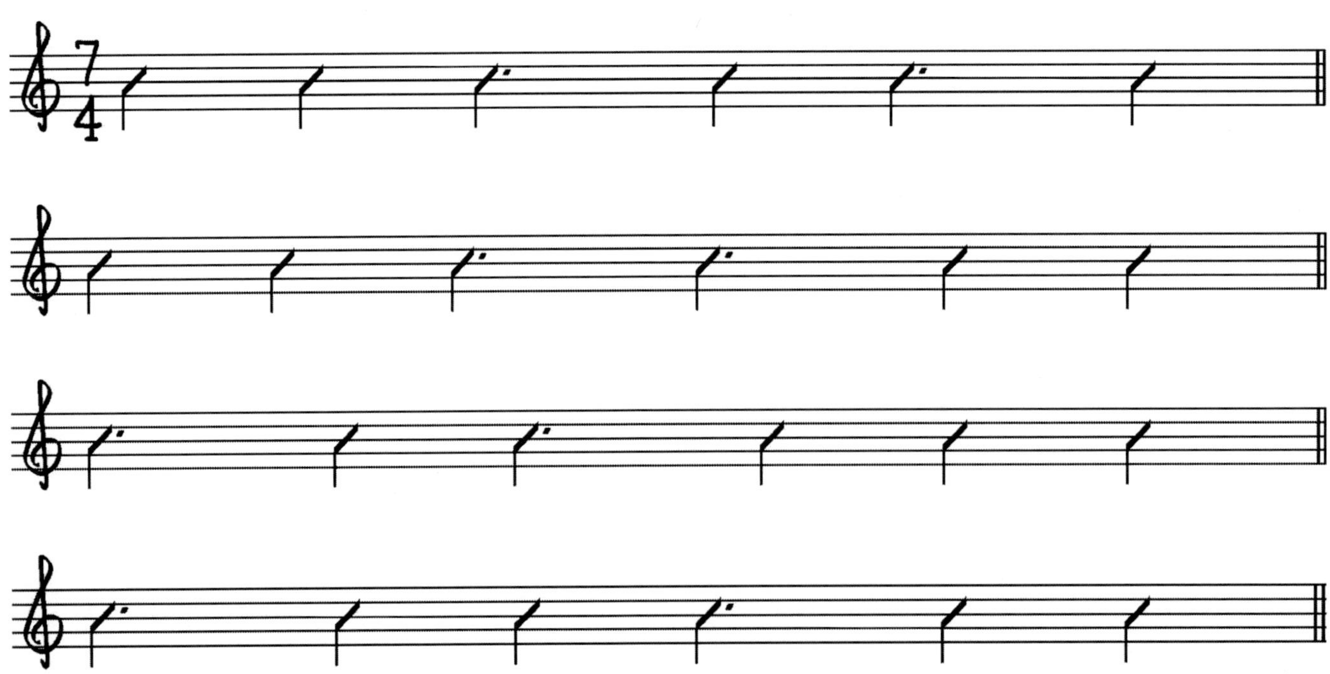

Grooves in 7

Here is the 4 and 3 clave as a bass line with a comping pattern. This meter works well with a samba feel and is used in my composition "Samba 7". Pianists and guitarists can try to play both parts simultaneously. Remember that we want the groove to sound continuous, rather than as if it is starting over at each downbeat. Work on the bass line first. Once you feel comfortable with the comping rhythm, try to improvise using your own variations.

Example 48: "Samba 7" BT with bass and drums only

Example 48A: "Samba 7" with rhythm section plus guitar

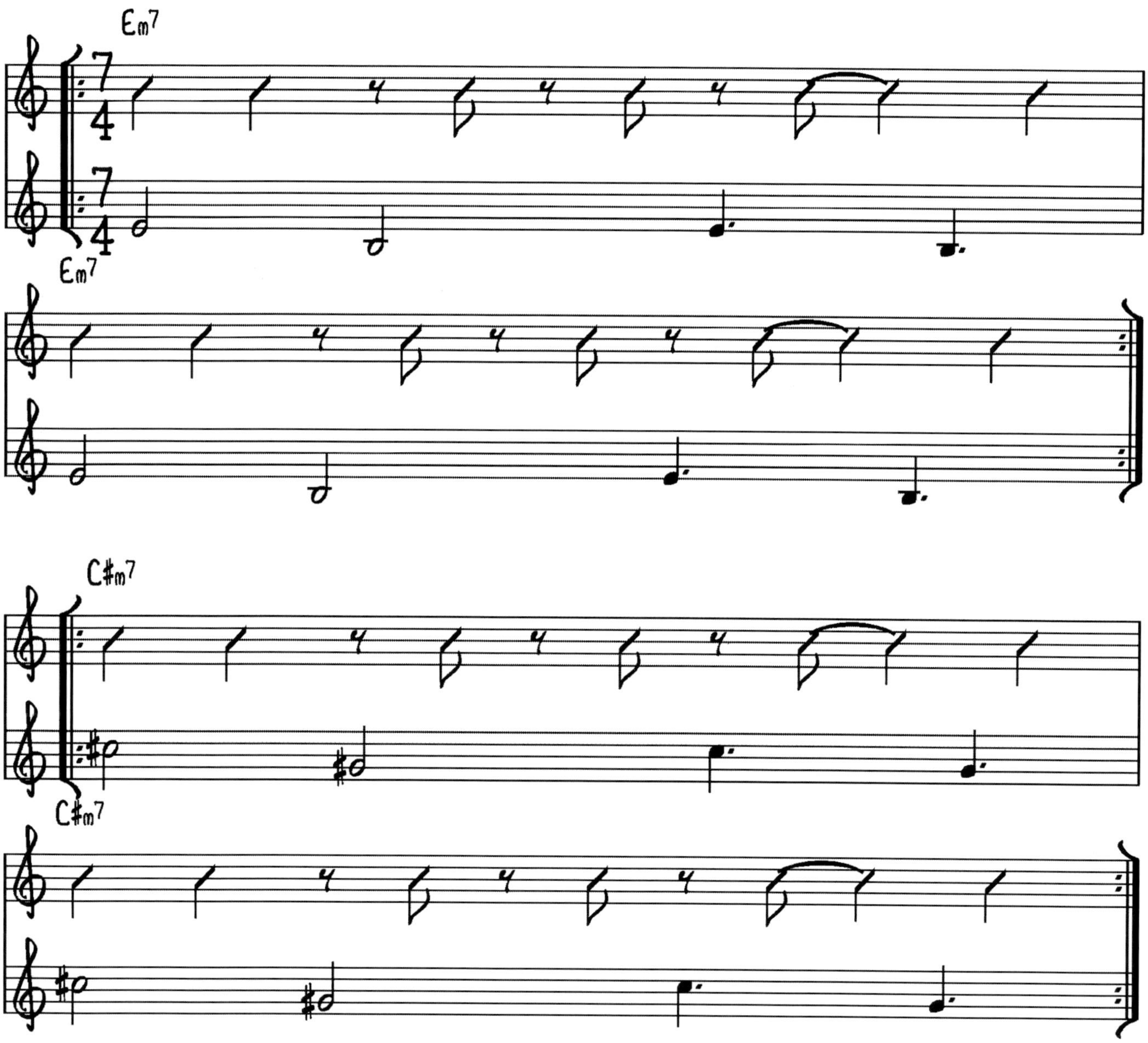

Variations with Rhythm Section

Here are 5 groups of various rhythms that can be used to get to know different ways of breaking up 7/4. Clap or play along with the recordings to get to know each one. The rhythms are played a few times by the guitar, then the backing track continues so that you can clap or play the rhythms by yourself.

Example 49 Group 1

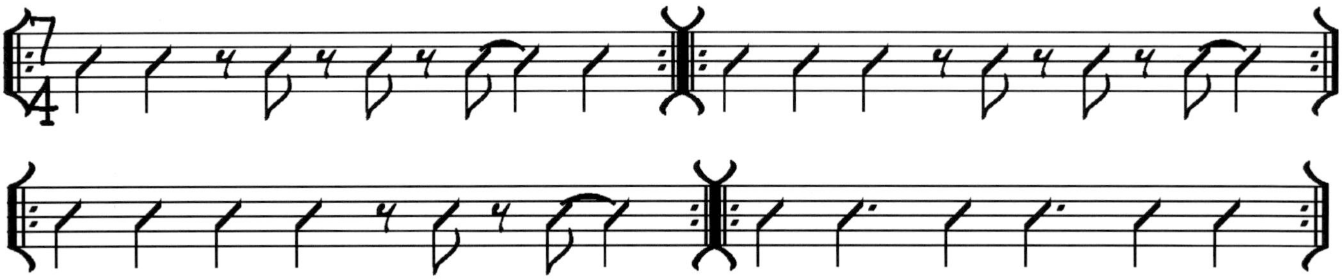

Example 49A Group 2

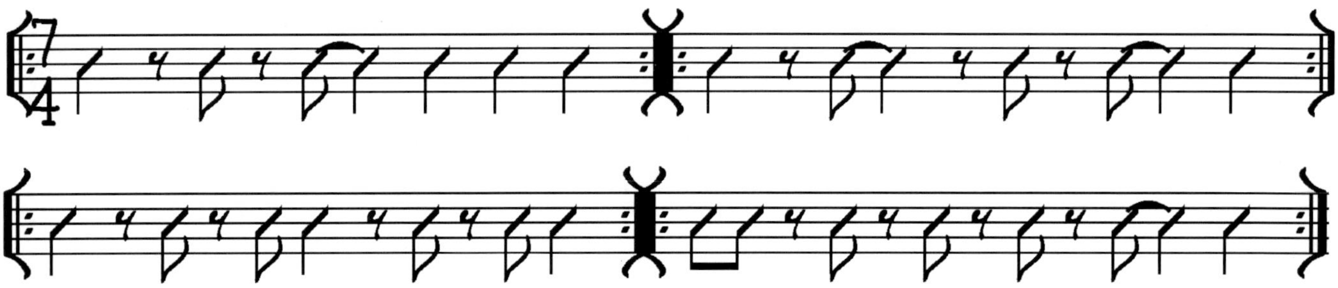

Example 49B Group 3

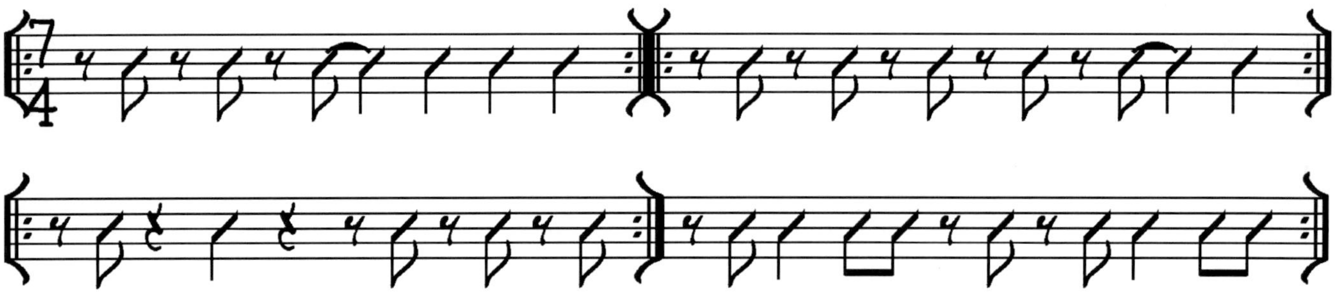

Example 49C Group 4

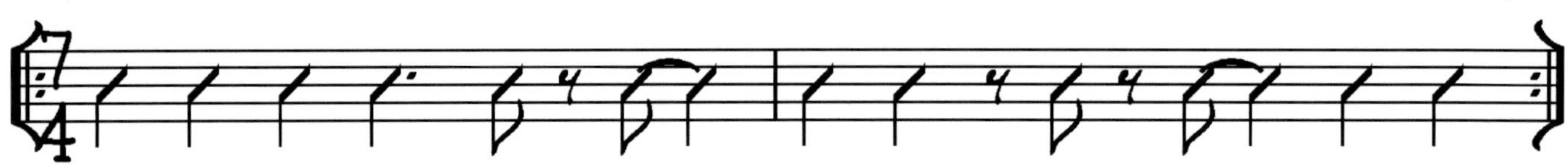

<u>Example 49D Group 5</u>

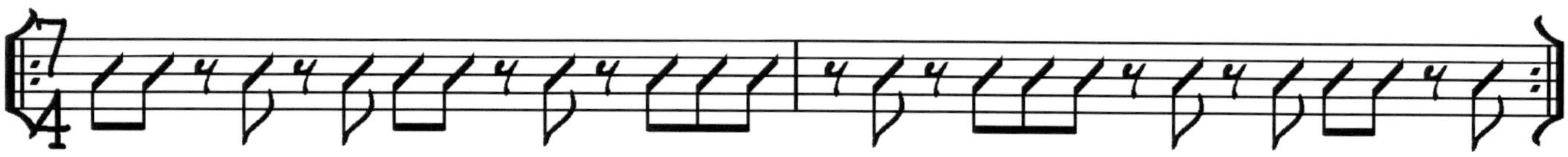

The next two examples use the same chart as Example 48, but at a faster tempo.

<u>Example 50: "Samba 7" up-tempo with bass and drums only</u>

<u>Example 50A: "Samba 7" up-tempo with rhythm section</u>

<u>Example 51: Dotted-quarter pattern in 7/4</u>

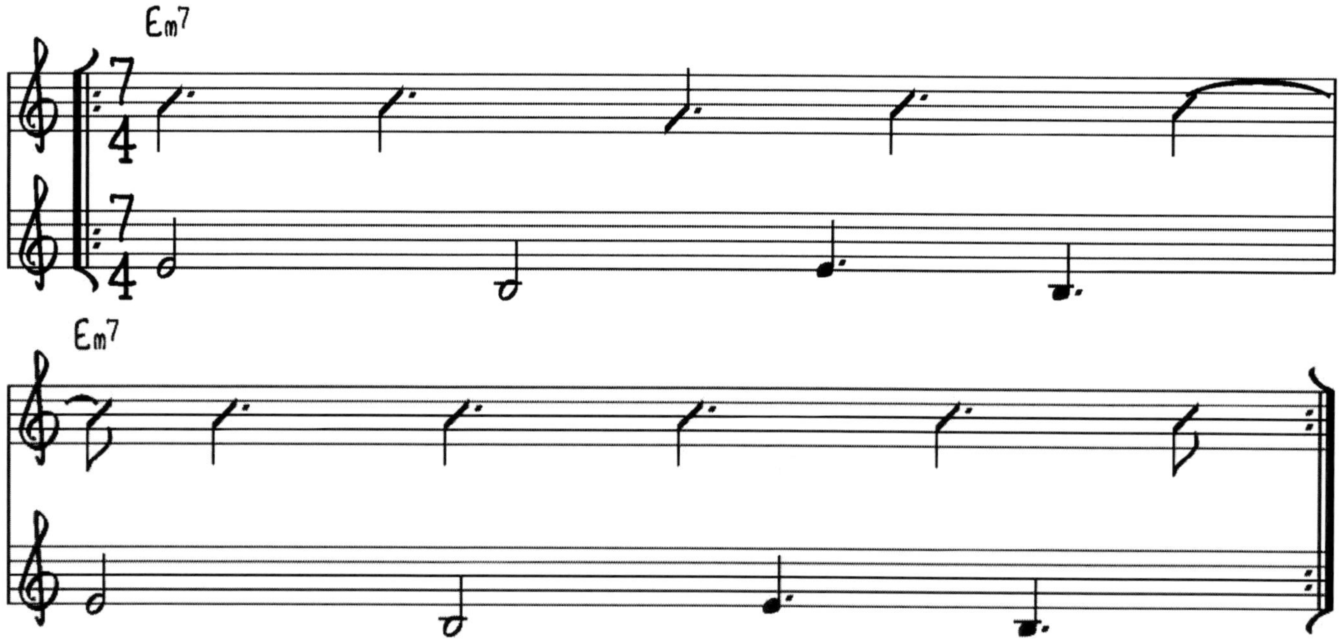

<u>Example 52: Pattern grouped in fives</u>

Two-measure comping pattern using groups of five 8th notes. (Play over 4 and 3 clave.)

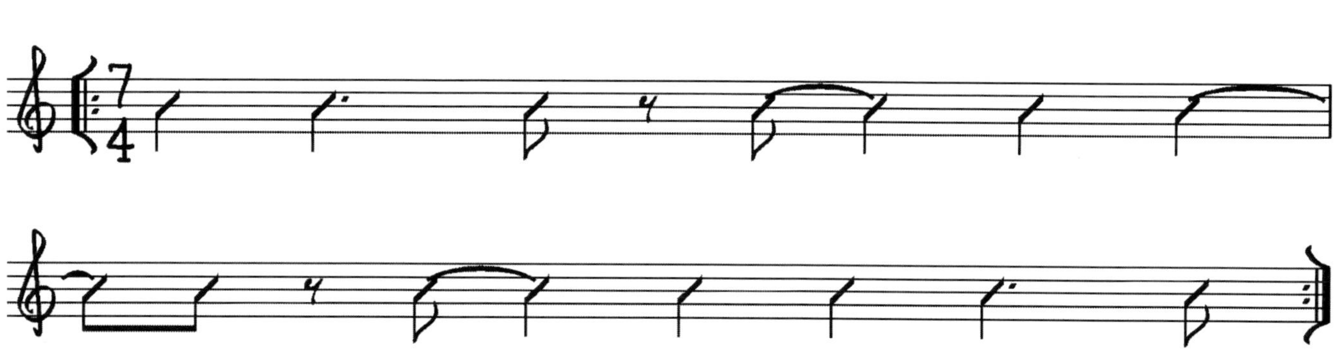

Example 53: 7/4 clave variation

Here is a variation of the 4 and 3 clave in which the third note is delayed by an 8th.

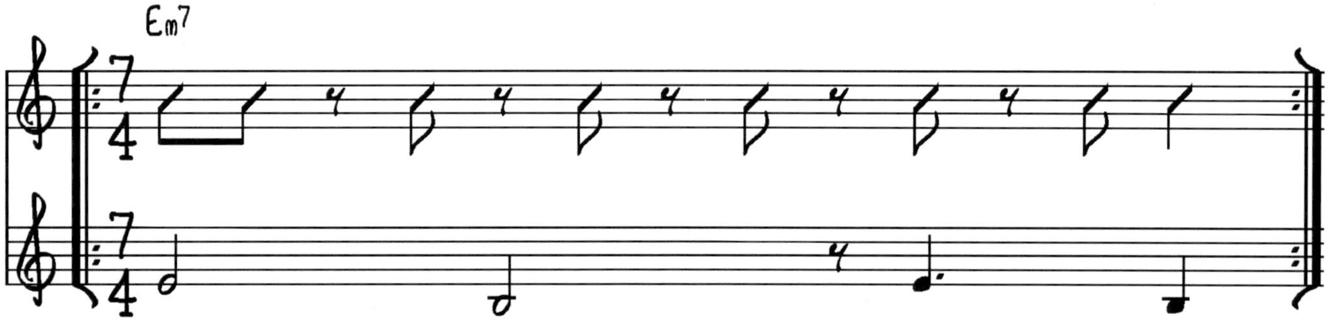

Example 54

Here's the retrograde clave of 3 and 4.

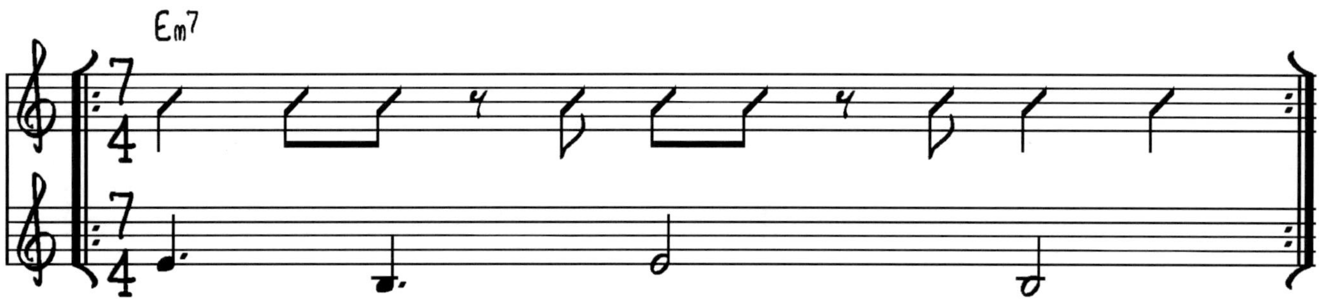

Example 55: Two-measure 7/4 groove

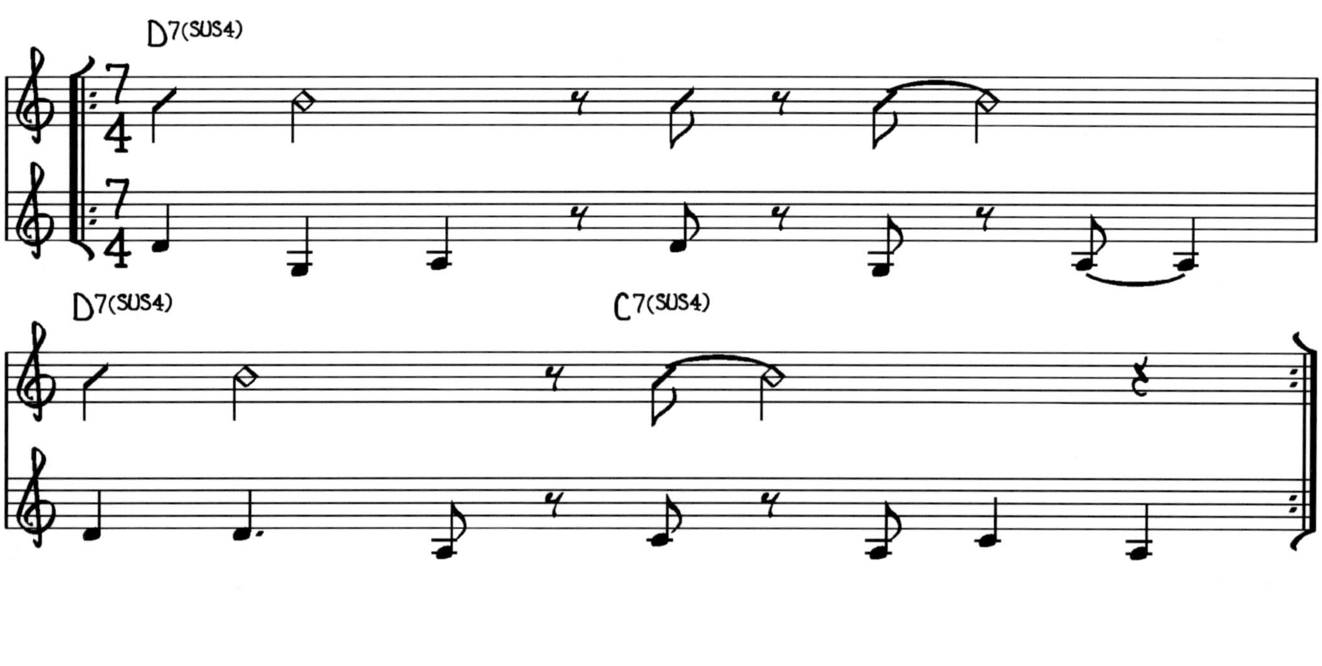

This page has been left blank to avoid an awkward page turn.

Example 56: "Blues in 7/4" with bass and drums only

Example 56A: "Blues in 7/4" with rhythm section

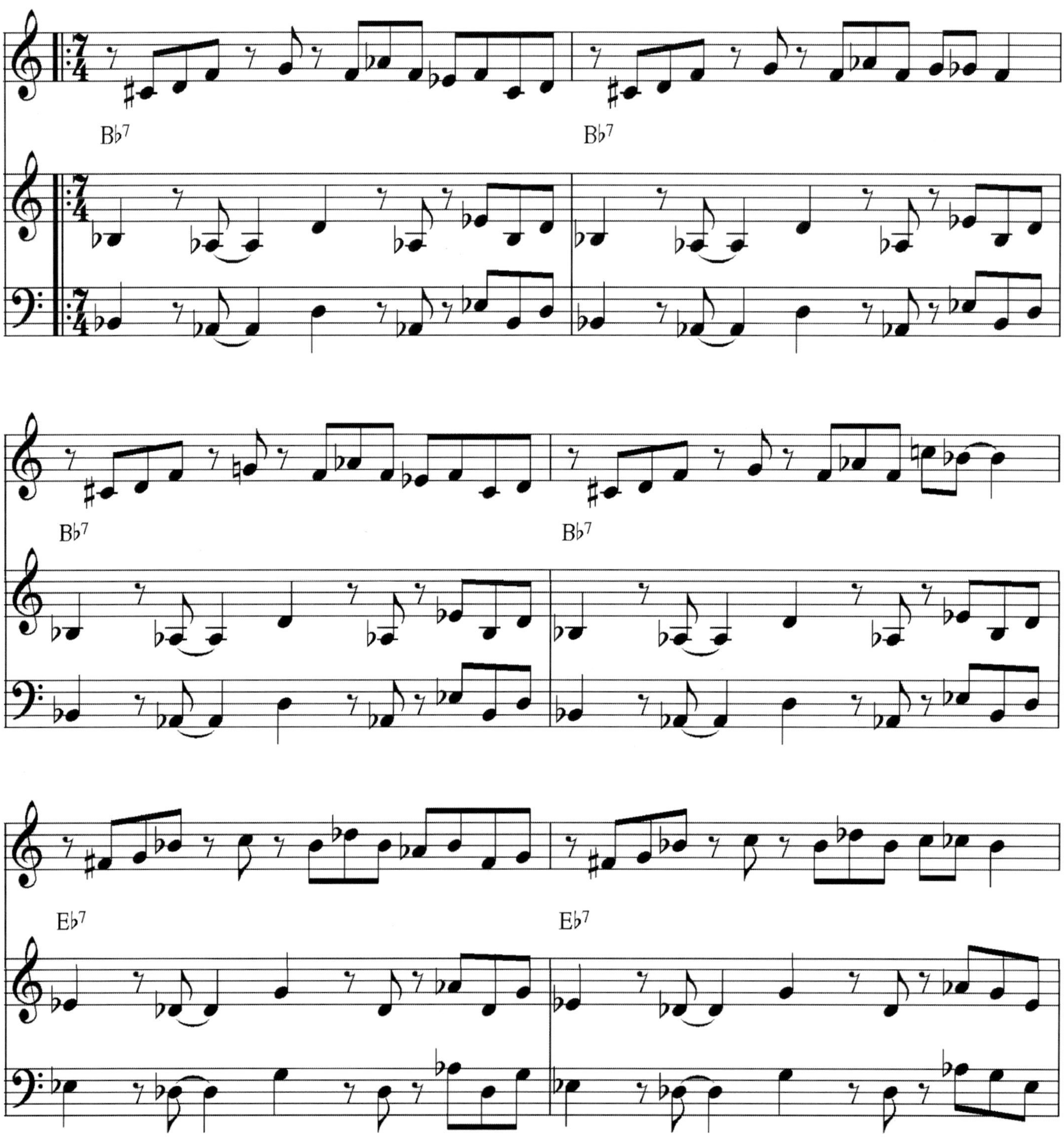

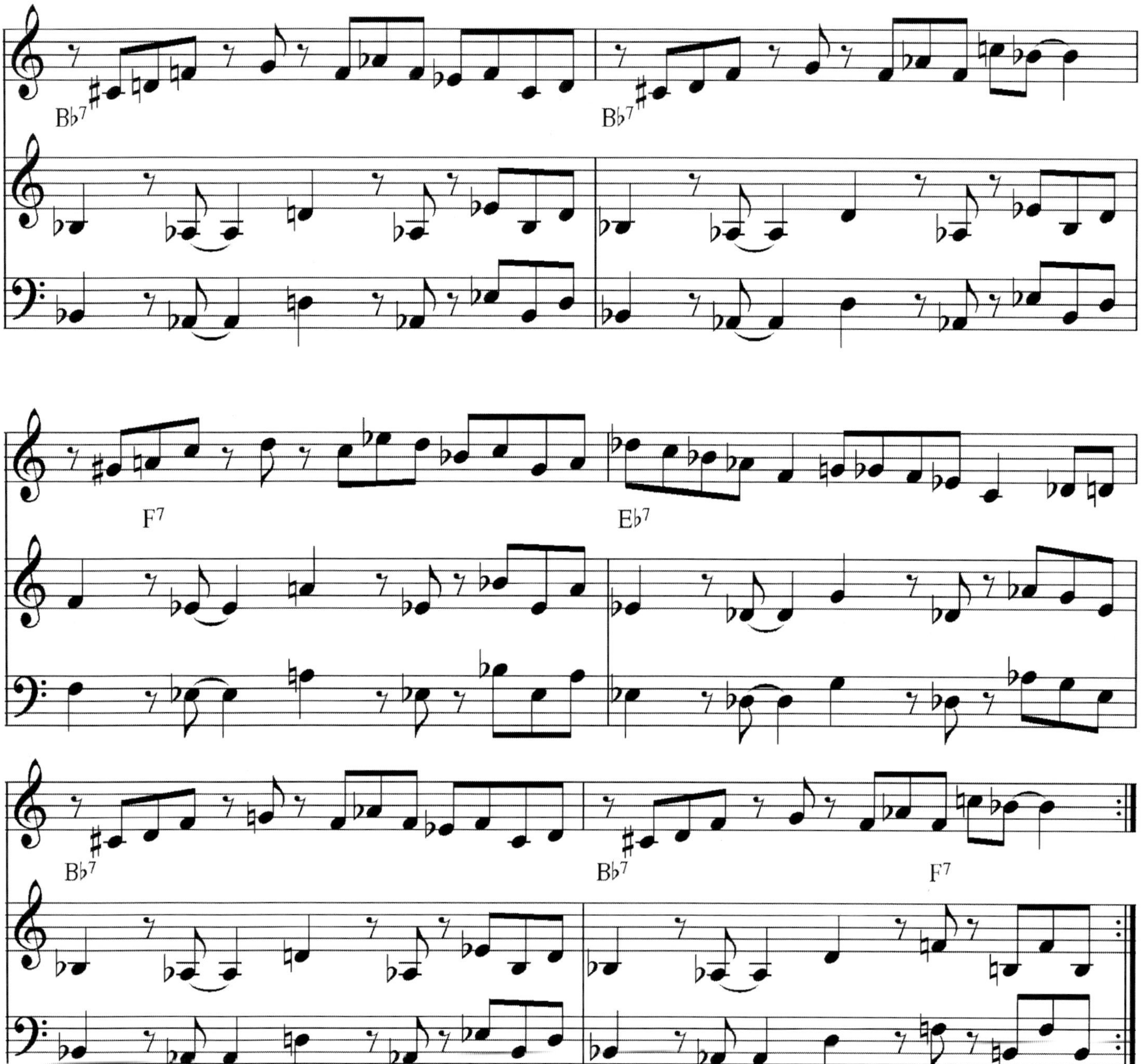
B♭7
B♭7
F7
E♭7
B♭7
B♭7
F7

Example 57 (BT)

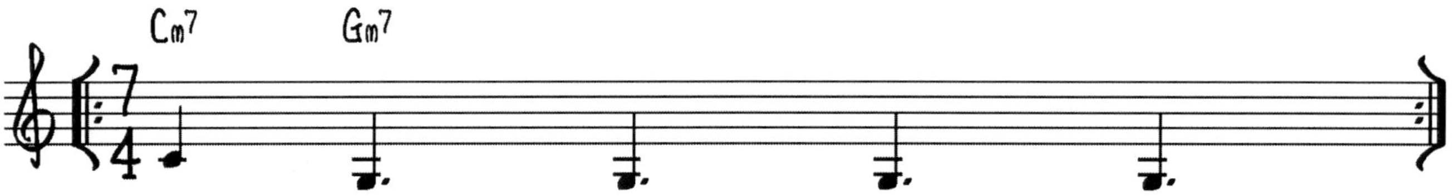

Example 58: Slow Swing feel with rhythm section

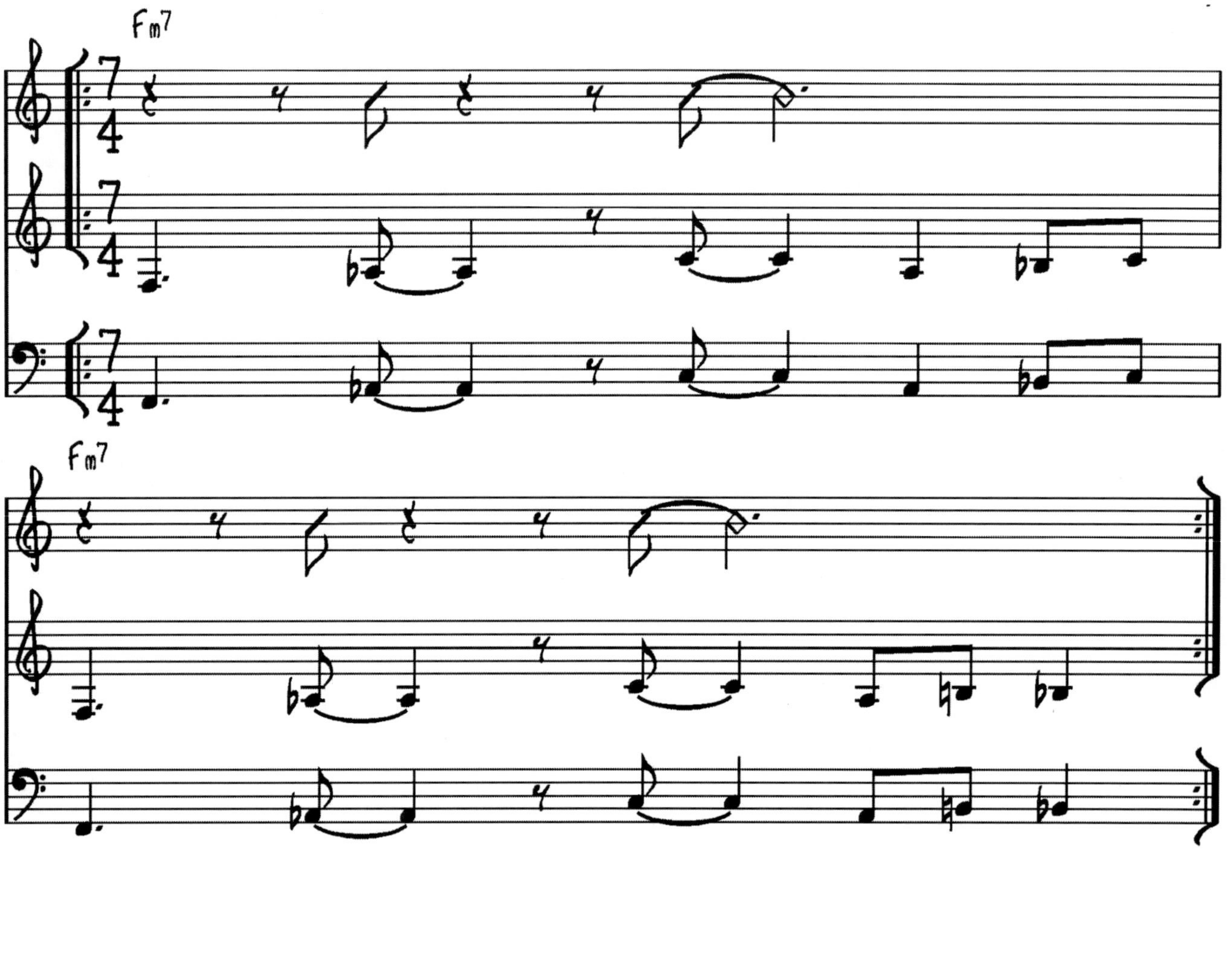

7/4 Patterns with No Downbeat:

Example 59

Here it can be helpful to play the chord or bass drum on the downbeat while getting to know the pattern.

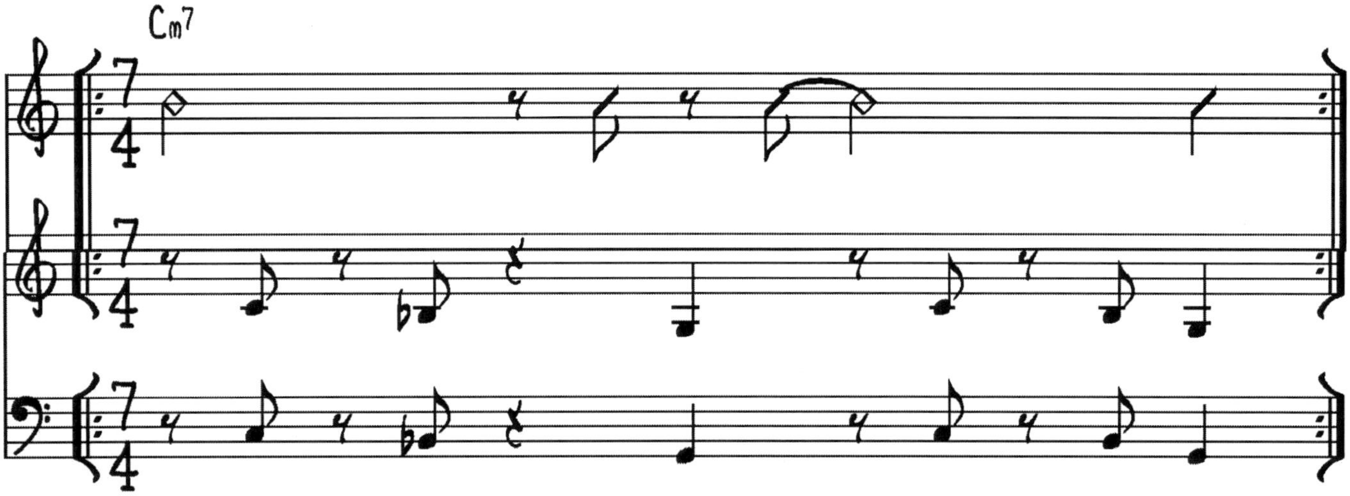

Example 60

Chords are played on beat one.

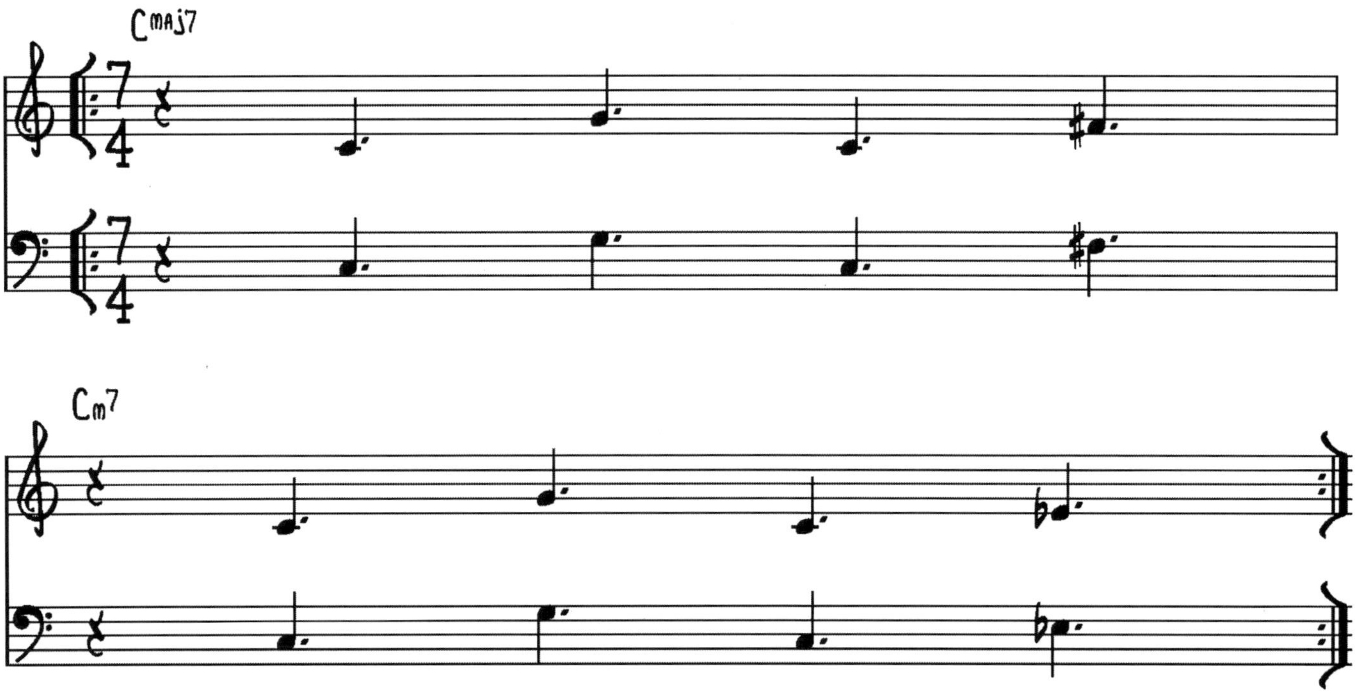

Example 61 with rhythm section:

Here we have a tied note at the end of the pattern that bypasses the downbeat.

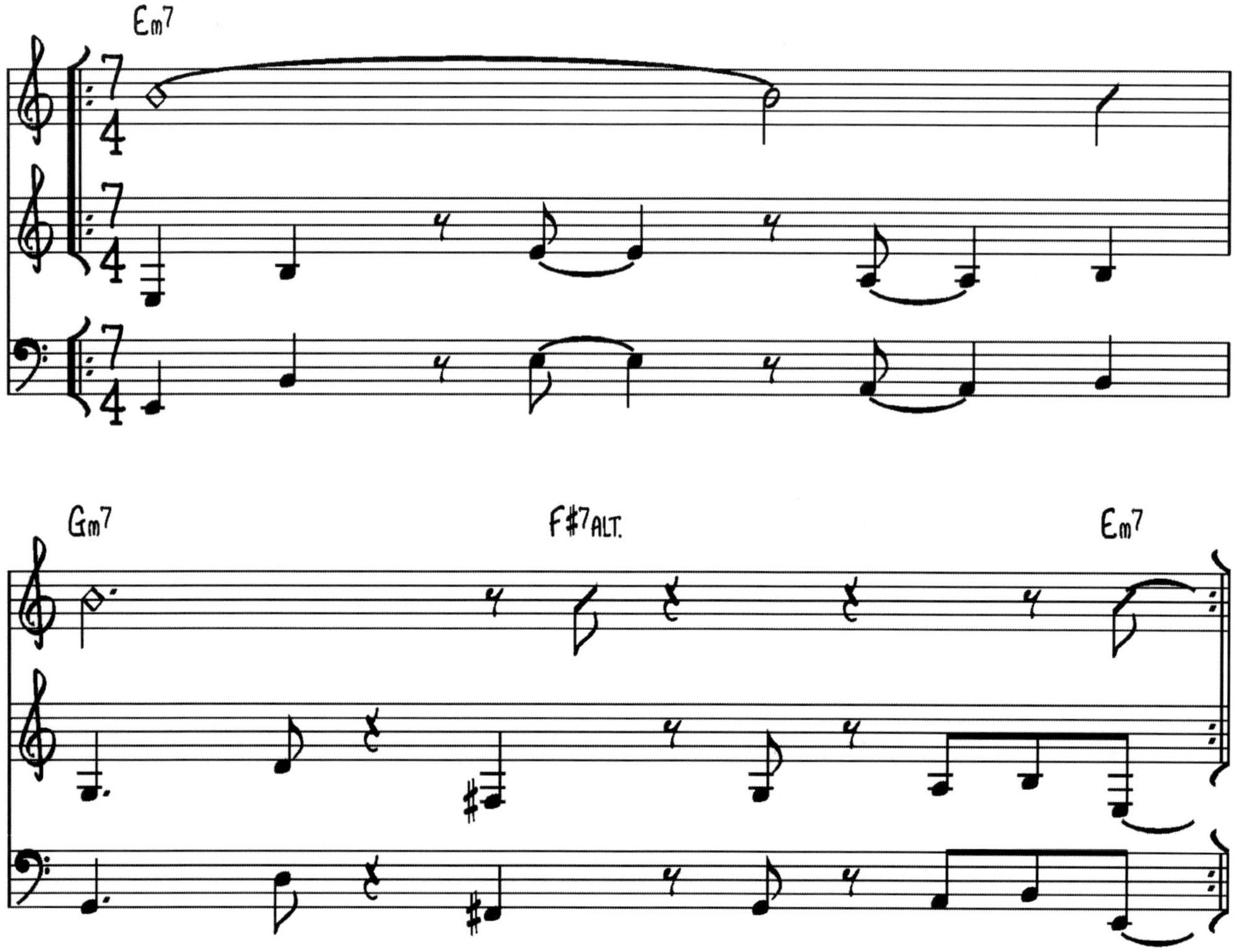

More Examples in 7/4

Example 62: (BT)

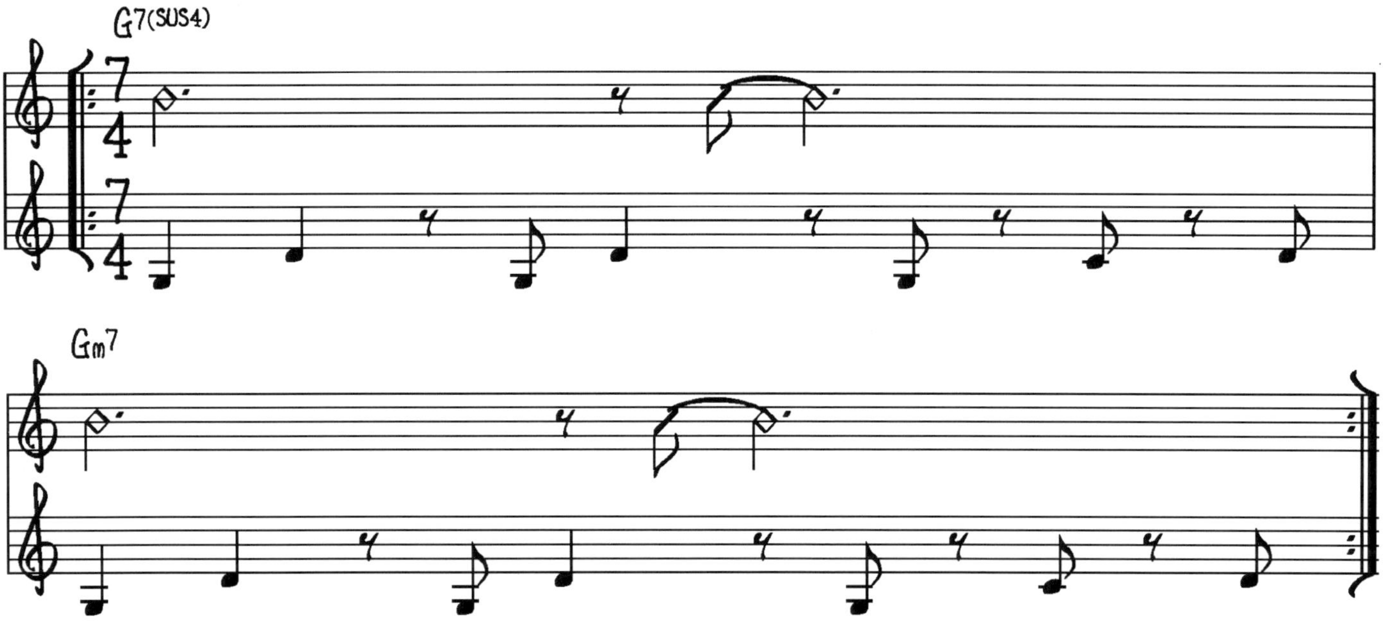

Example 63: Funk groove in 7/4 (BT)

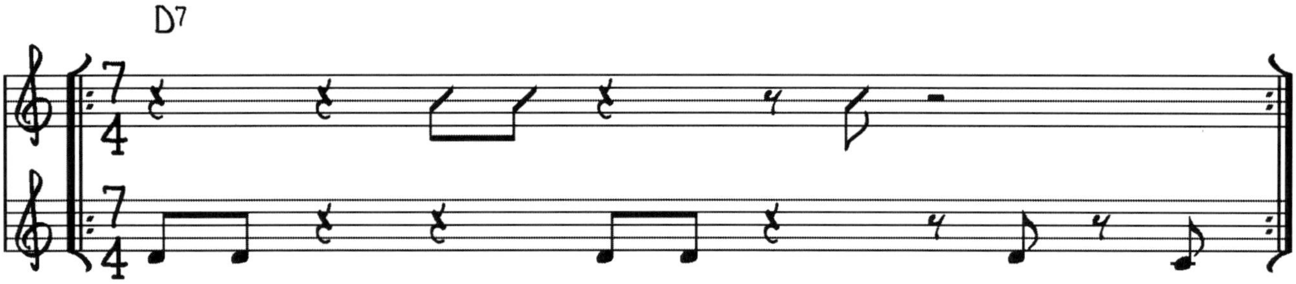

7/4 with standard chord changes:

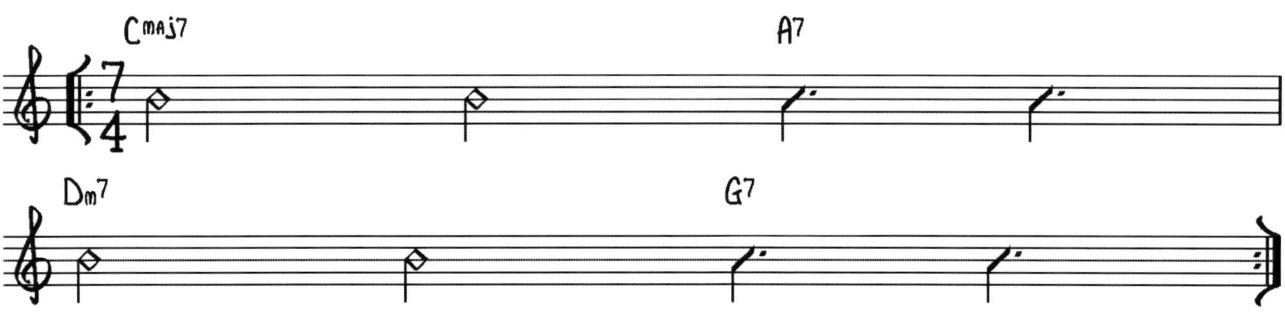

Example 64: 7/4 groove with 3 layers

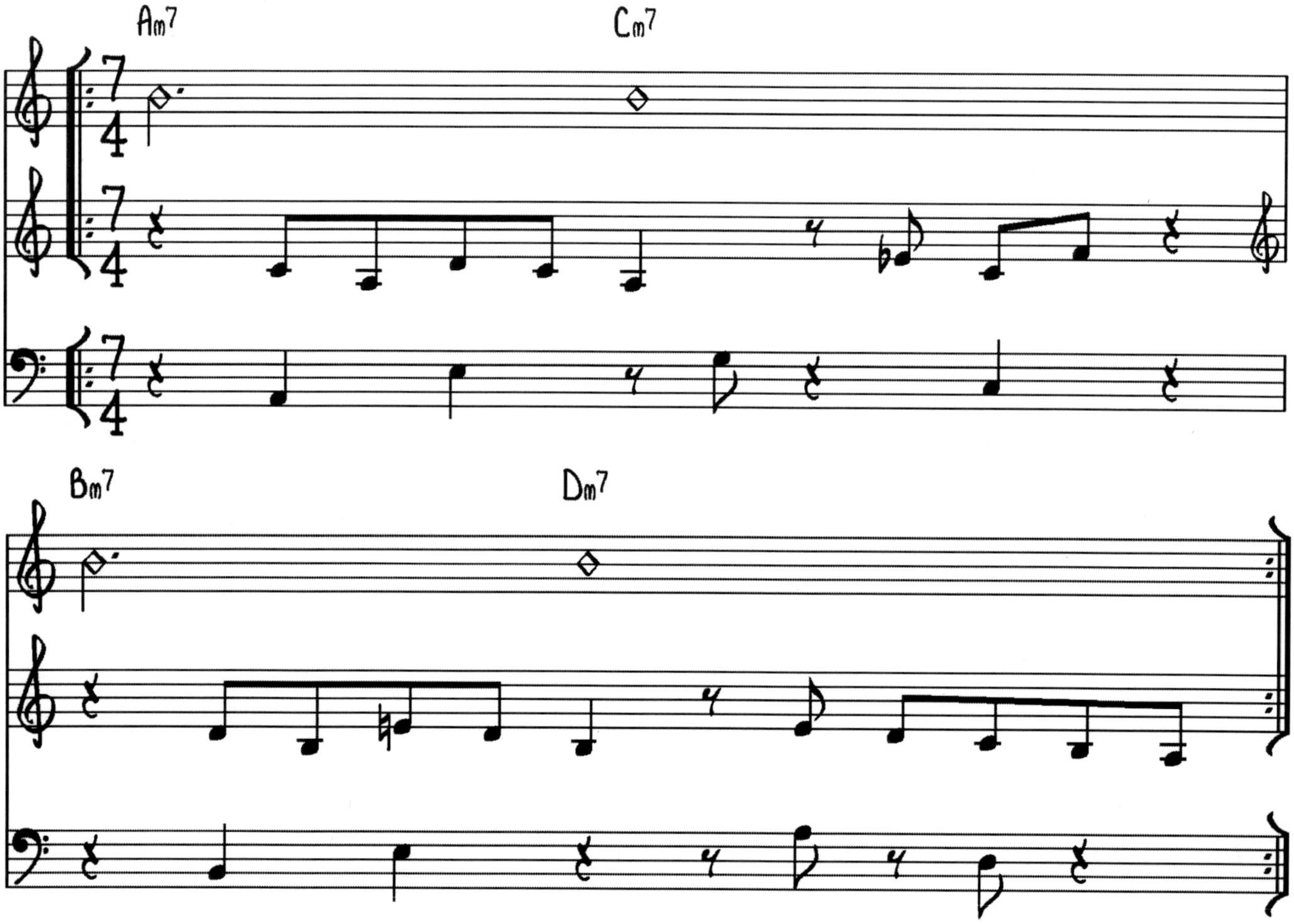

9. NINES

The ways in which we can divide the meter become more varied as the numbers get higher. The most common claves for nine are 2 / 2 / 2 / 3 and 2 / 2 / 3 / 2.

This pattern is common in Turkey and Bulgaria.

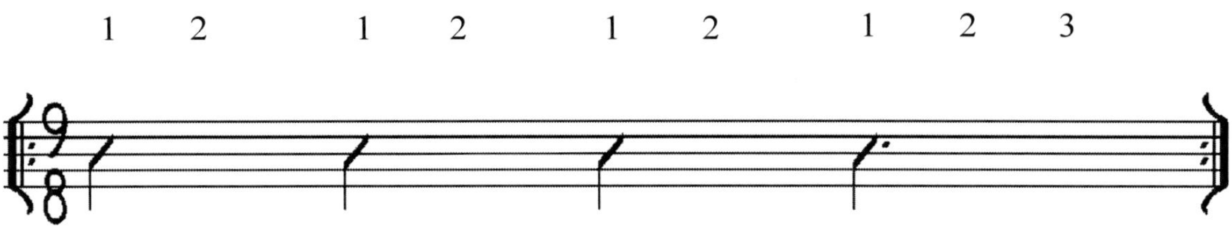

Example 65: Modal vamp with two rhythms (BT)

A common syncopation is created by superimposing three dotted quarter notes on top of this pattern. Try tapping each rhythm separately before combining them. You can also improvise over this simple modal vamp.

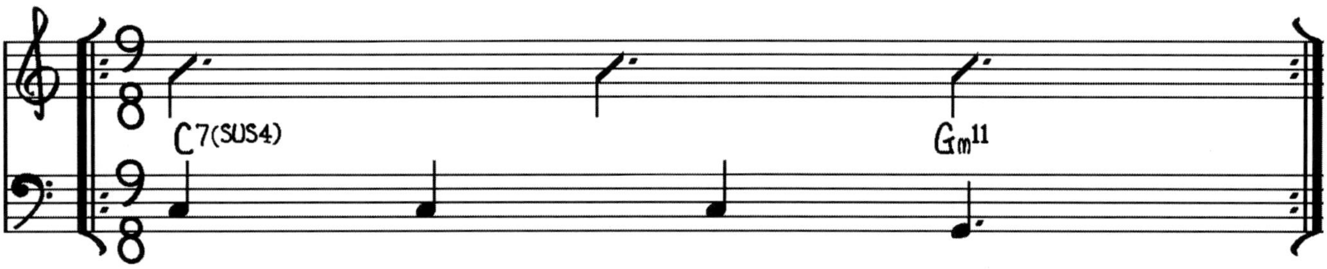

Example 66: 9/8 Balkan rhythm

This 9/8 rhythm found in the Balkan region is short   short – long – short.

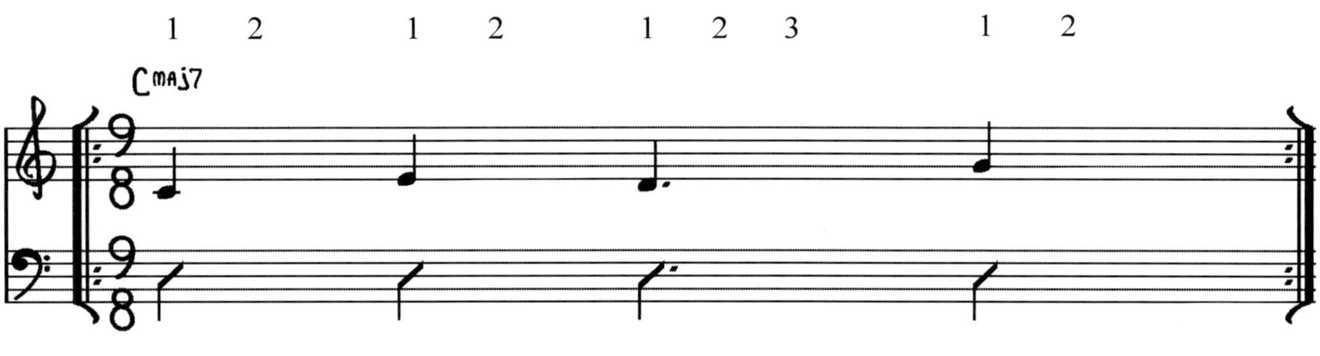

Variations:

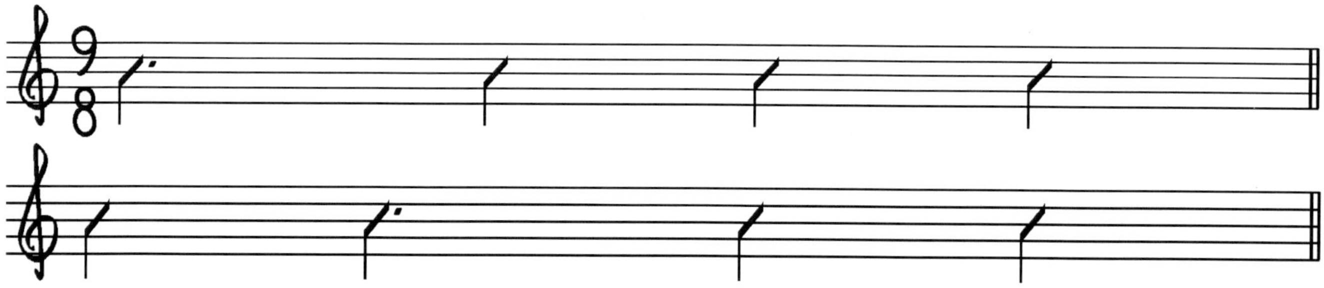

As the meter becomes longer, it is more likely that the groove can be divided into what feels like two measures of various meters. This breakdown can help us to navigate the new rhythm.

Example 67: Modal vamp in 9/4 (BT)

Feels like 5 and 4

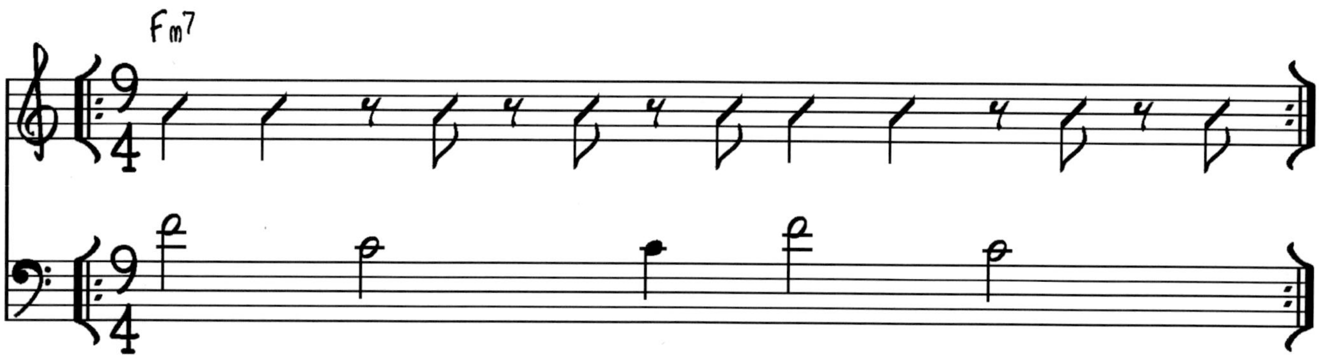

Example 68: Three-part invention in 9/4

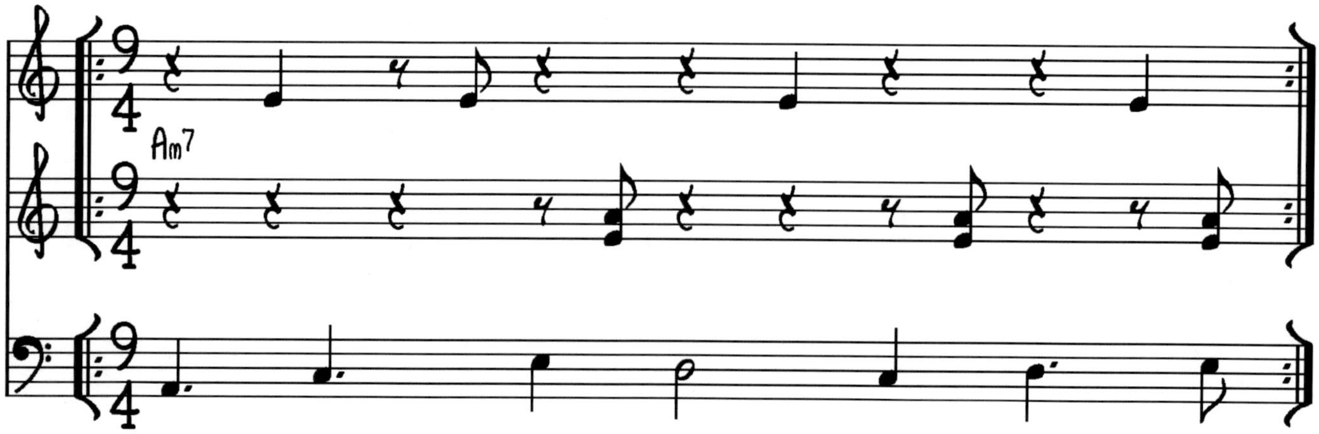

This page has been left blank to avoid an awkward page turn.

Example 69: "Minor Blues in 9/4" with bass and drums

Example 70: "Minor Blues in 9/4" with rhythm section

This meter can be broken into 4 and 5, or 3 and 6.

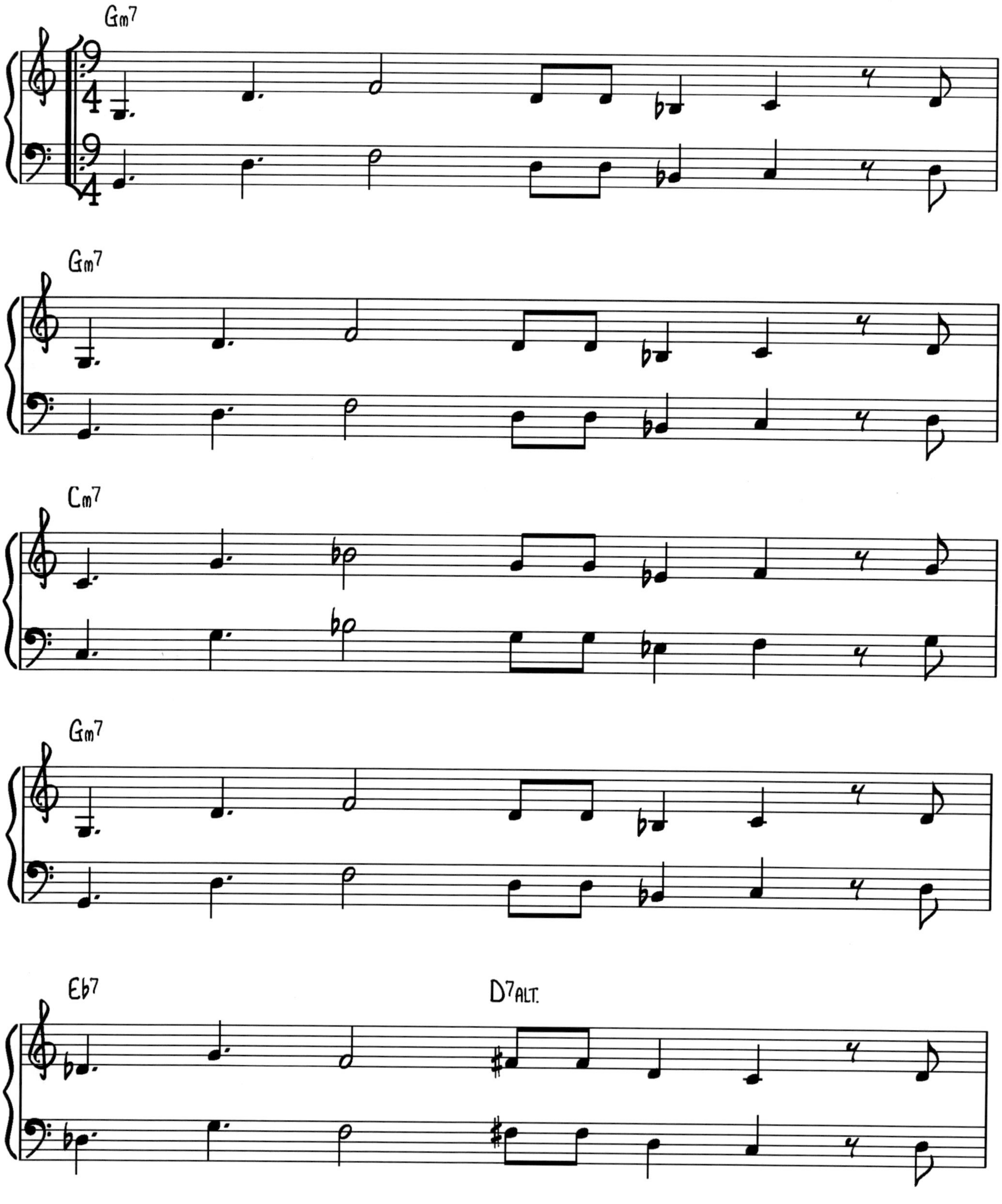

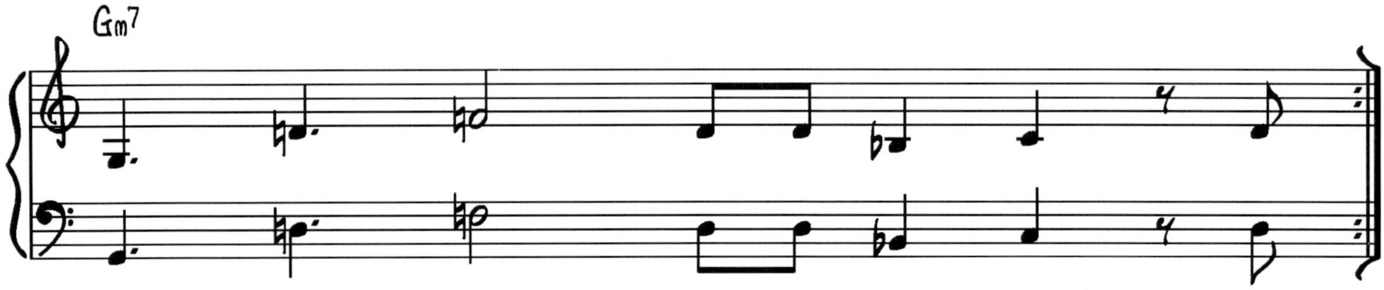

Example 71 Swing feel with rhythm section

Feels like 5 and 4.

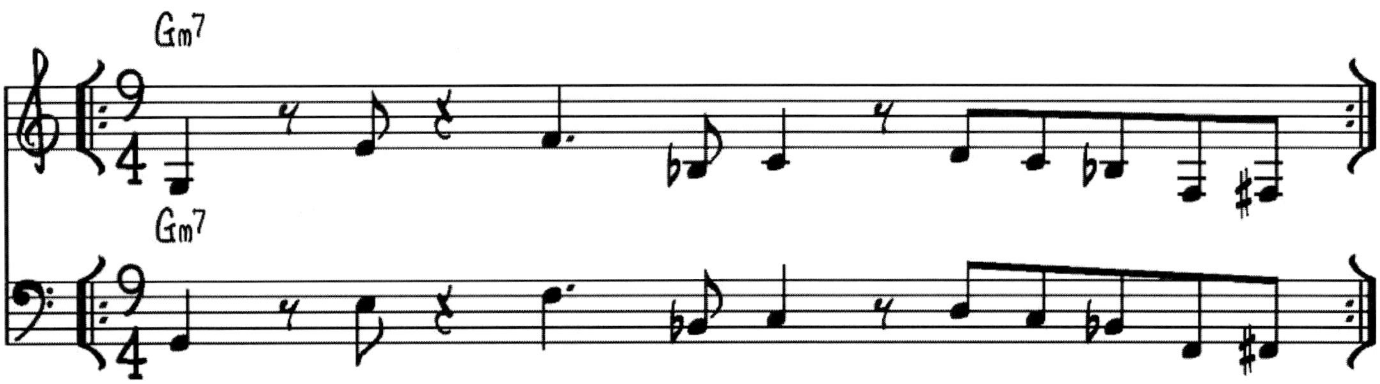

Example 72 with rhythm section

This example uses the same bass line as Example 71, but with a straight-8th note groove and a displaced comping pattern.

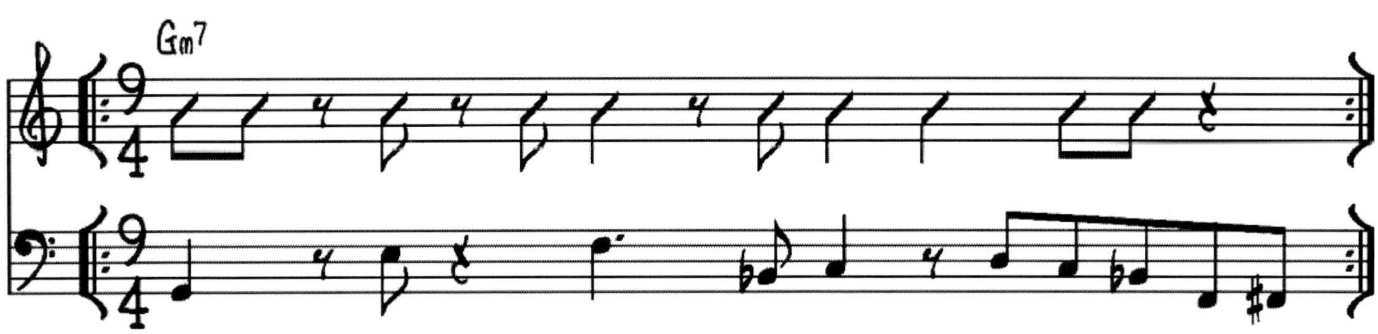

Here is another example of a comping pattern spaced evenly across the bar without starting on the downbeat. This can be very effective in creating the feeling of two different time feels simultaneously. If we begin with the upper symmetrical rhythm by itself, and then add the lower rhythm (as the backing track does), it has a surprising effect for the listener.

Example 73: Groove with symmetrical chord pattern - with rhythm section

Feels like 4 and 5. The track begins with chords only.

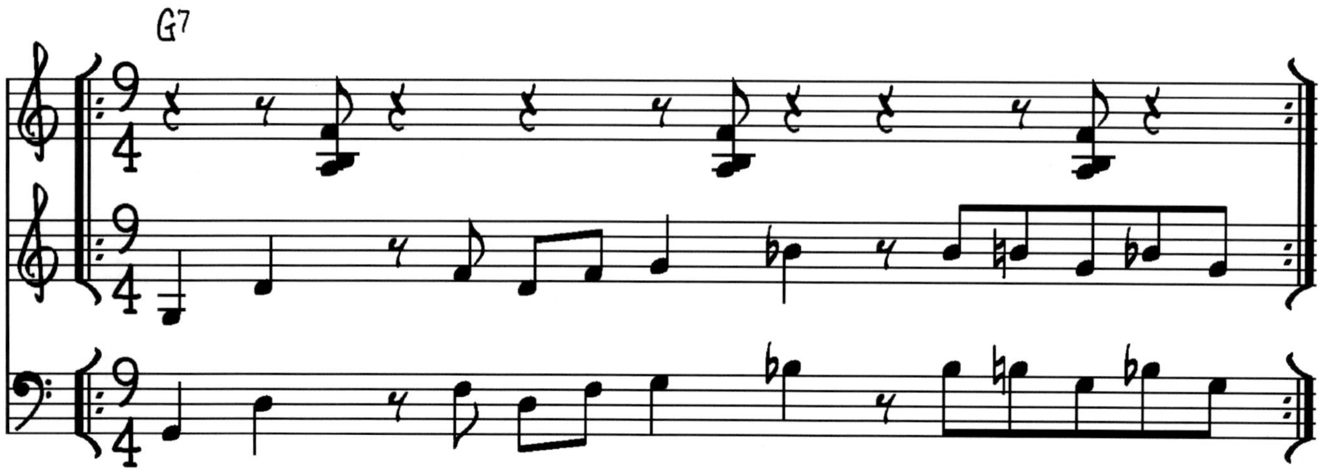

Example 74: 9/4 groove with chord changes and rhythm section

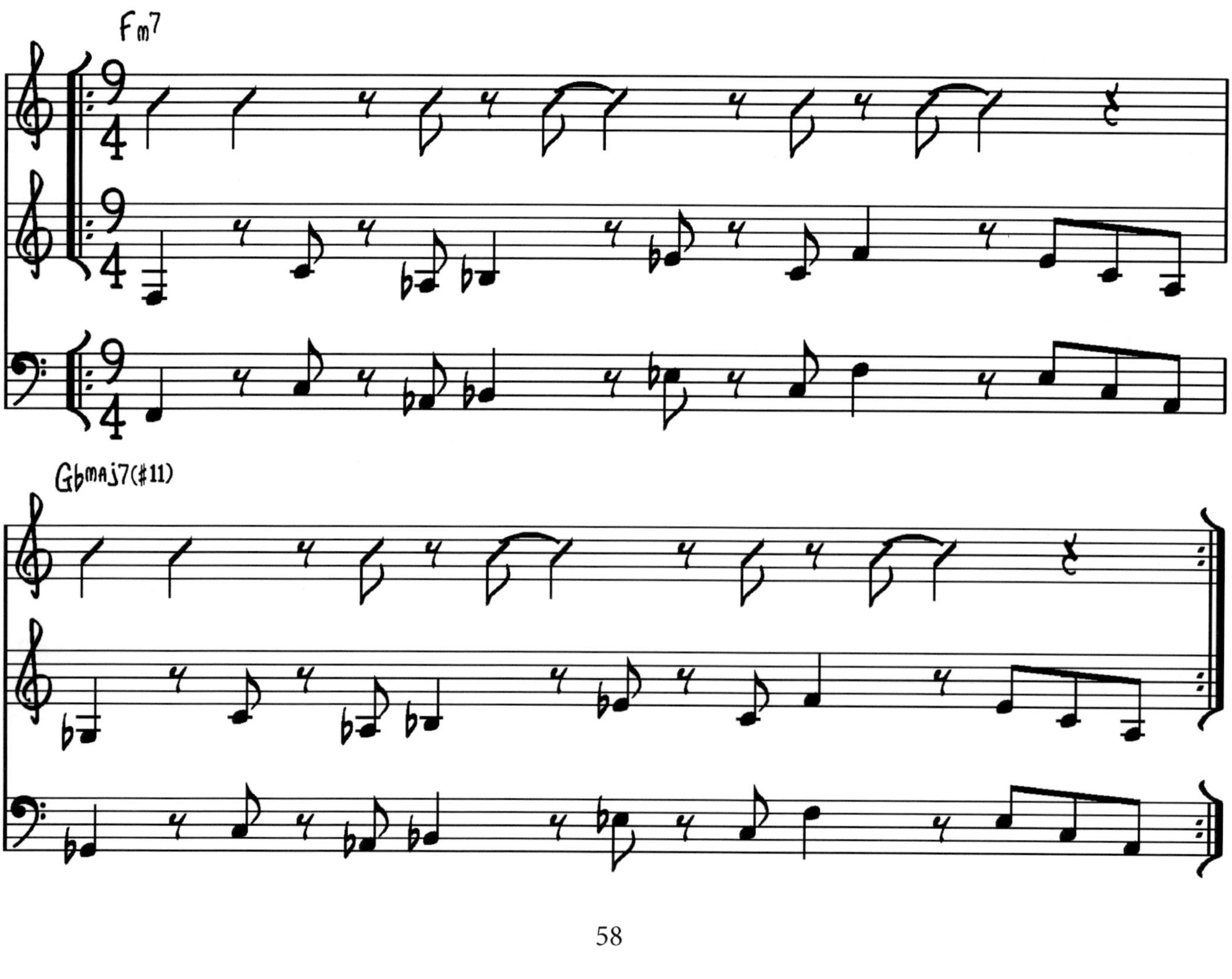

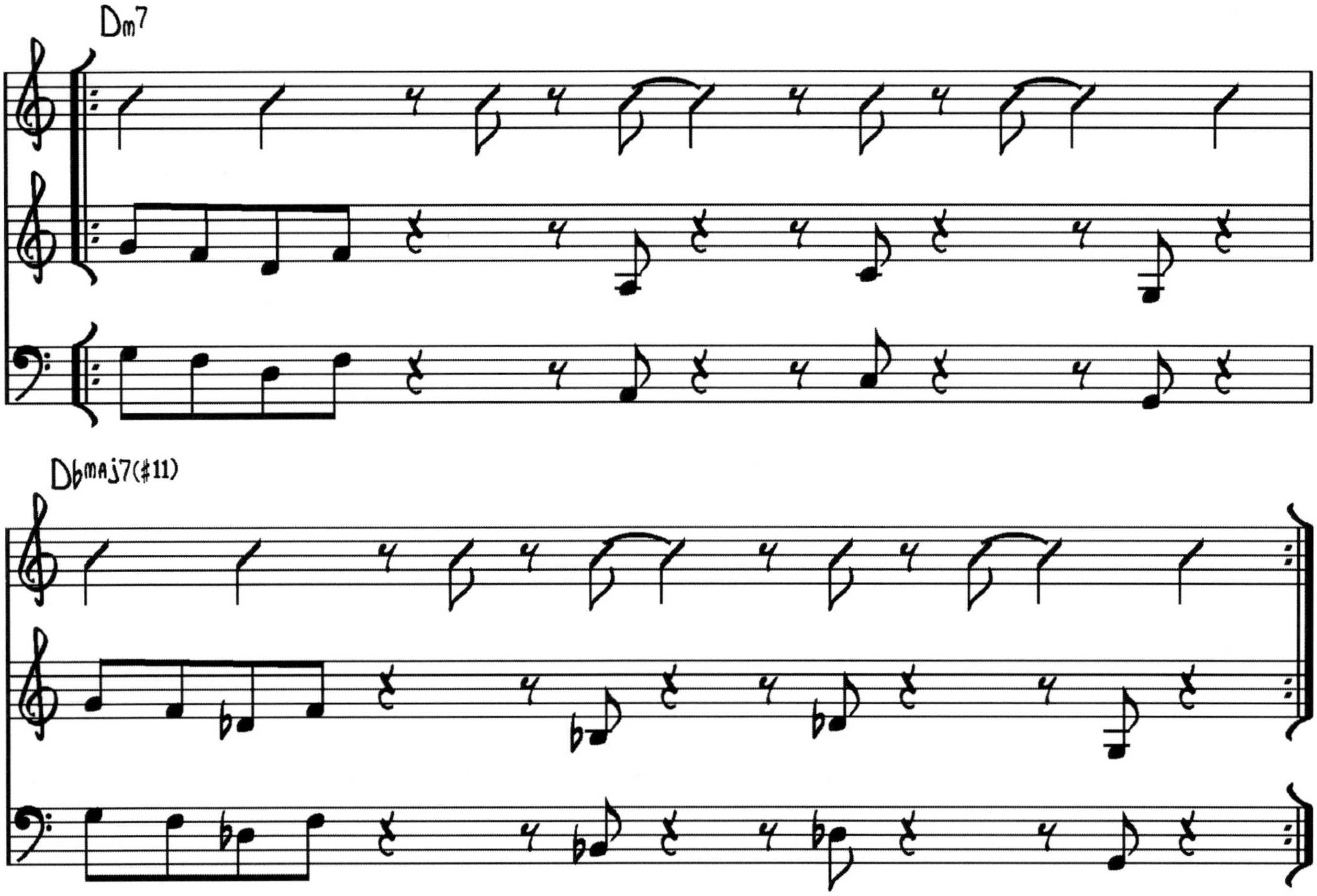
Dm7
D♭maj7(♯11)

10. TENS

Example 75: 10/4 groove with rhythm section

The larger even-numbered meters are less common because they are often split into two measures. For example 10/4 could be two bars of 5/4. In this example, the division feels more like 6 and 4. The choice of how to write ideas like this usually comes down to where the composer wants the downbeat to be felt.

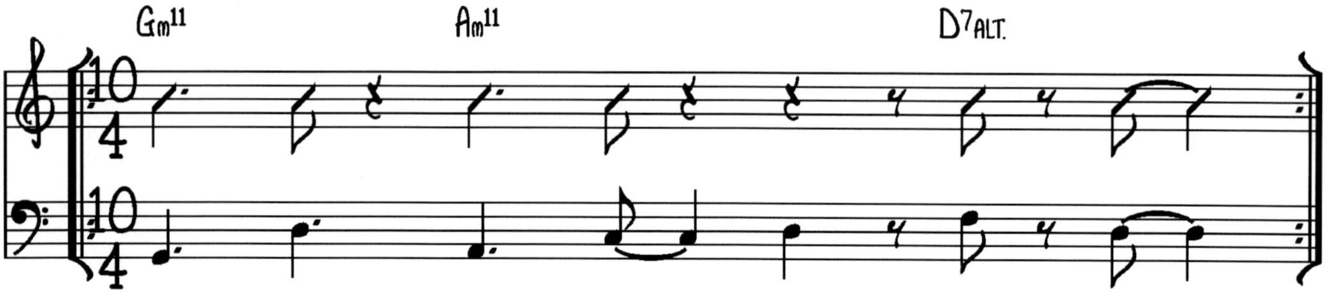

Example 76: 10/4 groove (BT)

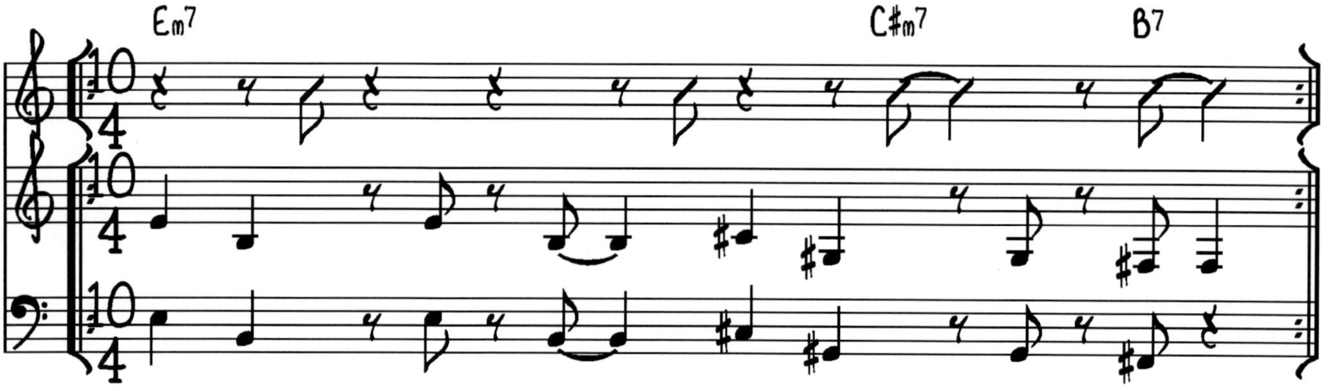

11. ELEVENS

This common rhythm from the Balkan region breaks the measure in half with a dotted quarter.

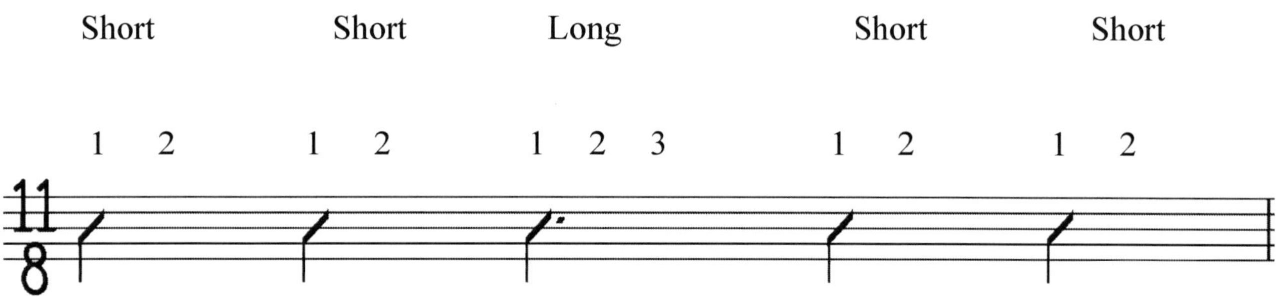

Example 77: 11/8 rhythm with three variations

Here is the same 11/8 rhythm divided in 3 different ways to create a layered groove.

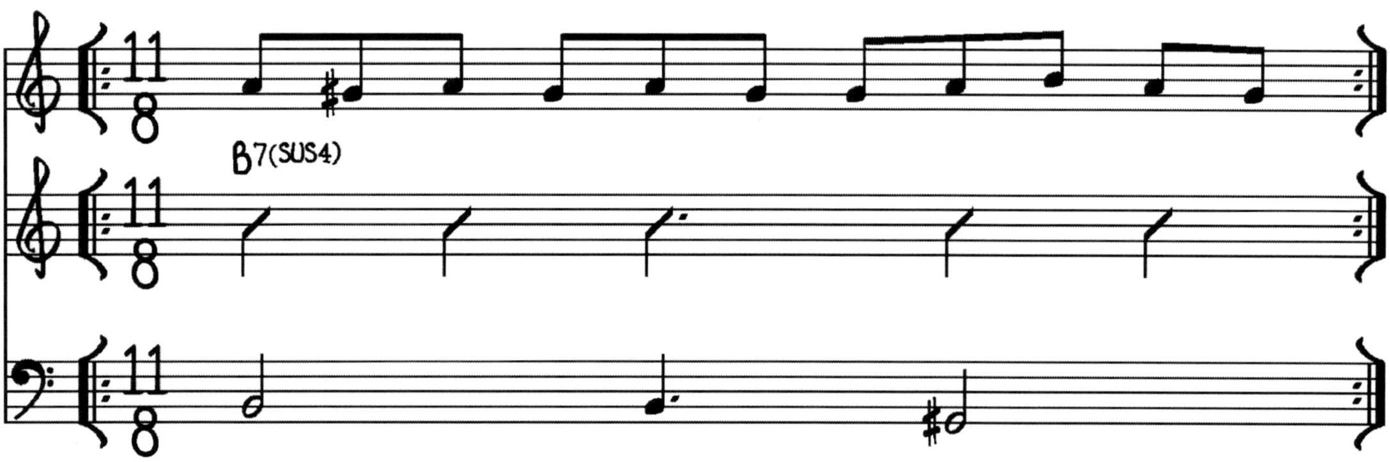

Example 78: 11/8 with two layers

Here's the same lower rhythm with a syncopated upper layer.

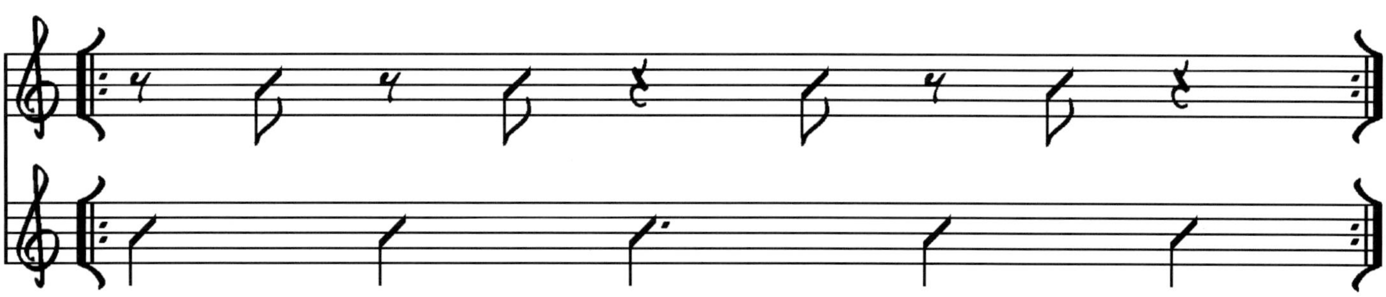

Example 79: 11/8 groove

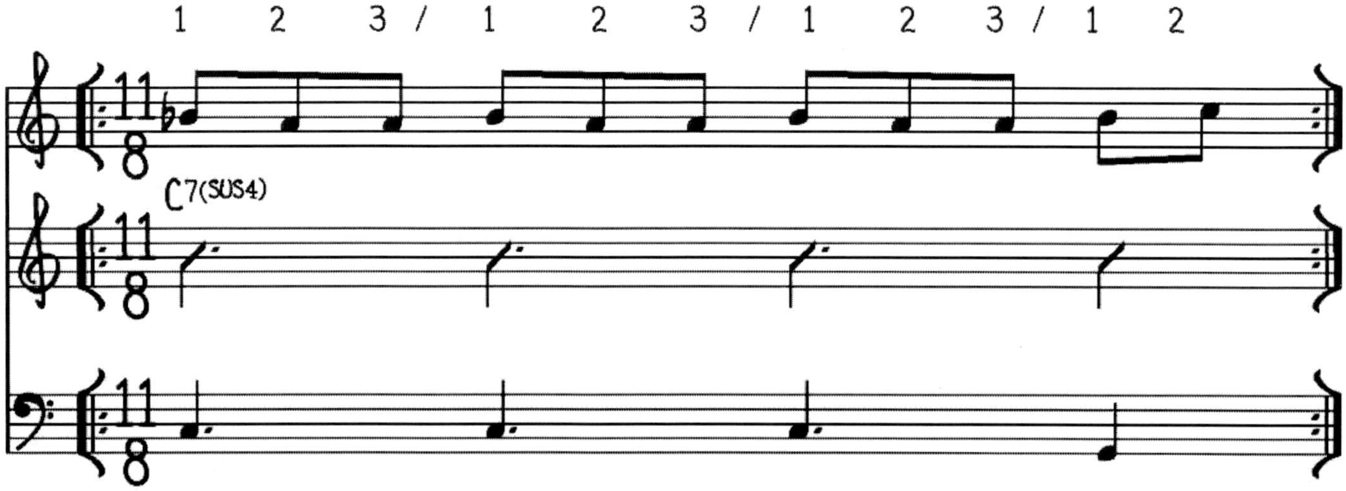

More variations:

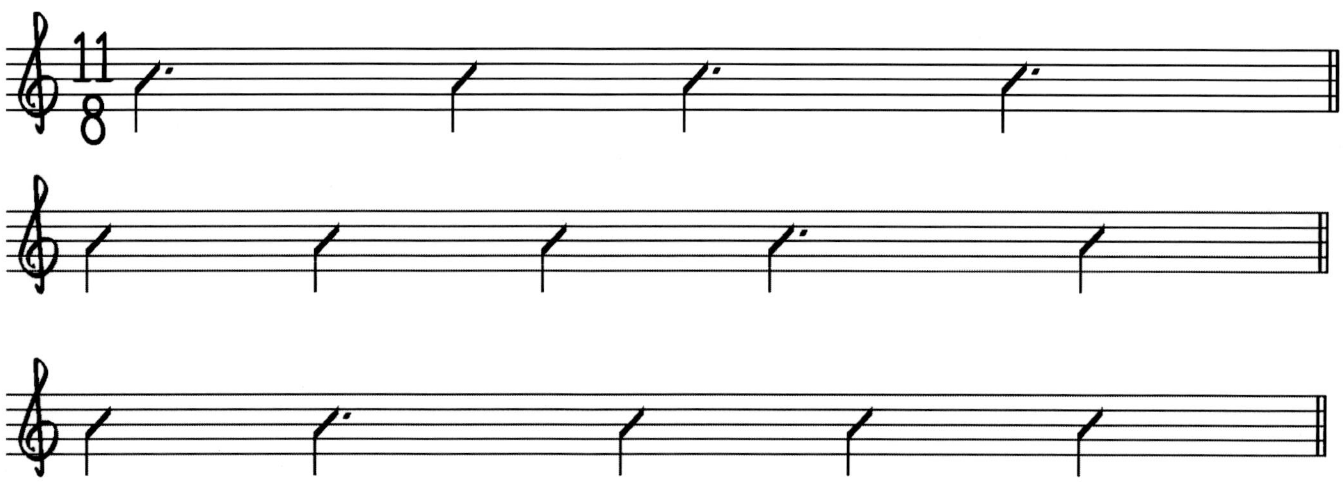

Example 80: 11/4 modal groove (BT)

This one feels like 5 and 6.

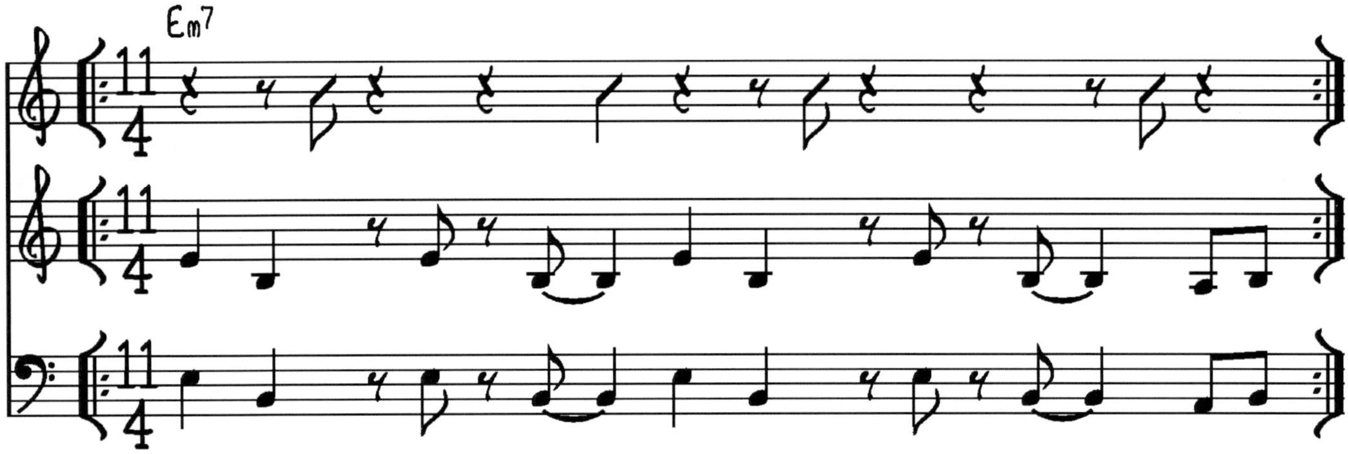

Example 81 with rhythm section

Here is the same rhythmic pattern as Example 80 but with additional chord changes.

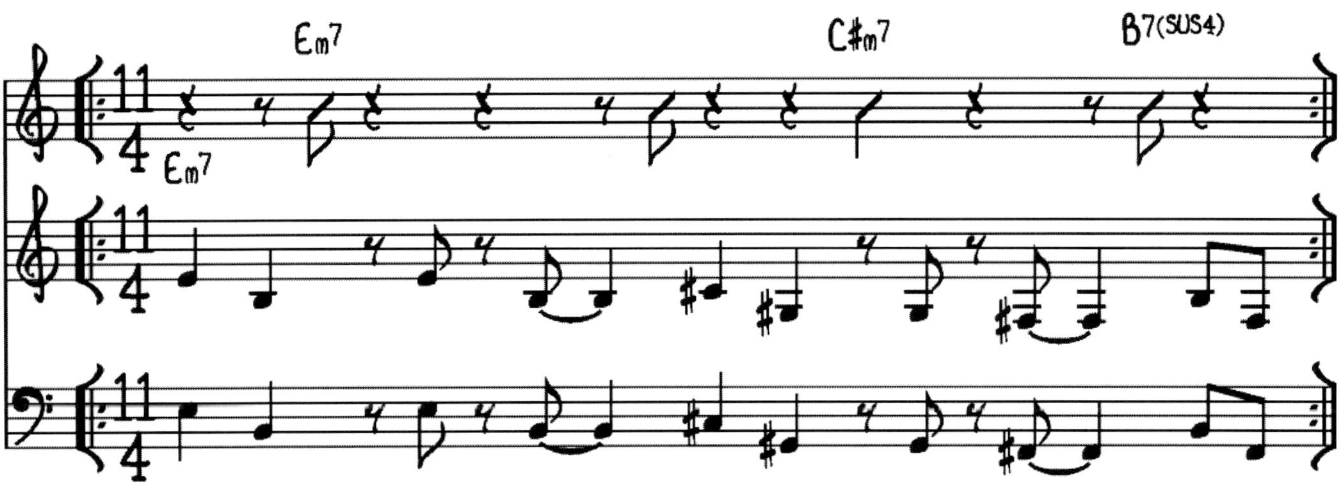

Example 82: 11/4 Modal vamp (BT)

Here, the 11/4 meter feels like 4 / 4 / 5.

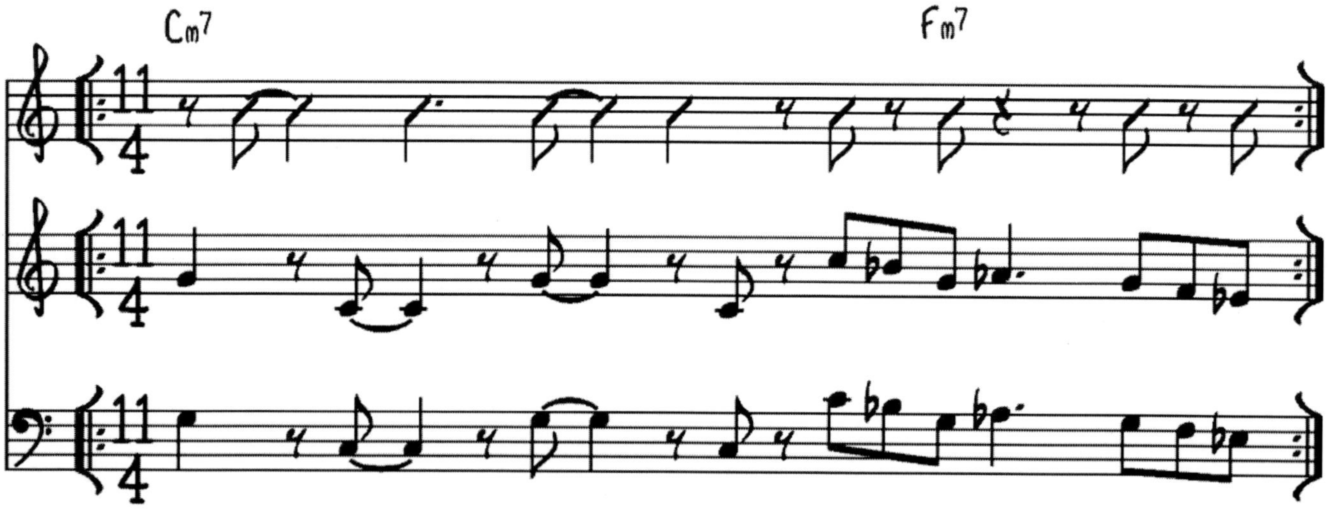

Example 83: 11/4 swing feel with rhythm section

This example can be felt as 6 and 5.

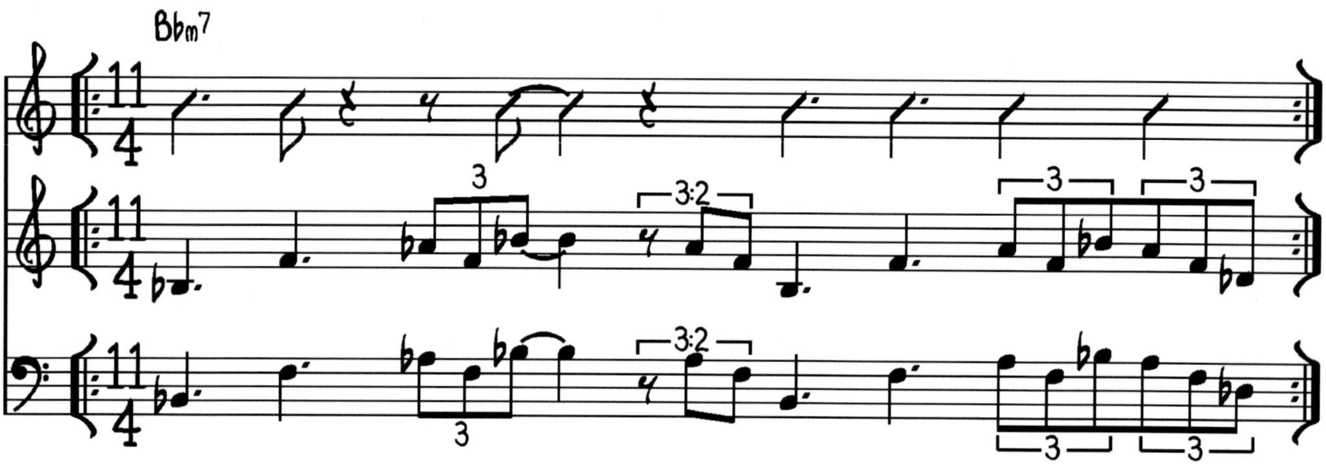

Example 84: Modal groove in 11/4 (BT)

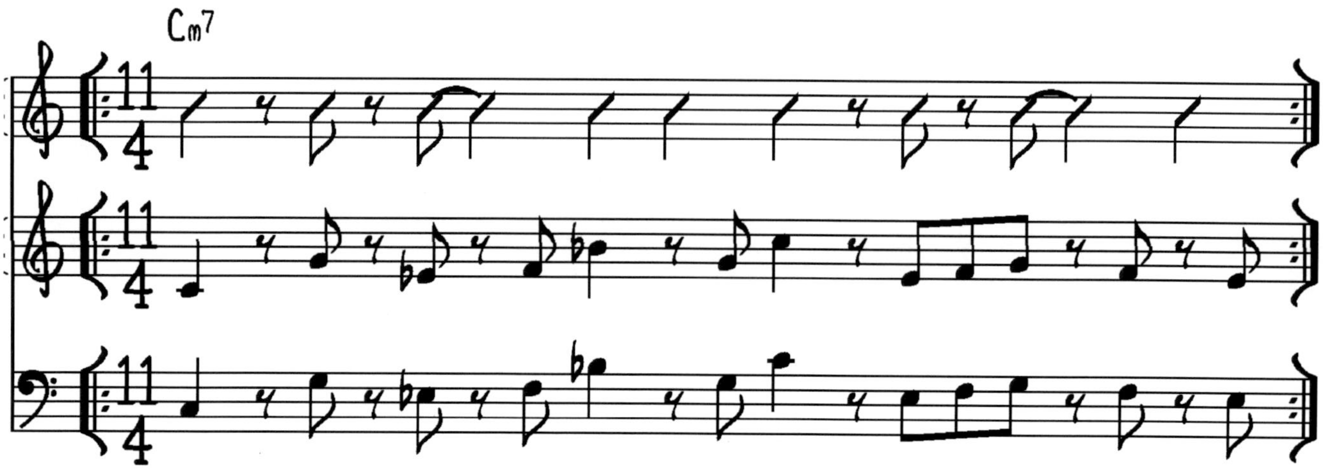

Example 85: Groove in 11/4 with chord changes and rhythm section

Here's another 11/4 that feels like 6 and 5.

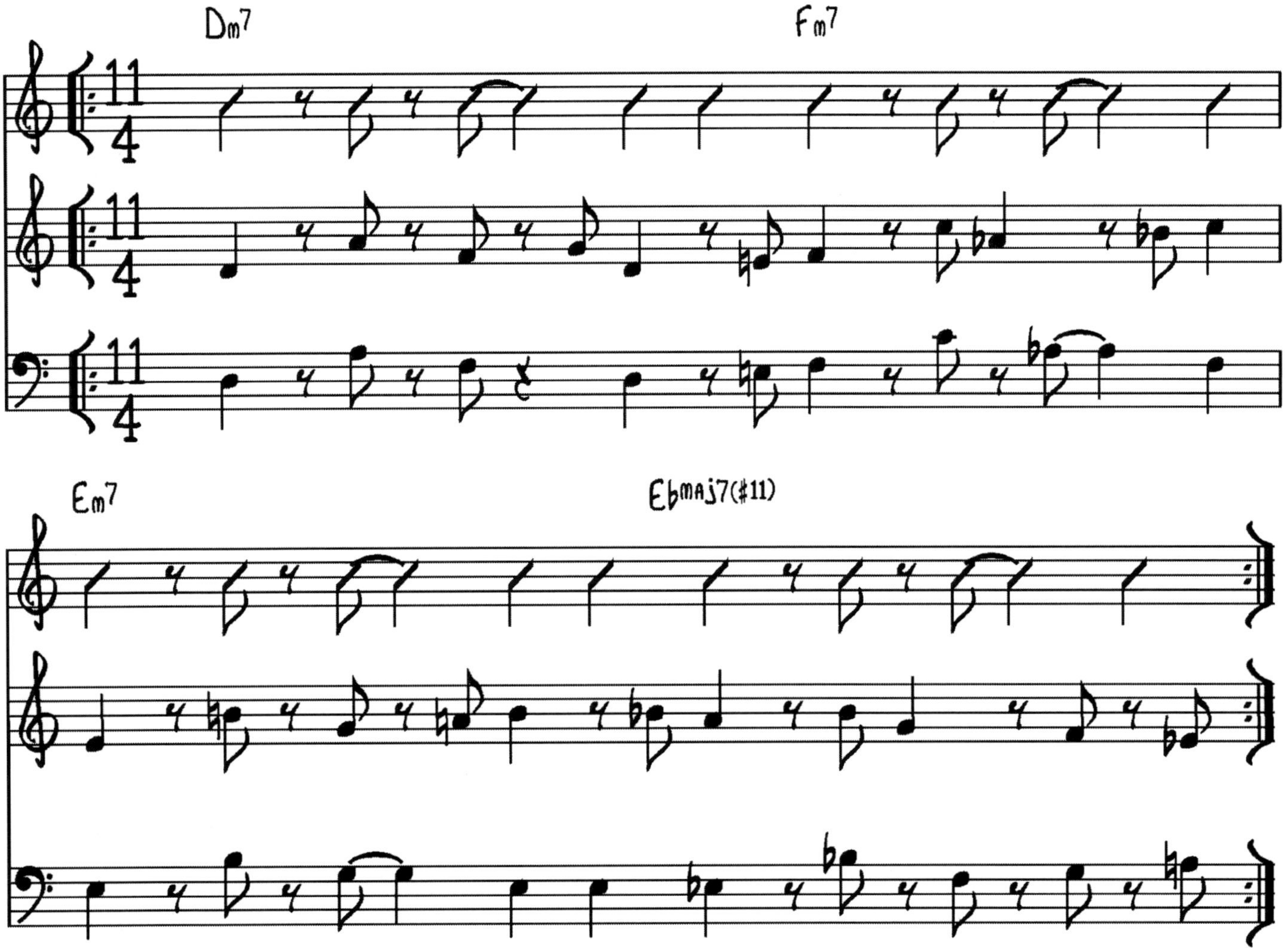

12. THIRTEENS

The higher-numbered meters can be challenging to grasp. Using melodic groupings can help us understand these longer rhythms. Start with simple scale groupings, like the two examples below. It can also help to have a larger and smaller subdivision to feel the pattern. The first using quarters and dotted quarters, the second using 8th notes with accents. Clap and count through each example before playing it.

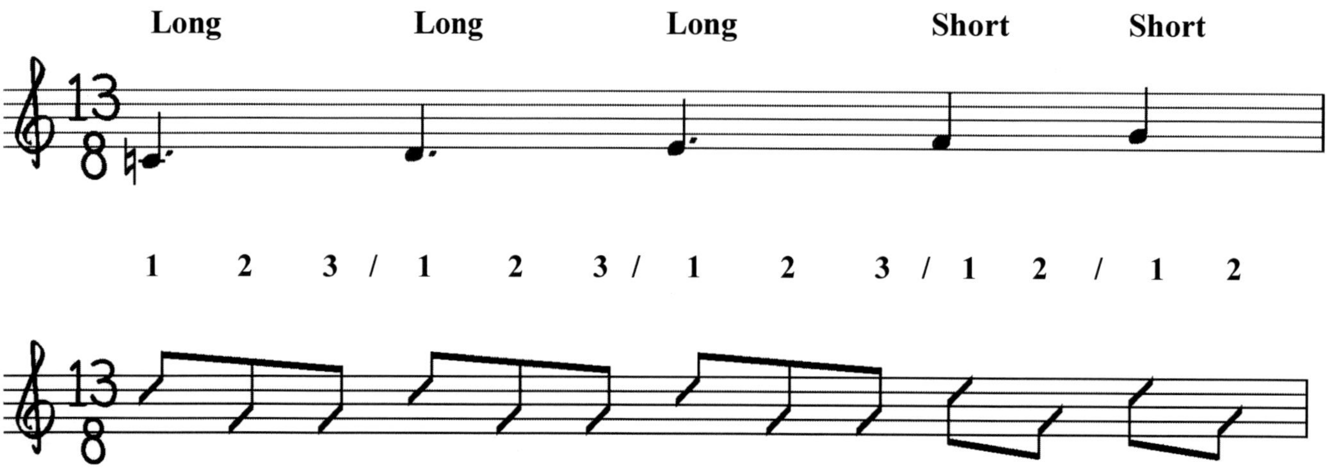

Example 86: Modal vamp in 13/8

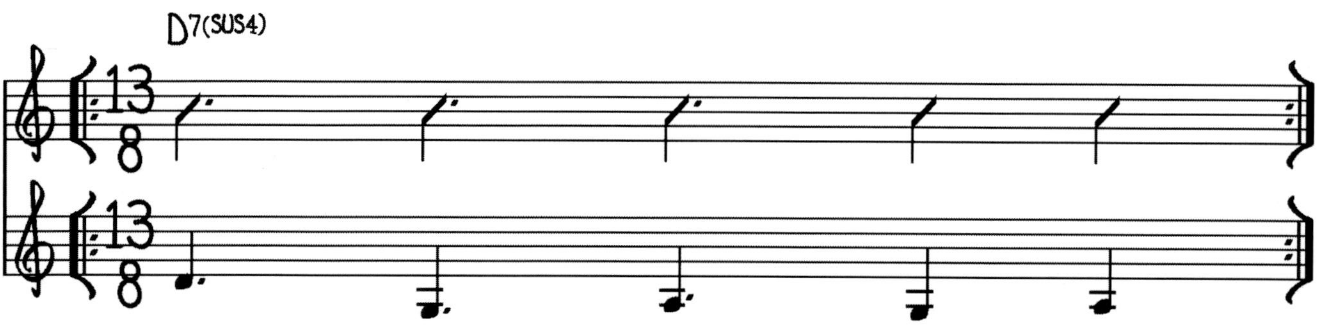

Example 87: 13/8 variation

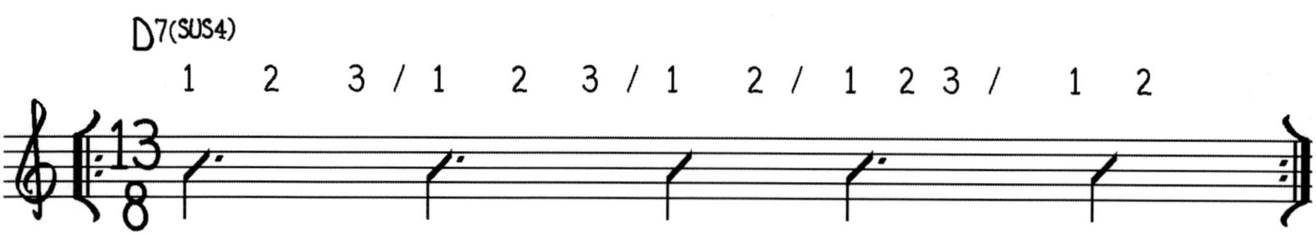

Clap or play these variations in 13/8:

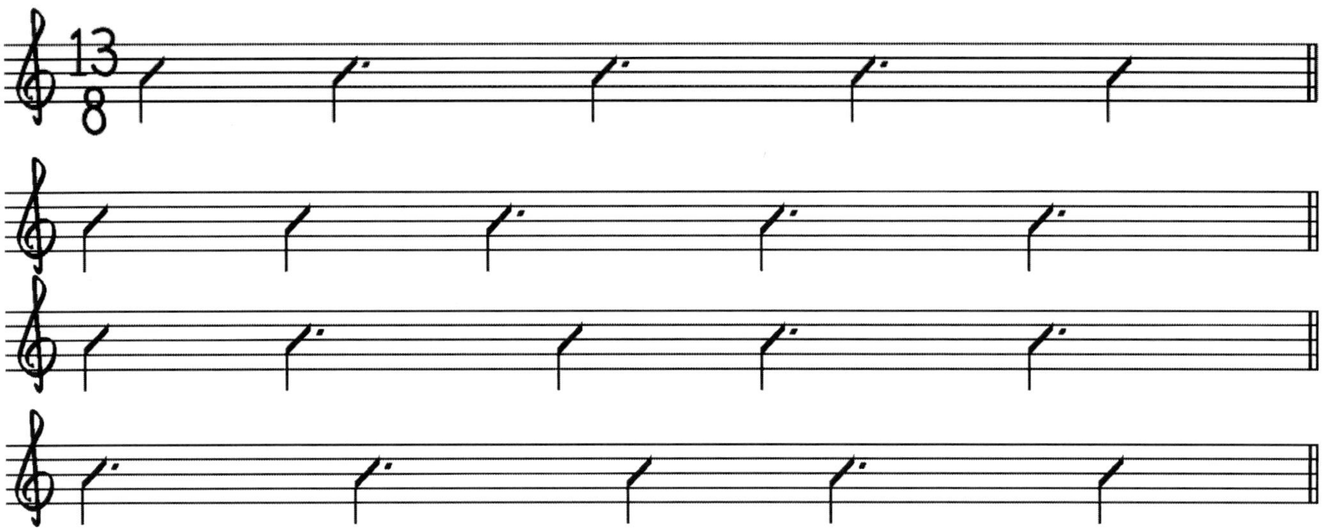

Example 88: 13/4 groove with rhythm section

This 13/4 groove feels like 5 and 8.

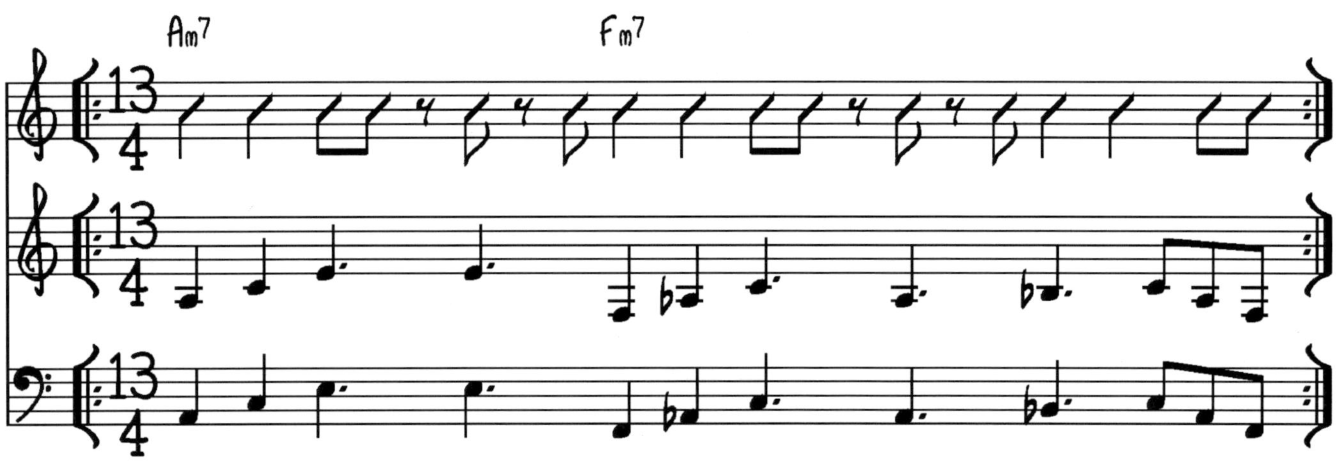

Example 89 with rhythm section

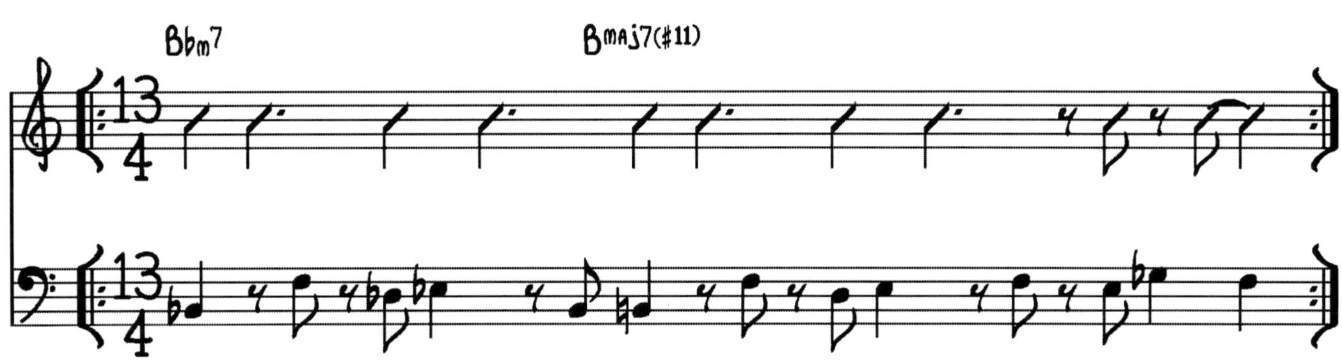

13.FIFTEENS AND SEVENTEENS

Clap and count these examples of rhythmic divisions in 15/8. Remember that you can break these rhythms down into short beats and long beats.

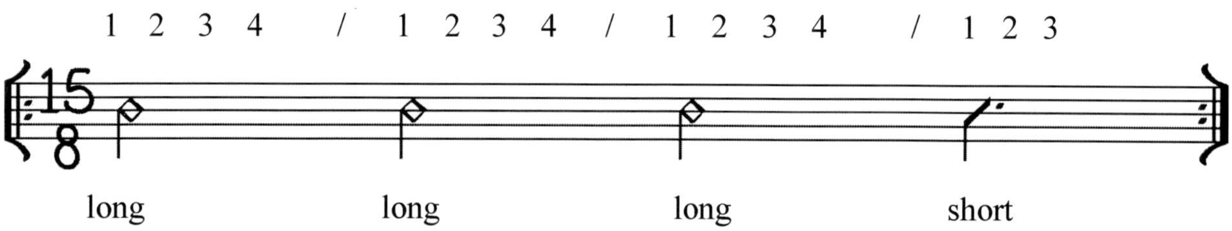

Clap or play these variations of 15/8.

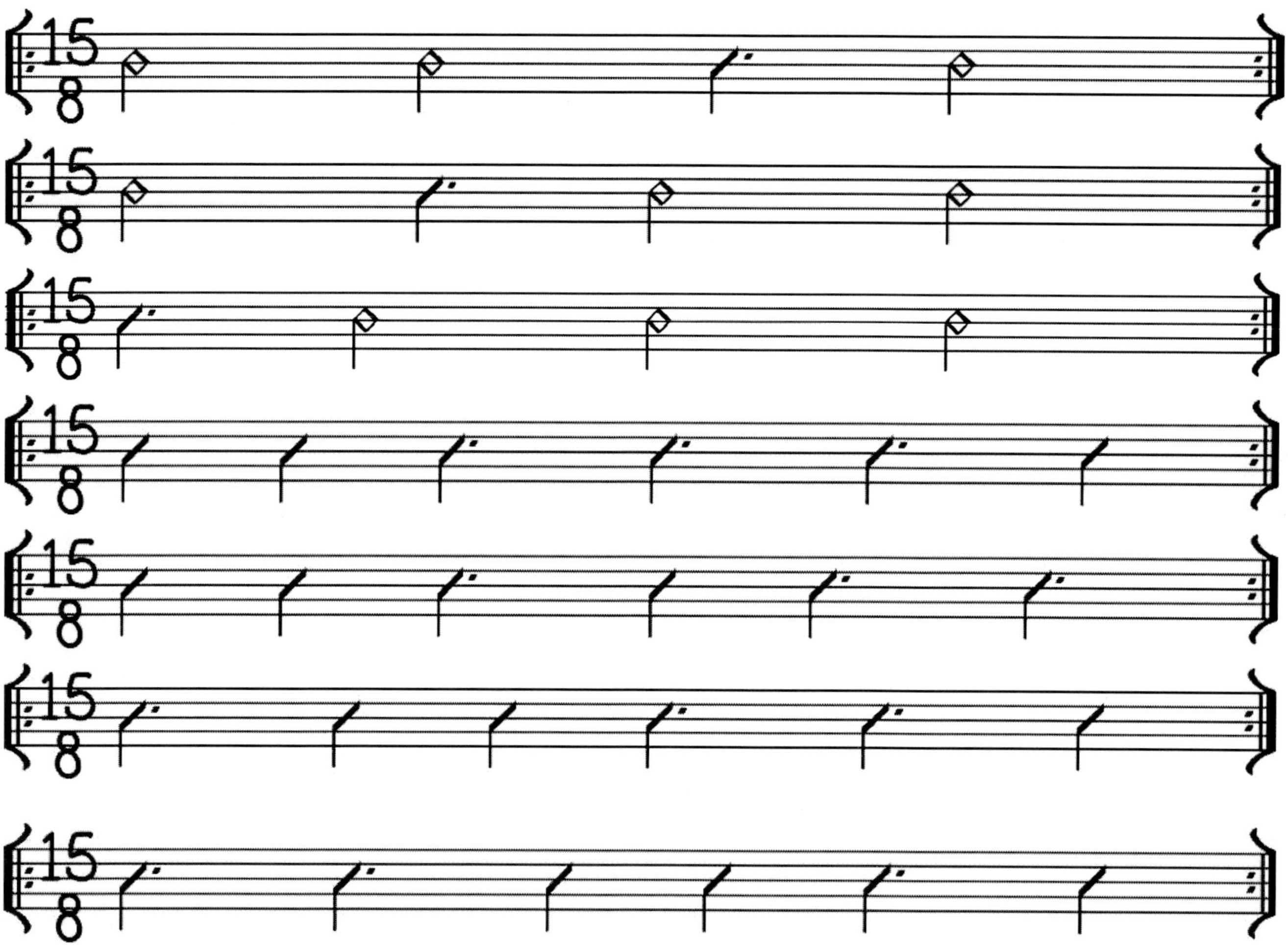

Example 90: Modal vamp (BT)

Feels like 4 / 4 / 7

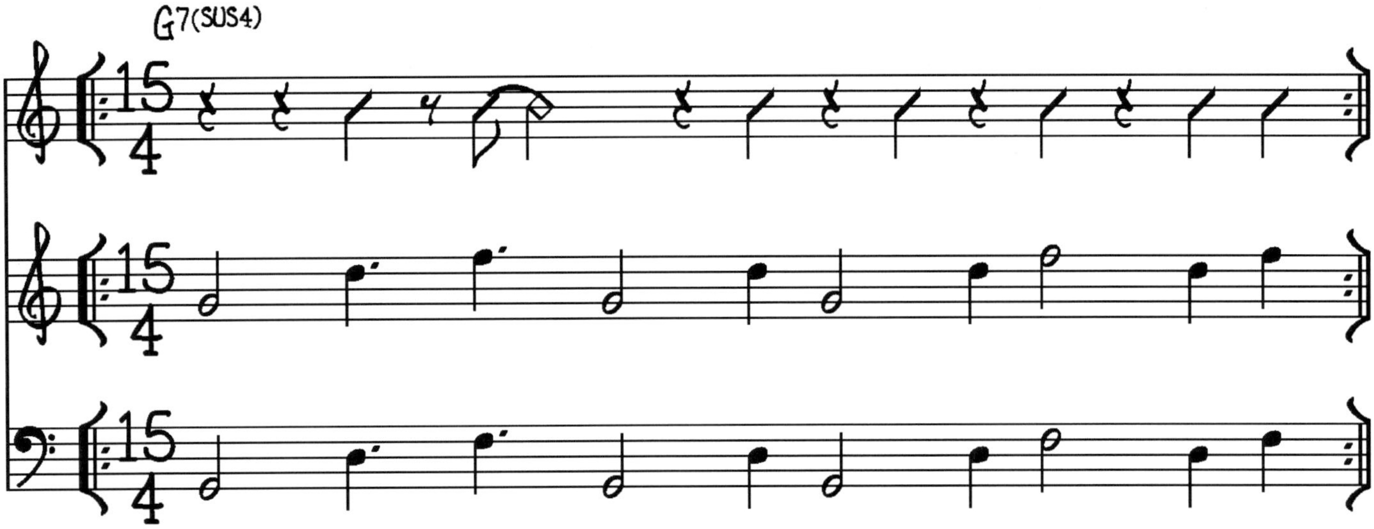

Example 90A: 15/4 vamp (BT)

Feels like 8 and 7

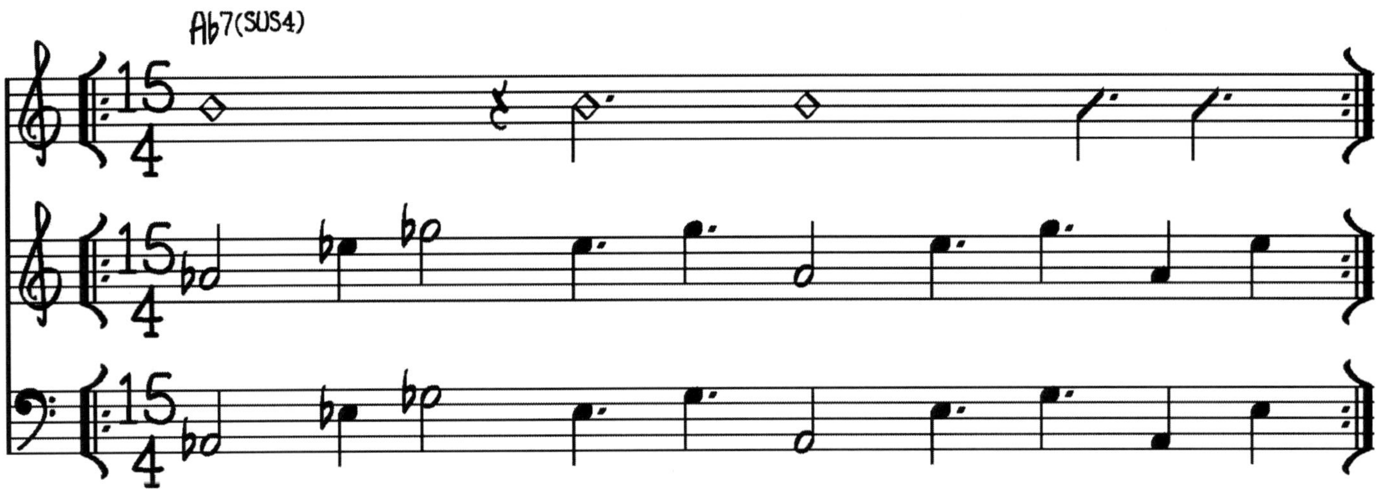

Example 90B: bass line in 15/4 (BT)

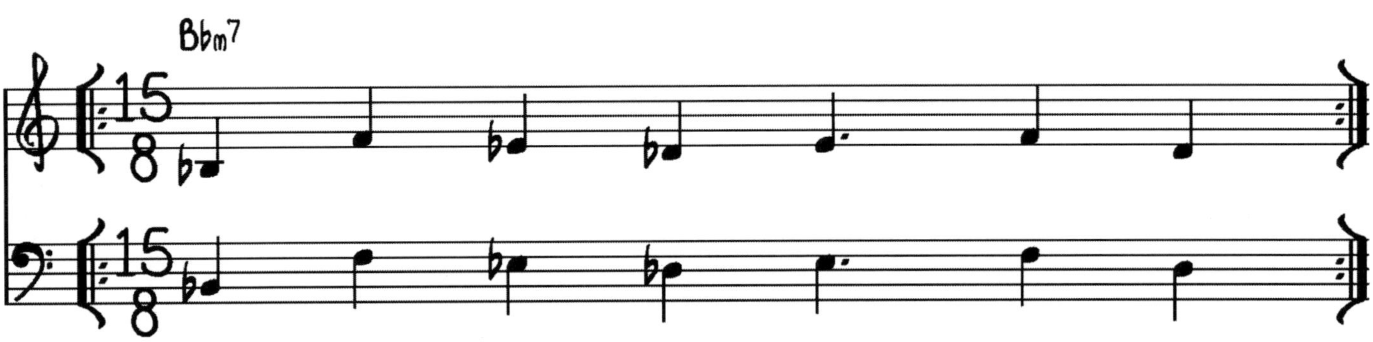

Example 91: 15/8 groove (BT)

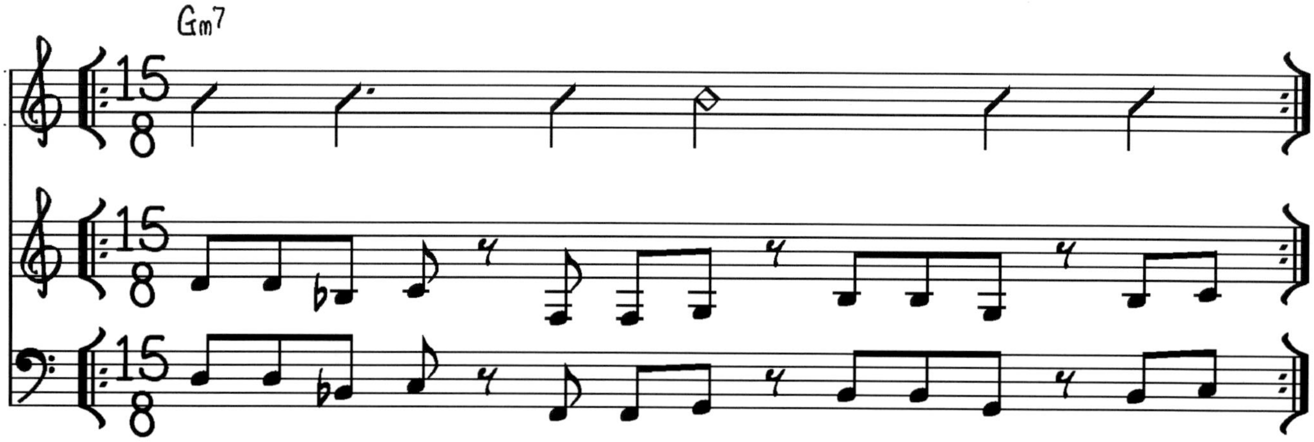

Example 92: Bass line in 15/4 (BT)

This 15/4 bass line can be felt as 4 / 5 / 7.

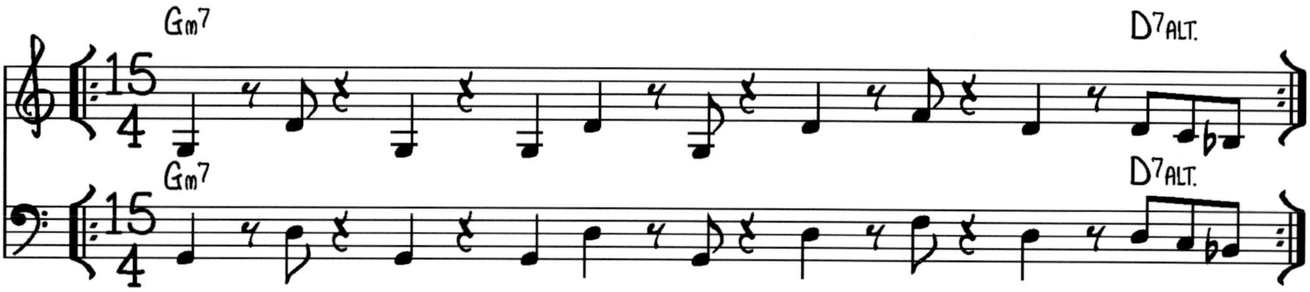

Example 93 with rhythm section

Here is the same pattern as Example 92 but with additional chord changes.

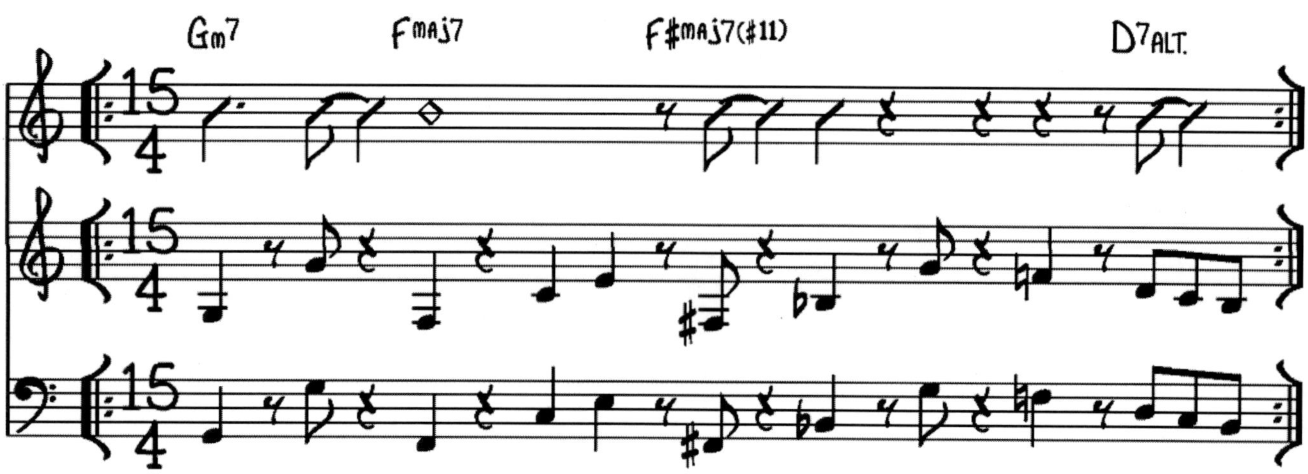

Example 94: 15/4 Swing feel with rhythm section

Swing feel

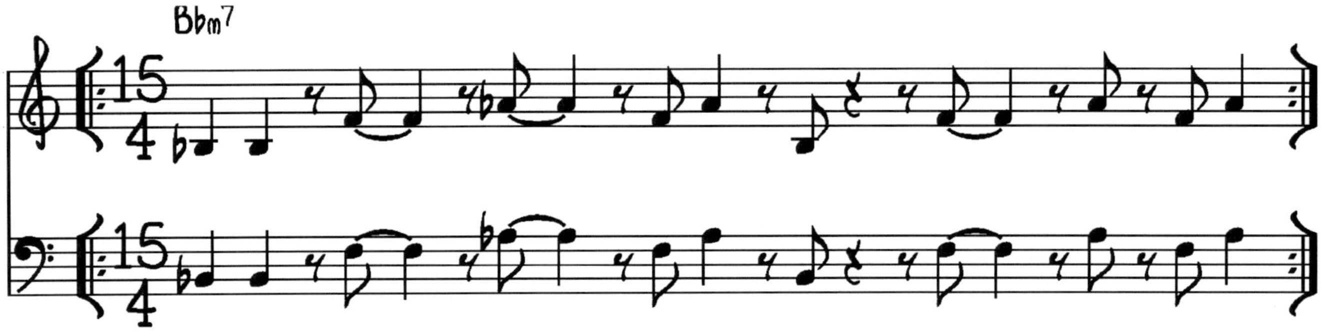

Clap or play these rhythms in 17/8 while counting.

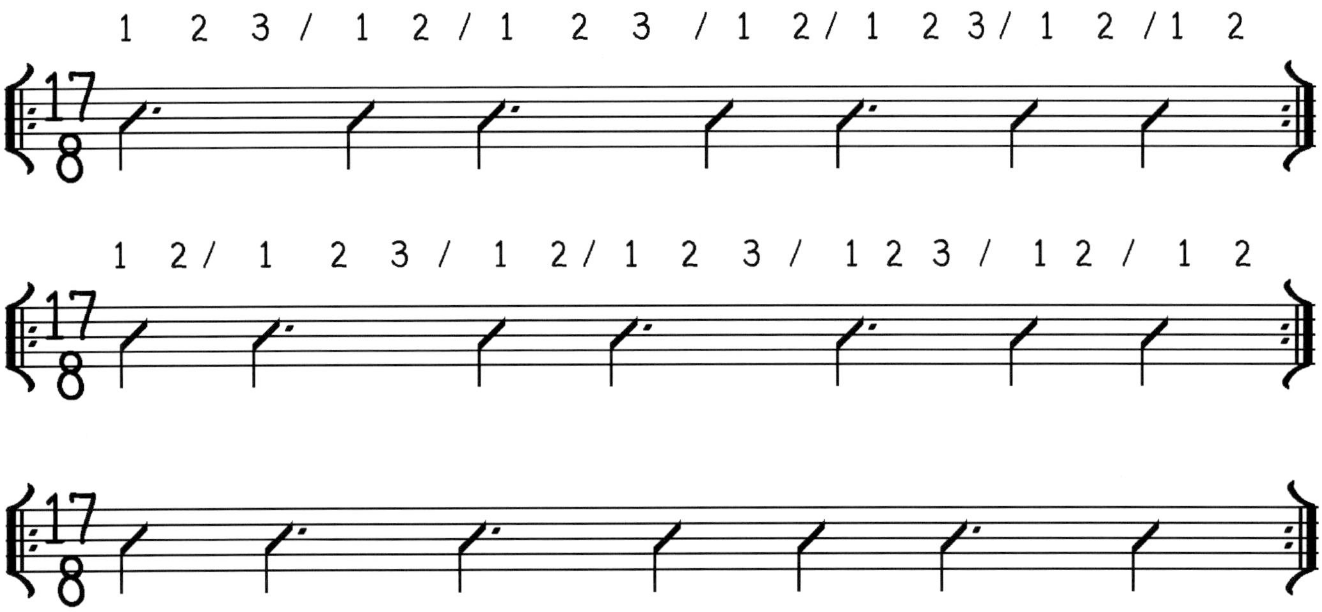

Example 95: Modal groove in 17/8 (BT)

This one feels like 6 / 6 / 5.

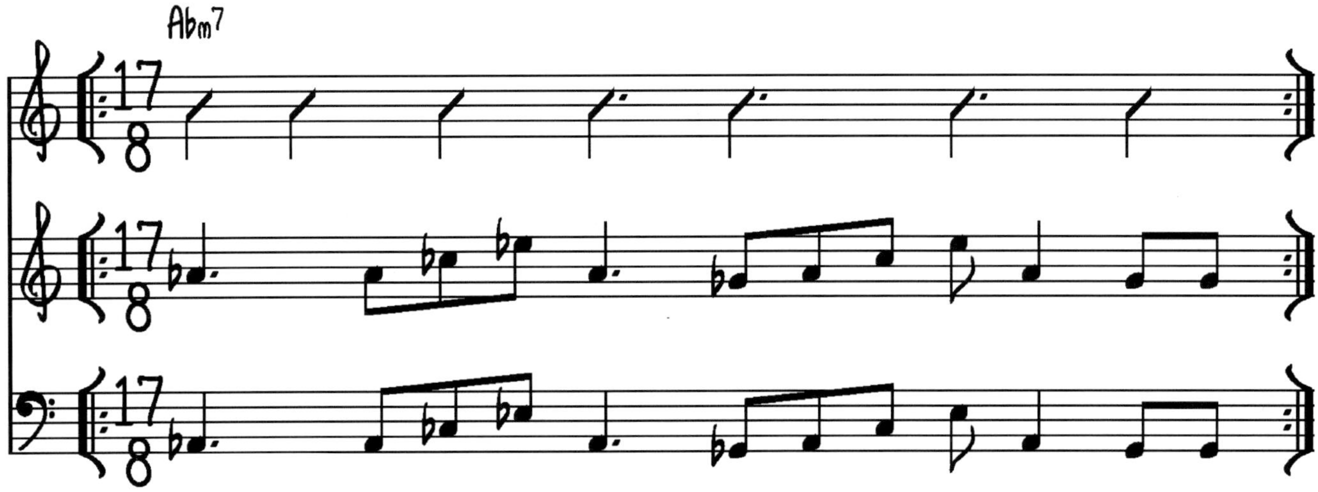

Example 96 with rhythm section

Feels like 5 / 5 / 7

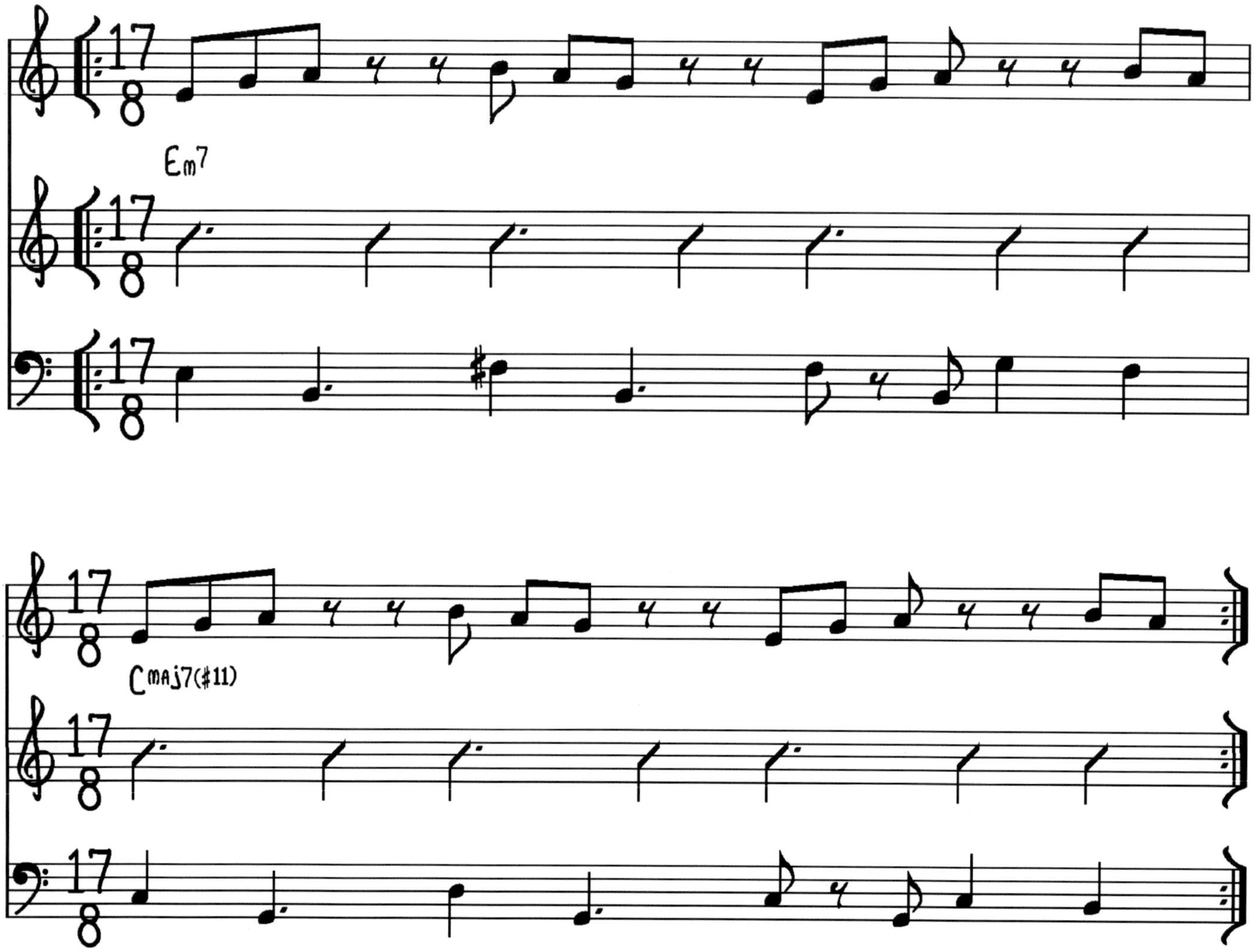

Example 96A

Feels like 6 / 6 / 5

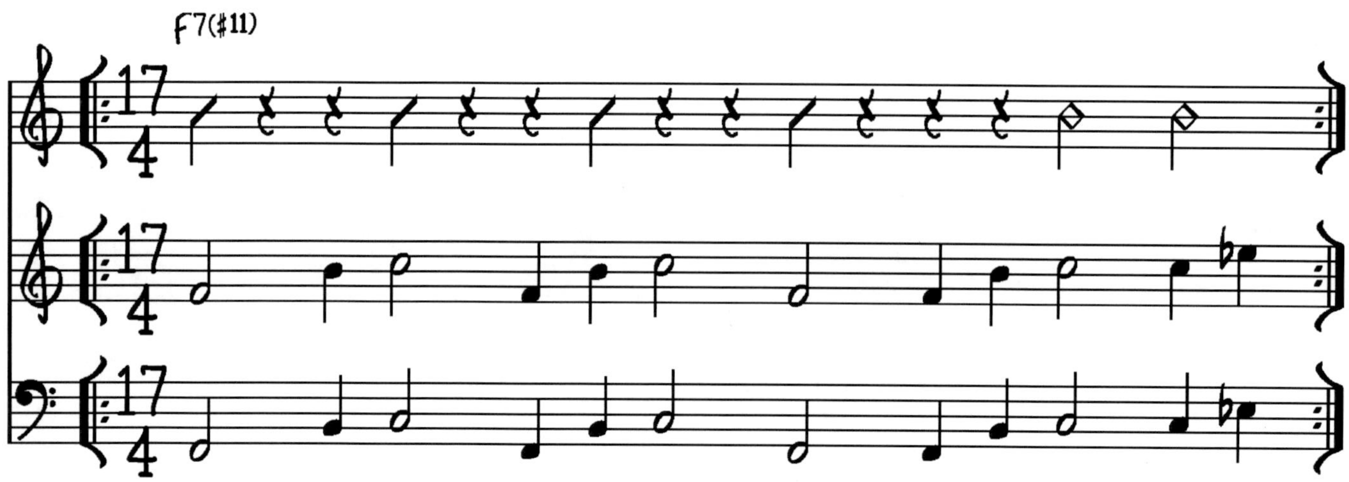

14. MIXED METERS

It has become more and more common for jazz composers to use multiple, shifting meters within the same composition. This results in new rhythmic landscapes which can be a real challenge for the improviser. We can use chord changes, bass lines, and clave-like patterns to help feel this new structure. Just as we had to learn to play in one meter, we now want to learn what this shifting rhythmic structure feels like. In this case we usually need to start by breaking the structure down and counting. Once we begin to feel the contour of this new pattern, we can begin to take some chances with trying to play over it without counting.

You will make plenty of mistakes where you "fall off" the structure, or at least experience a feeling of precariousness. That is quite natural and is an important part of the process. Slowly, you will begin to physically "understand" the pattern and start to shape your lines in a way that connects to the underlying rhythms. When finding your way, try not to be overly concerned with accuracy. A dancer can't expect to land perfectly the first few times they try a new jump. Even so, it is important to take the leap without knowing exactly where you will land. Falling down is an important part of the learning process as you find your footing.

Combining 3/4 and 4/4

Here is an excerpt from my composition "Uneasy". Two bars of 4/4 and two bars of 3/4 equals an even fourteen beats. Keep the swing accent of 2 and 4 the same throughout the pattern. The bottom rhythm is where the metronome pulse or accent should be placed. It is easiest to think of this as B minor with chromatic motion.

Example 97: "Uneasy" with rhythm section

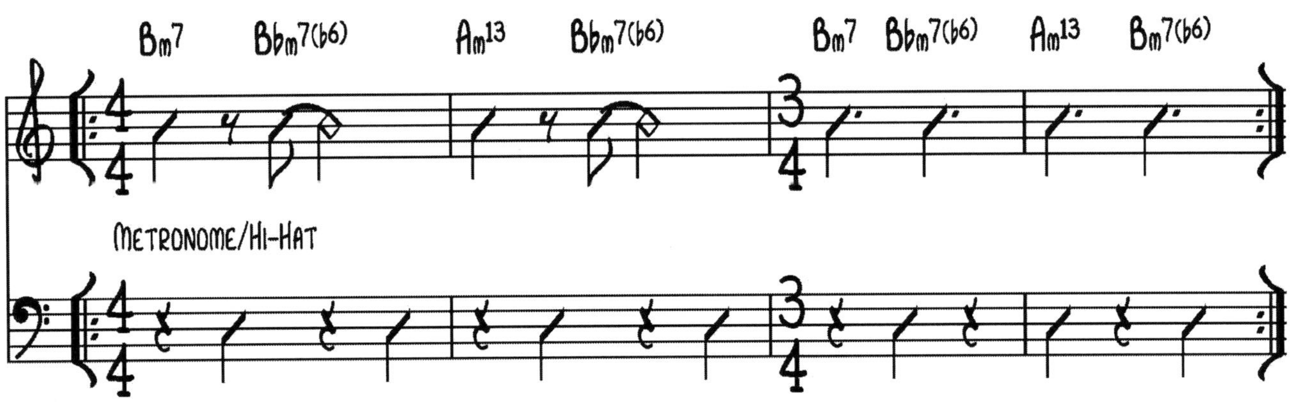

Combinations Beginning with 3/4:

Example 98 with rhythm section

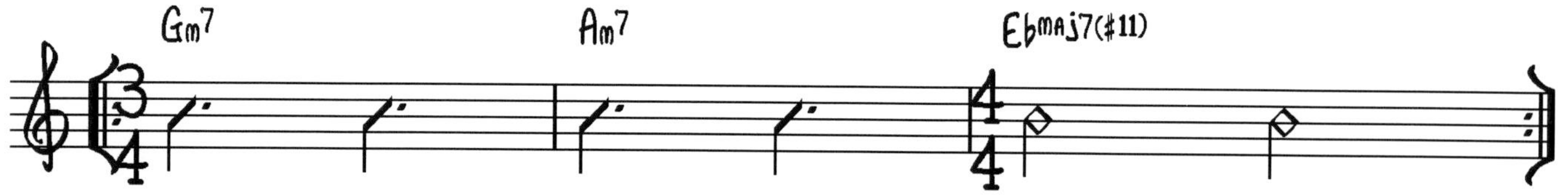

Example 99: (BT)

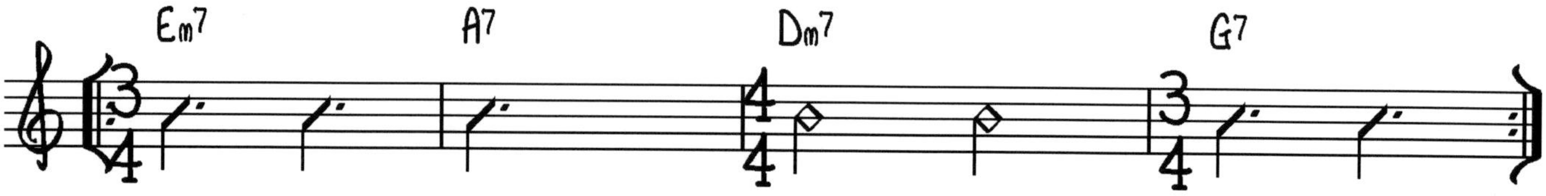

Example 100: Mixed-meter swing feel with rhythm section

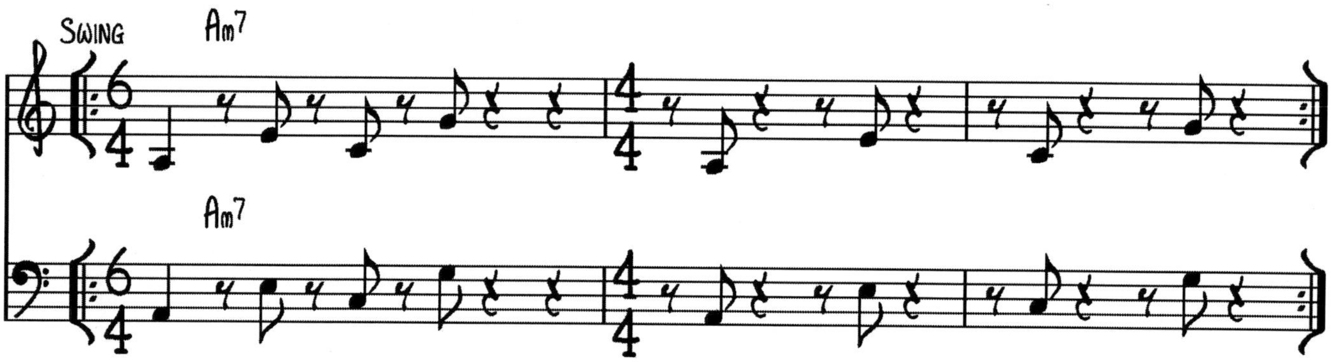

Combinations beginning with 5/4:

Example 101

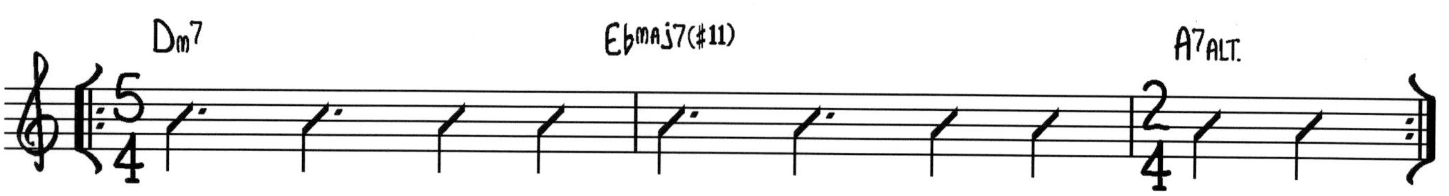

Example 102 (BT)

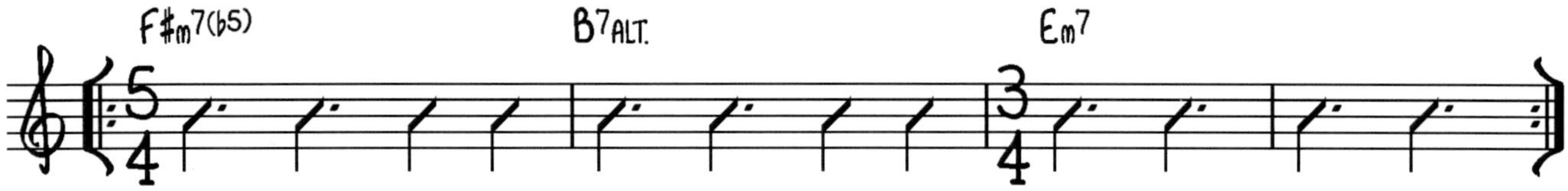

Example 103 with rhythm section

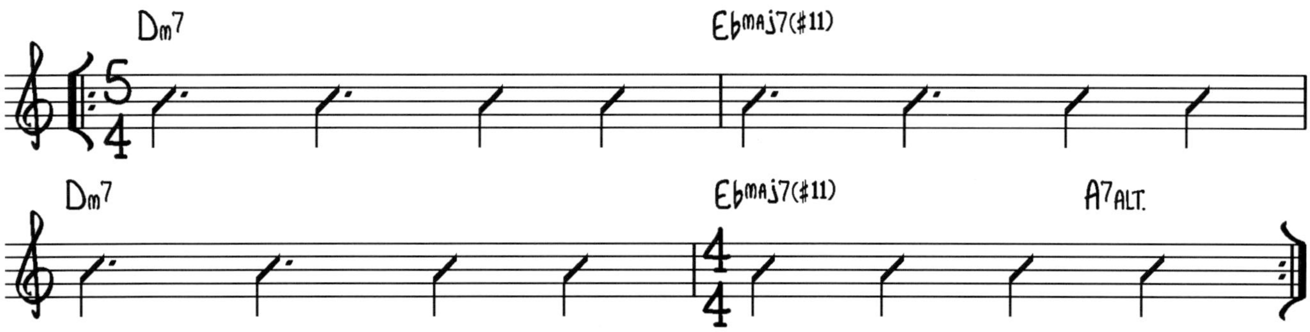

Example 104

This line feels like 3 / 4 / 3 / 2, but could also be written in 12/4.

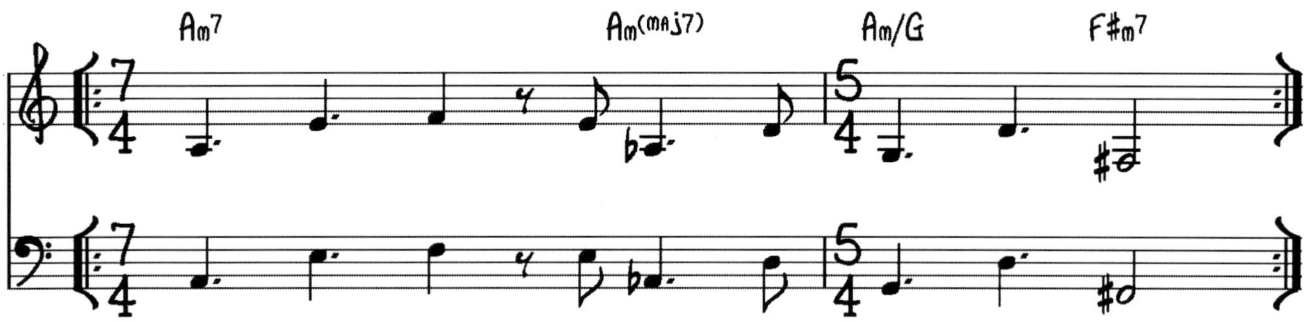

More difficult:

Example 105: "Slipping Glimpser" with rhythm section

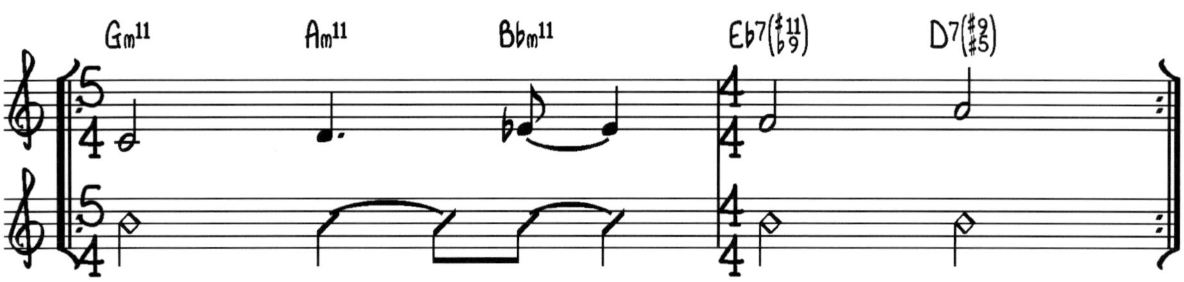

Example 106: "Real and Imagined" with rhythm section

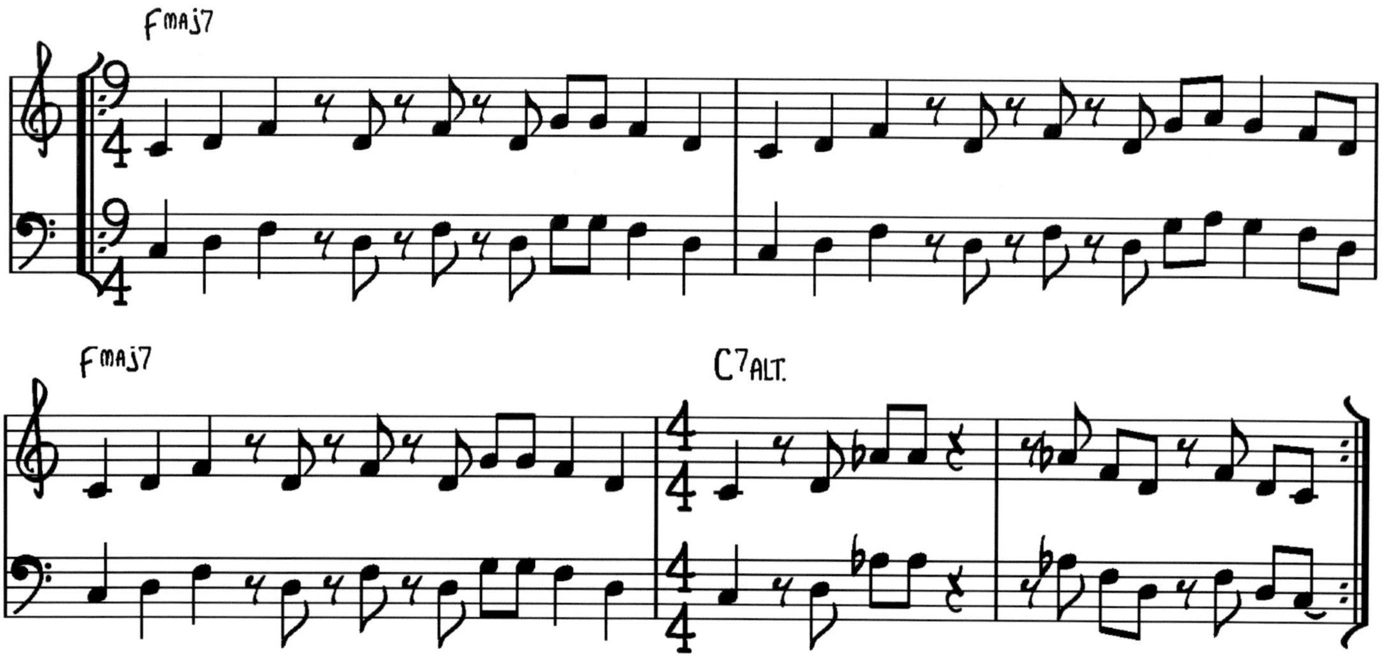

Example 107: "Thread" with rhythm section

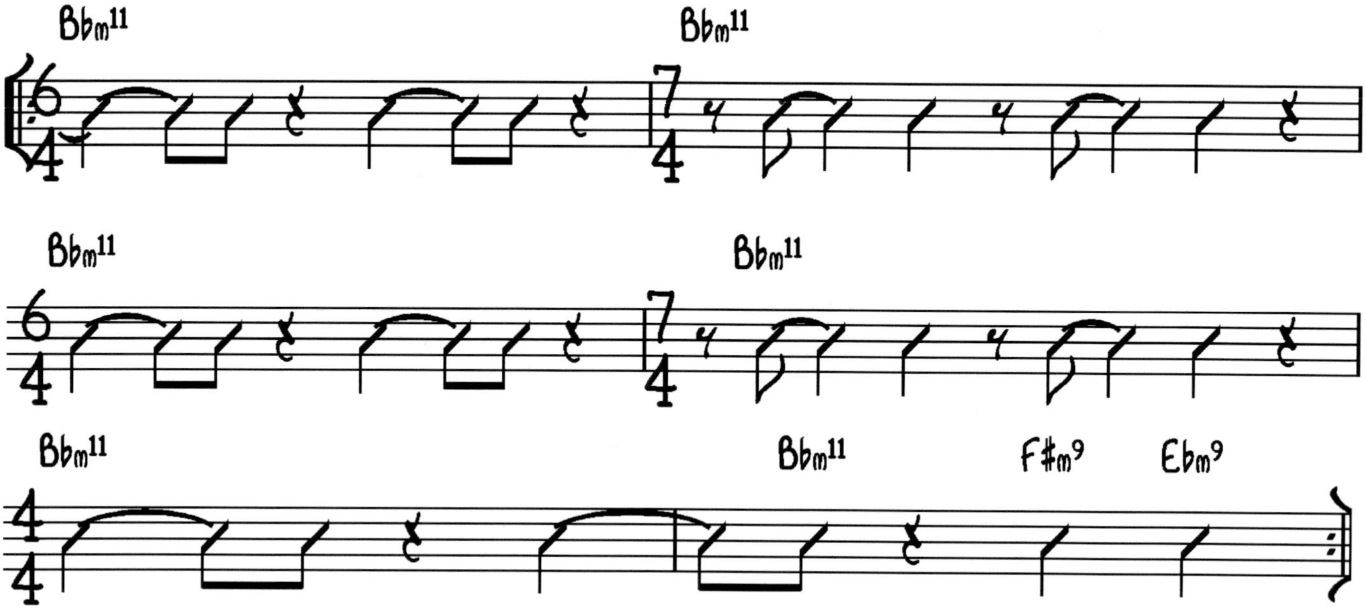

Example 108: "654" with rhythm section

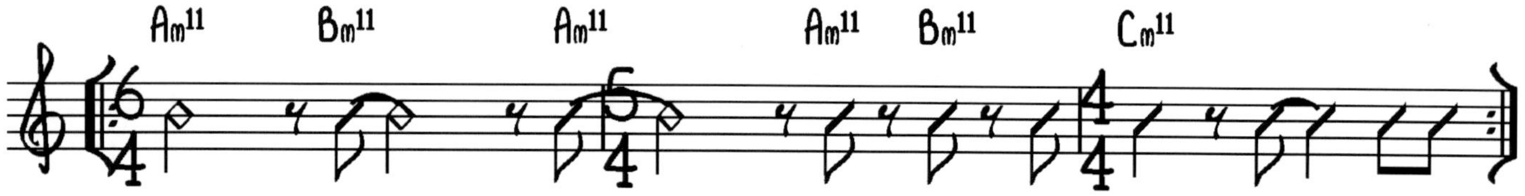

Simultaneous Meters:

Here is another excerpt from my composition "Real and Imagined". This piece overlaps 3/4 and 11/4. Record or have someone else play this four-bar vamp in 3/4.

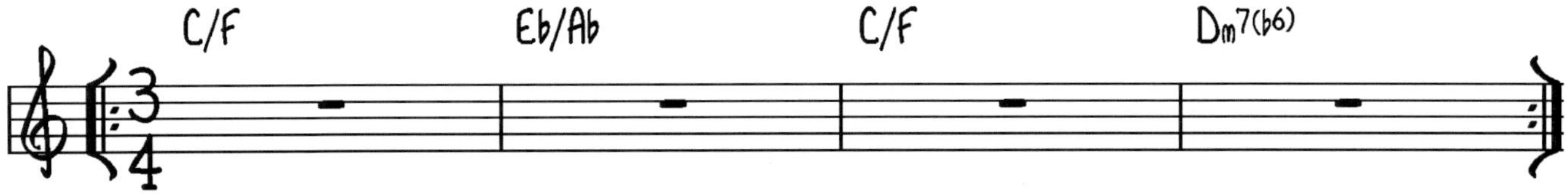

Play the above 3/4 vamp several times and then begin the 11/4 bass line (below) on the downbeat of the first measure of 3/4. Keep playing both parts simultaneously. The 11/4 line will move across the 3/4 groove to create shifting rhythmic layers. This is not yet a modulation. Keep the quarter note the same. It might help to listen to the recording on my record which is also called *Real and Imagined.*

Example 109: "Real and Imagined" 3/4 vamp plus 11/4 bass line

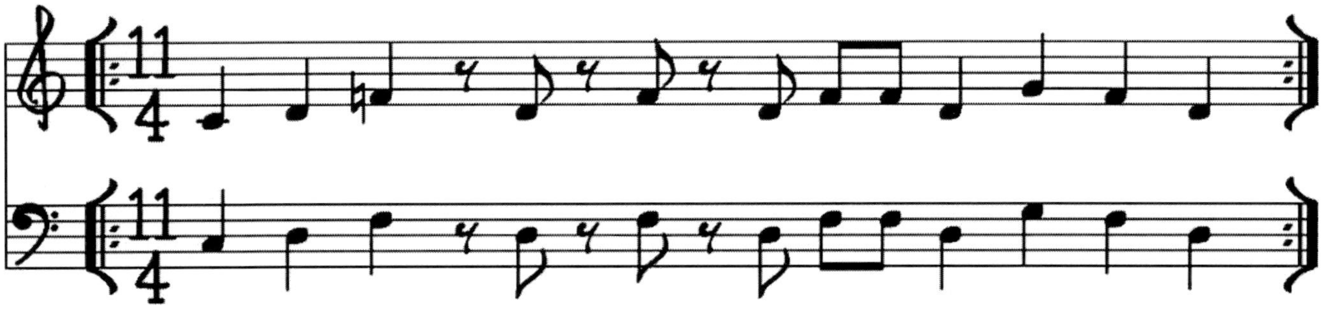

When I play this tune with my group, I do not have any set number of bars planned, so you do not have to wait for the two meters to line up mathematically. The person playing the 3/4 vamp eventually lets it fade out. Then the entire band transitions to 11/4. After that we would begin the 5-measure groove from Example 106.

15. POLYRHYTHMS

Getting to know polyrhythms is a good way to expand your rhythmic vocabulary and enhance your phrasing. It can take time to get to know these rhythms well enough to apply them in improvisation. Some may feel natural, while others will not. The following four sequences can be tapped along with a metronome, between your two hands, or played on your instrument.

- Begin by practicing each rhythm, one measure at a time, by itself before attempting the entire sequence. Don't move on before you feel you are playing each rhythm accurately.
- If you are playing these sequences on your instrument, it can be helpful to use a melodic pattern that corresponds to the number of notes in the top rhythm. For example, use a seven-note scale for 7 over 4.

Polyrhythm Sequence 1 in 4/4

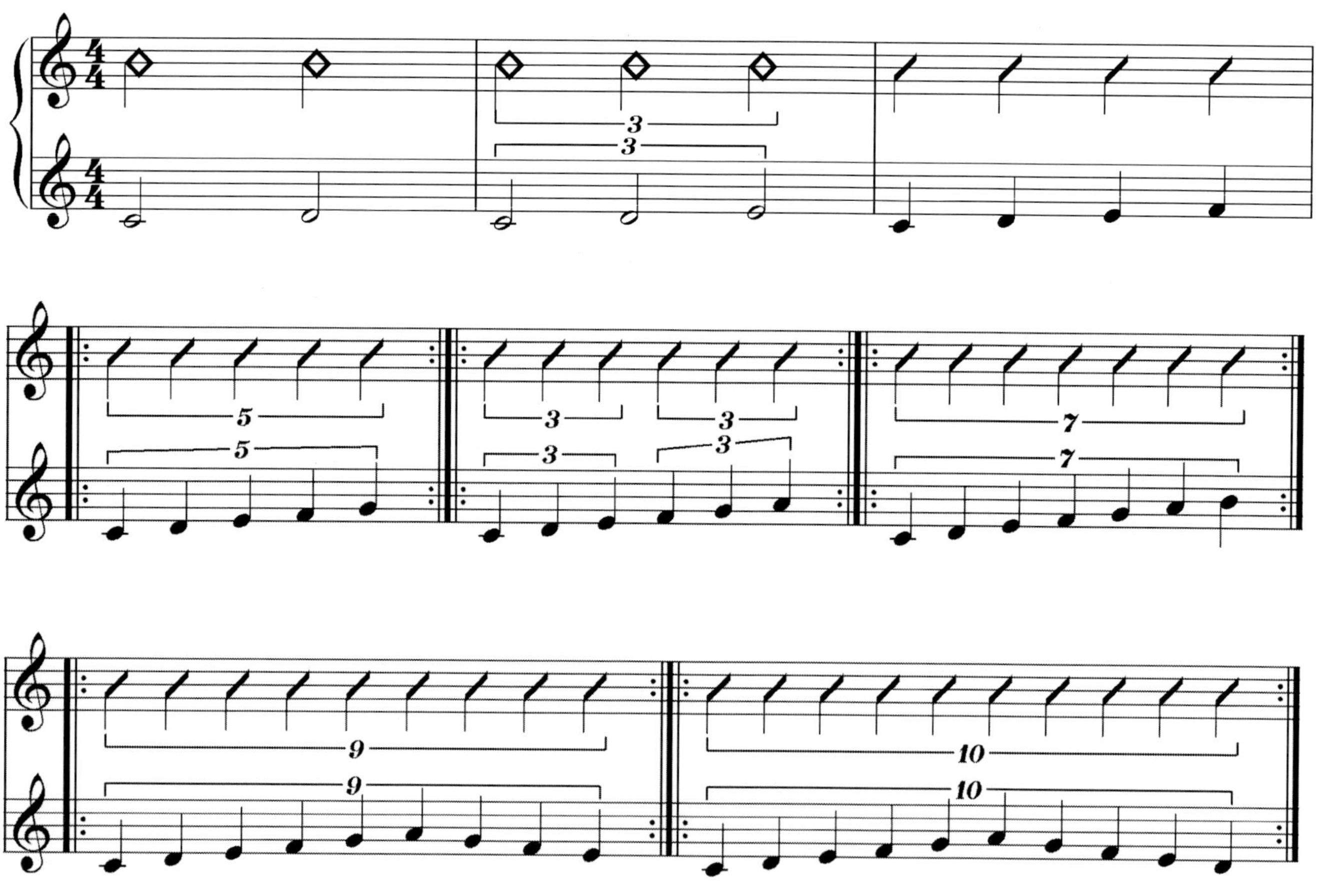

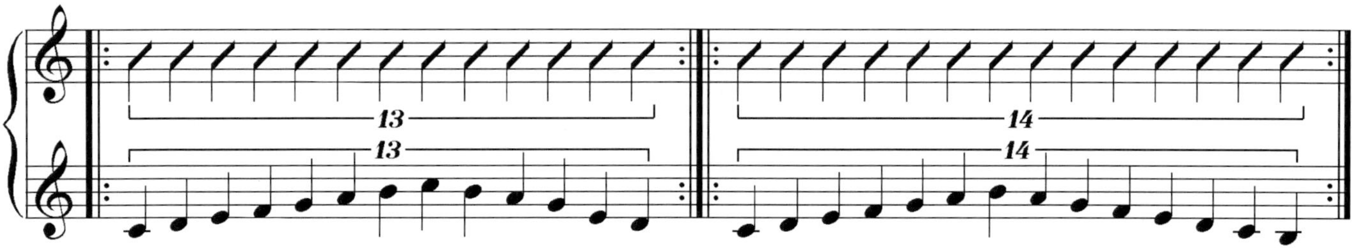

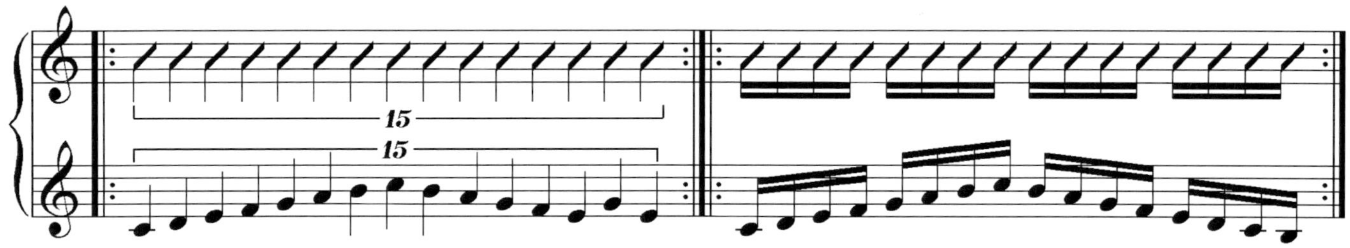

Polyrhythm Sequence 2: Four over Three

Like Triplet Exercise 2 on page 15, this exercise requires that the upper and lower rhythms trade places so that we can get to know it in more than one way. Once you have both parts in-hand, see if you can count them out loud while tapping or playing.

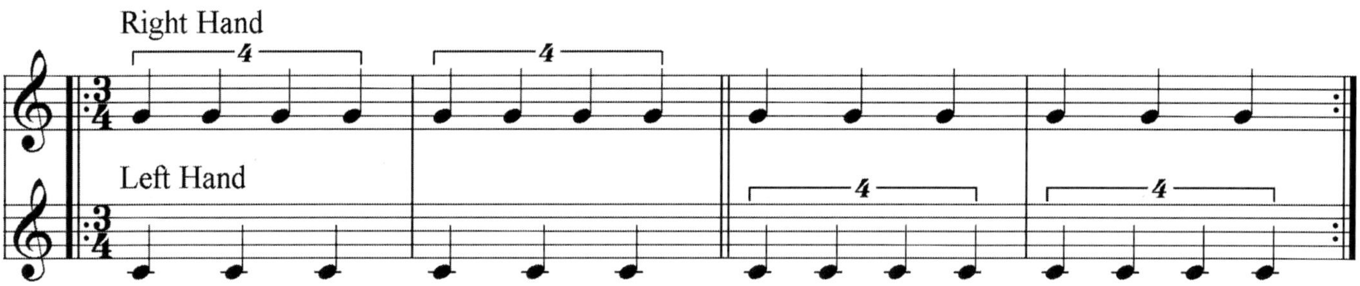

Groupings in Twos:

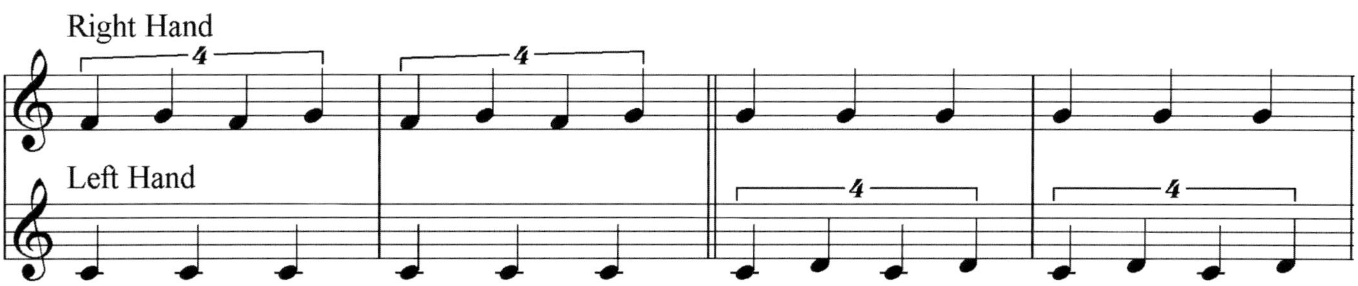

Groupings in Threes:

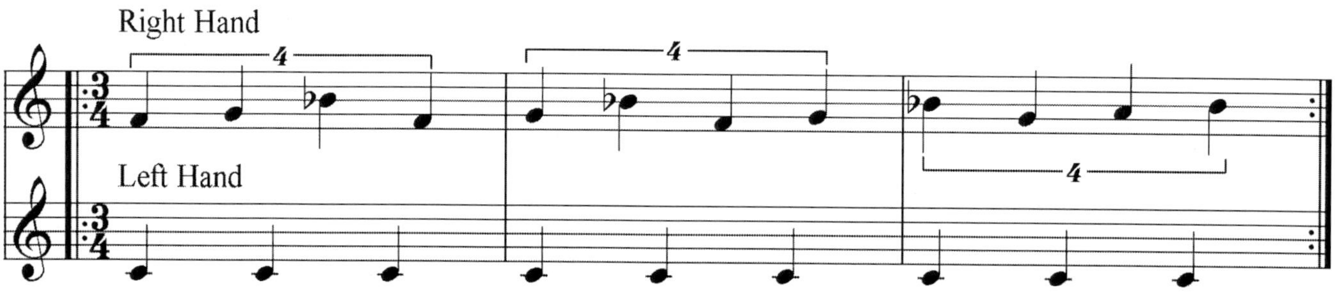

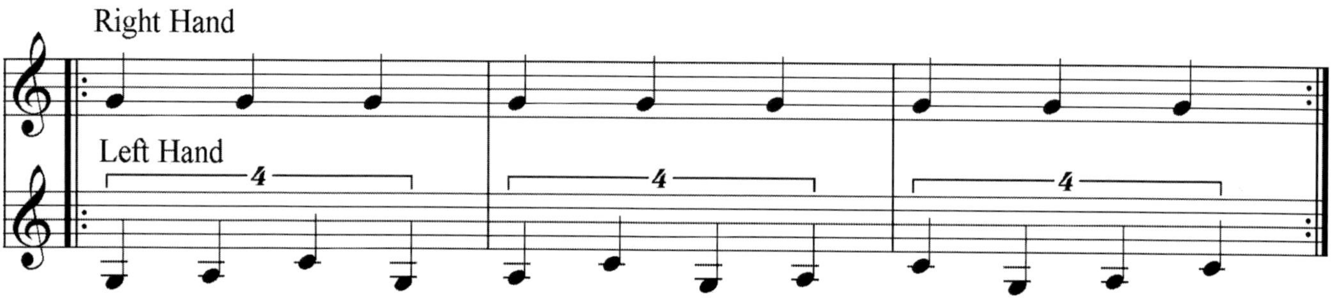

Polyrhythm Sequence 3: 3/4 and 5/4

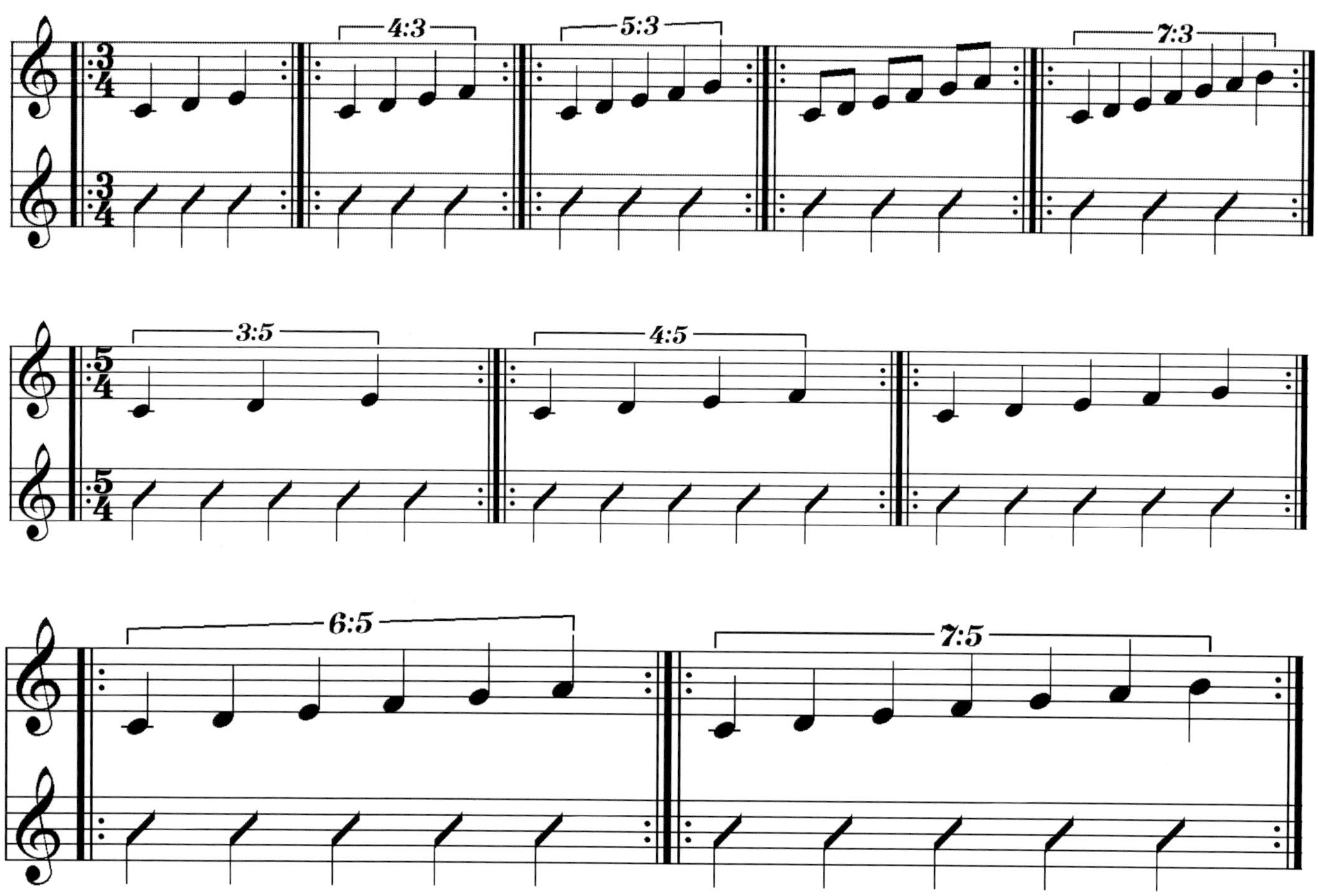

Polyrhythm Sequence 4

Here we transition between 6 over 4, and 4 over 3.

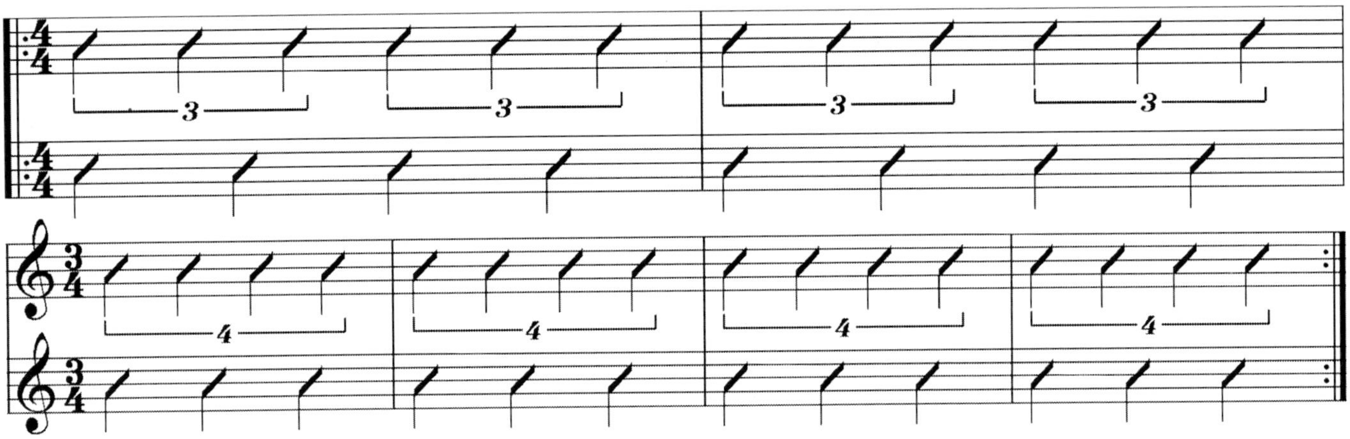

Keeping a Practice Journal

Keeping a long and short goal practice journal is a good method for structuring your practice time. Every time you sit down to practice you can check the list to know where you need to focus your efforts. You set your own pace and priorities.

Below is only an example of what might be included in a practice journal:

1. Time: With metronome set on beats 2 and 4, play sequence of quarters, 8ths and triplets. Then practice triplet groupings. (20-30 mins)
2. Scales: Warm up with intervallic exercises (3rds, 4ths, 5ths, 6th, 7ths through Lydian scales). (15 minutes)
3. Play arpeggios and 3rds and 7ths through All the Things You Are (15-20 mins)
4. Modes: Record vamp using Lydian dominant in several keys. Improvise using only 8th note with no rests, then solo melodically. (15 mins)
5. Songs: Practice and memorize melody and changes for “Confirmation”. (15-20 mins).
6. Compose and practice ii-V-I lines using both diminished and altered on the V. (20 mins)
7. Use metronome for soloing and comping on a slow swing standard (blues), a medium swing tune (Solar) and an up-tempo “Rhythm Changes” (like Oleo). Focus on time feel and flow. Record yourself and listen back to assess.
8. Sight-reading: Bach two-part invention, 5 pages in melodic rhythm book
9. Practice exercises in 7/4. Play over backing track.

You can change the amount of time you spend on any one thing as you wish. If you have one hour, try to cover at least 2 or 3 areas in your practice session. You can also get much more specific than the above list. Remember that it is good to be clear about your goals when you sit down to practice. Anything on your list that you don’t get to on a given day can be done in your next practice session. Update your list regularly.

Essential practice categories:

1. Rhythm - (Time/swing feel, consistency, tempos, metronome, polyrhythms, odd meters)
2. Harmony/Theory (Scales, chords, arpeggios, progressions)
3. Improvising (using the above information to actually "perform" in time in each practice session)
4. Memorization (standards, etc)
5. Sight-Reading
6. Ear training
7. Listening (recordings of the masters, all instruments, all time periods. Critical and analytical listening)
8. Transcription - Play it exactly like they play it. Then write it down.

List of Compositions

Compositions by Dave Allen from *Untold Stories* – Fresh Sound Records - 2006

Samba 7 (Example 48)
Momentum (Example 36)

Compositions by Dave Allen from *Real and Imagined* – Fresh Sound Records - 2008

Real and Imagined (Examples 106 and 109)
Slipping Glimpser (Example 105)

Compositions by Dave Allen from *The Sky Above Her* – Fresh Sound Records - 2019

Pulsion (Examples 27 and 28)

Unreleased Compositions

Quarantine #1 (Example 98)
Quarantine #2 (Example 102)
Thread (Examples 30 and 107)
654 (Example 108)

MOMENTUM

Vamp 1st bar bass line Intro/outro

Dave Allen

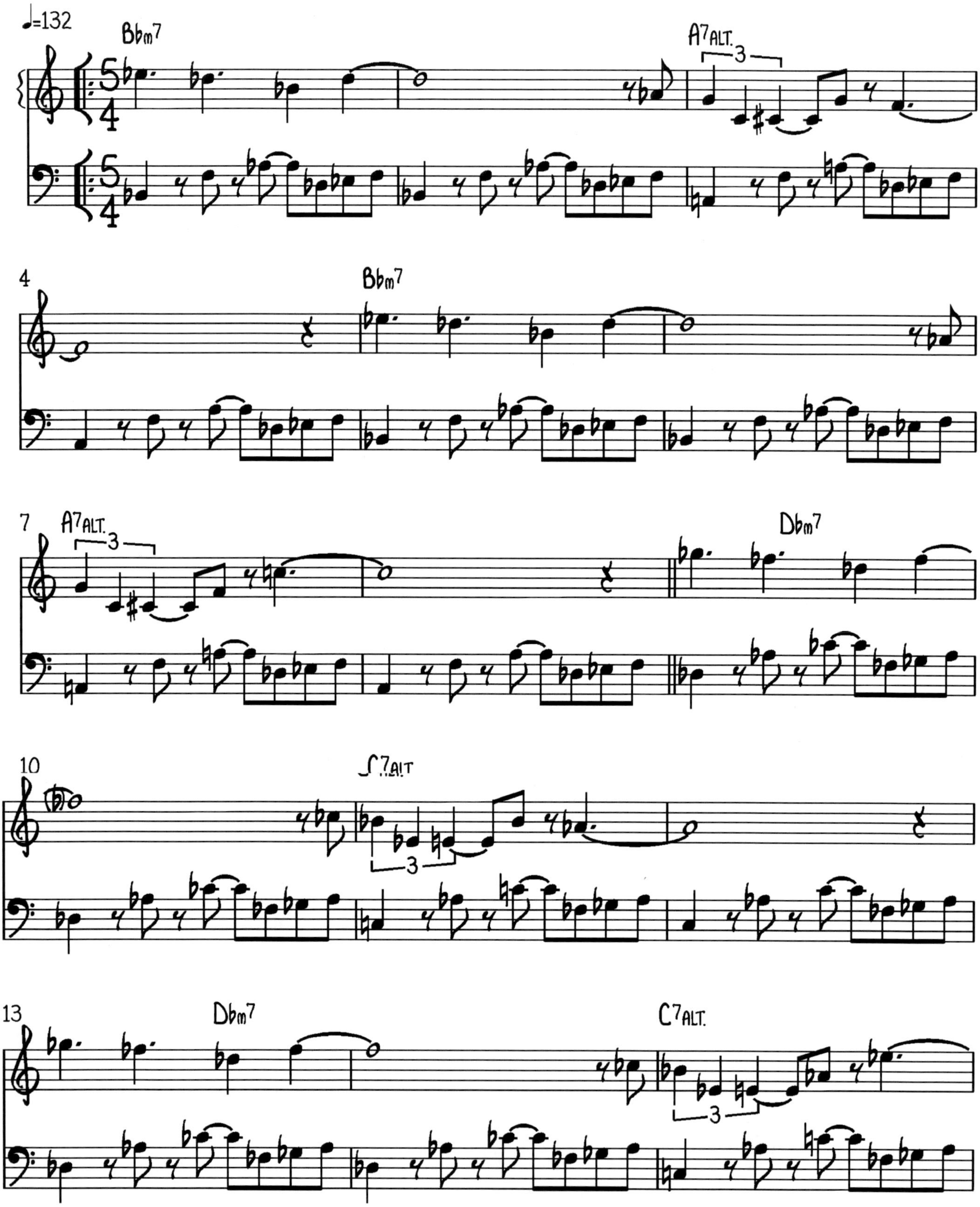

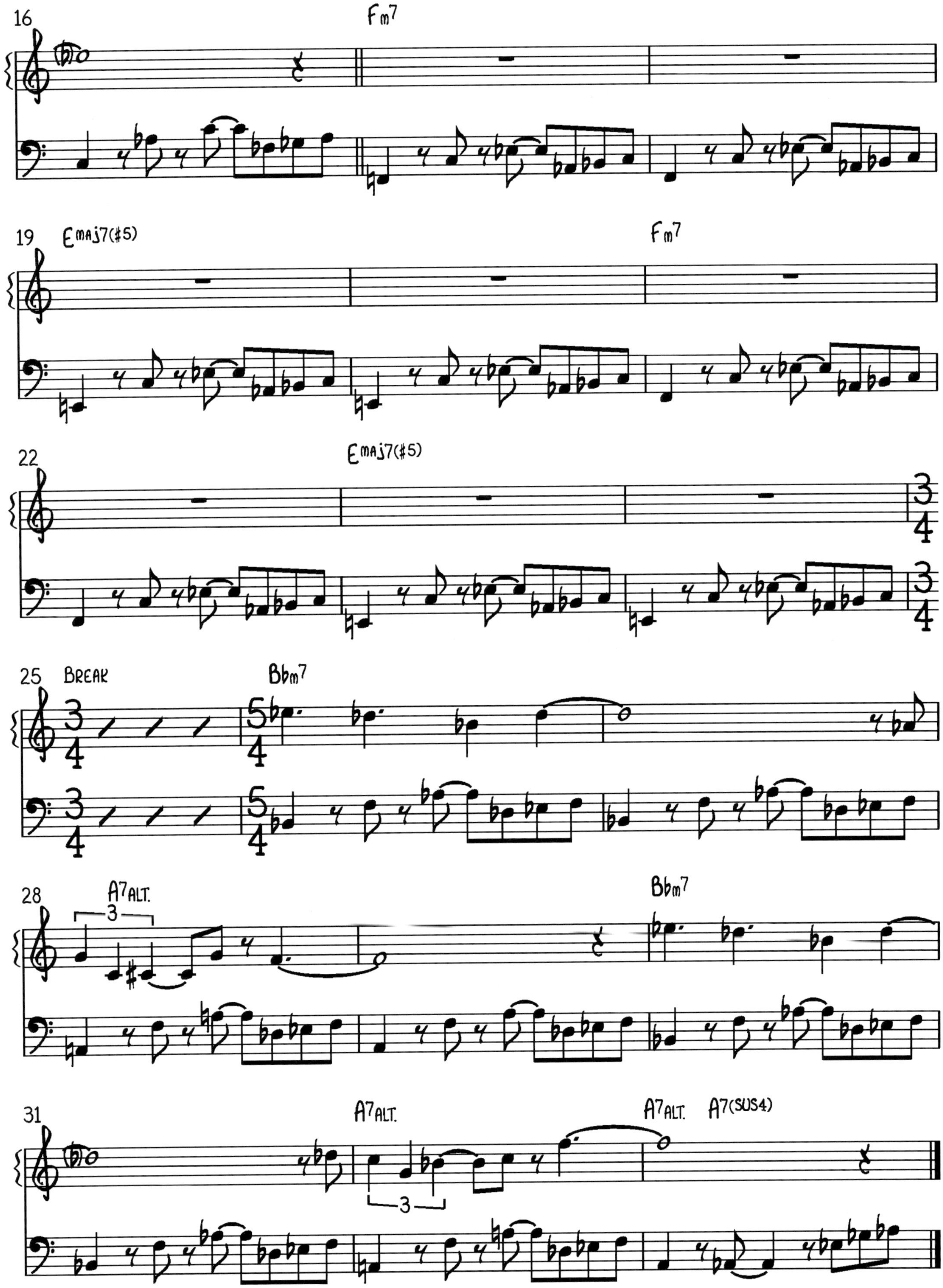
16
Fm7
19
Emaj7(#5)
Fm7
22
Emaj7(#5)
25
BREAK
Bbm7
28
A7ALT.
Bbm7
31
A7ALT.
A7ALT.
A7(SUS4)

SAMBA 7

DAVE ALLEN

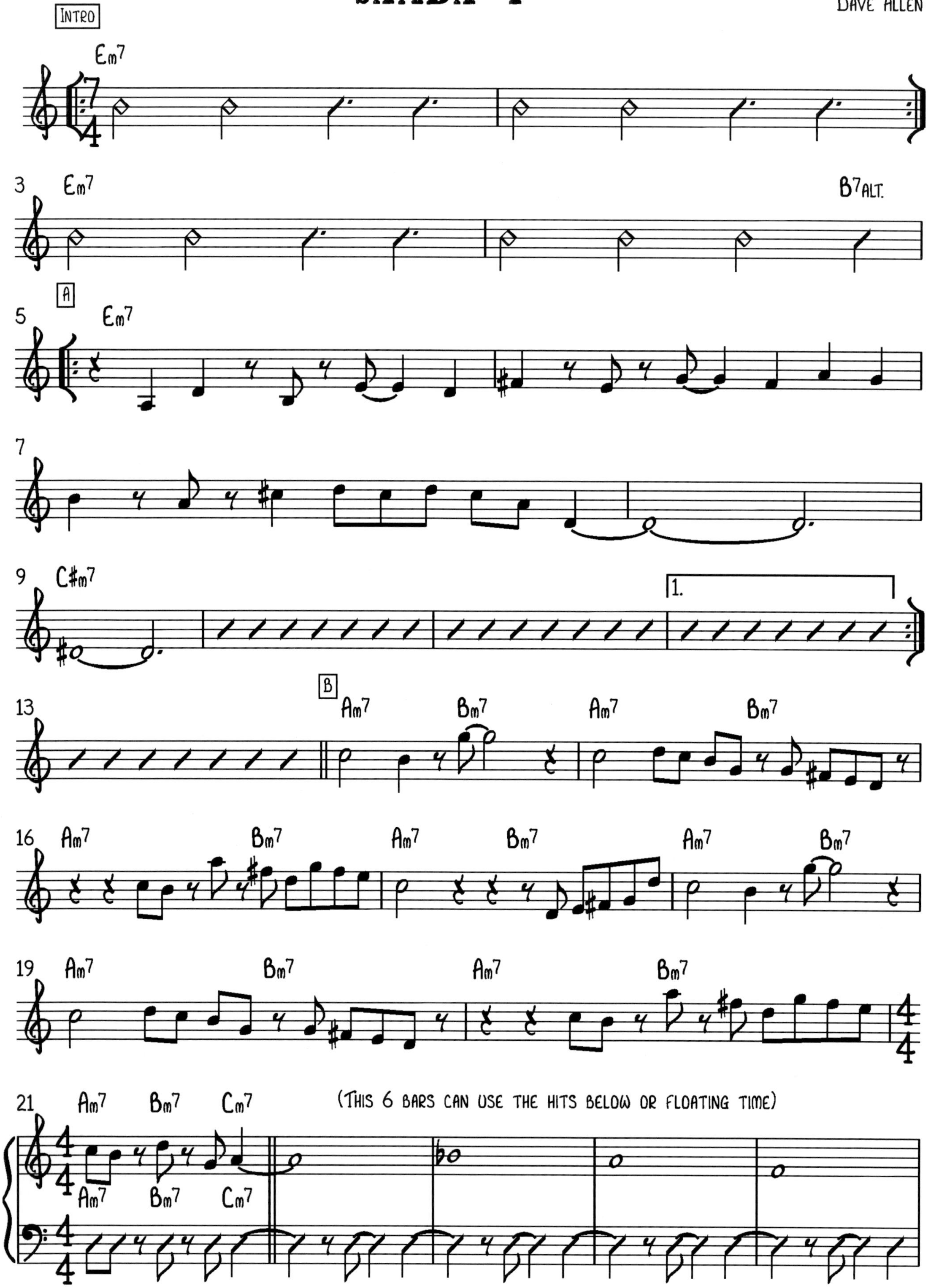

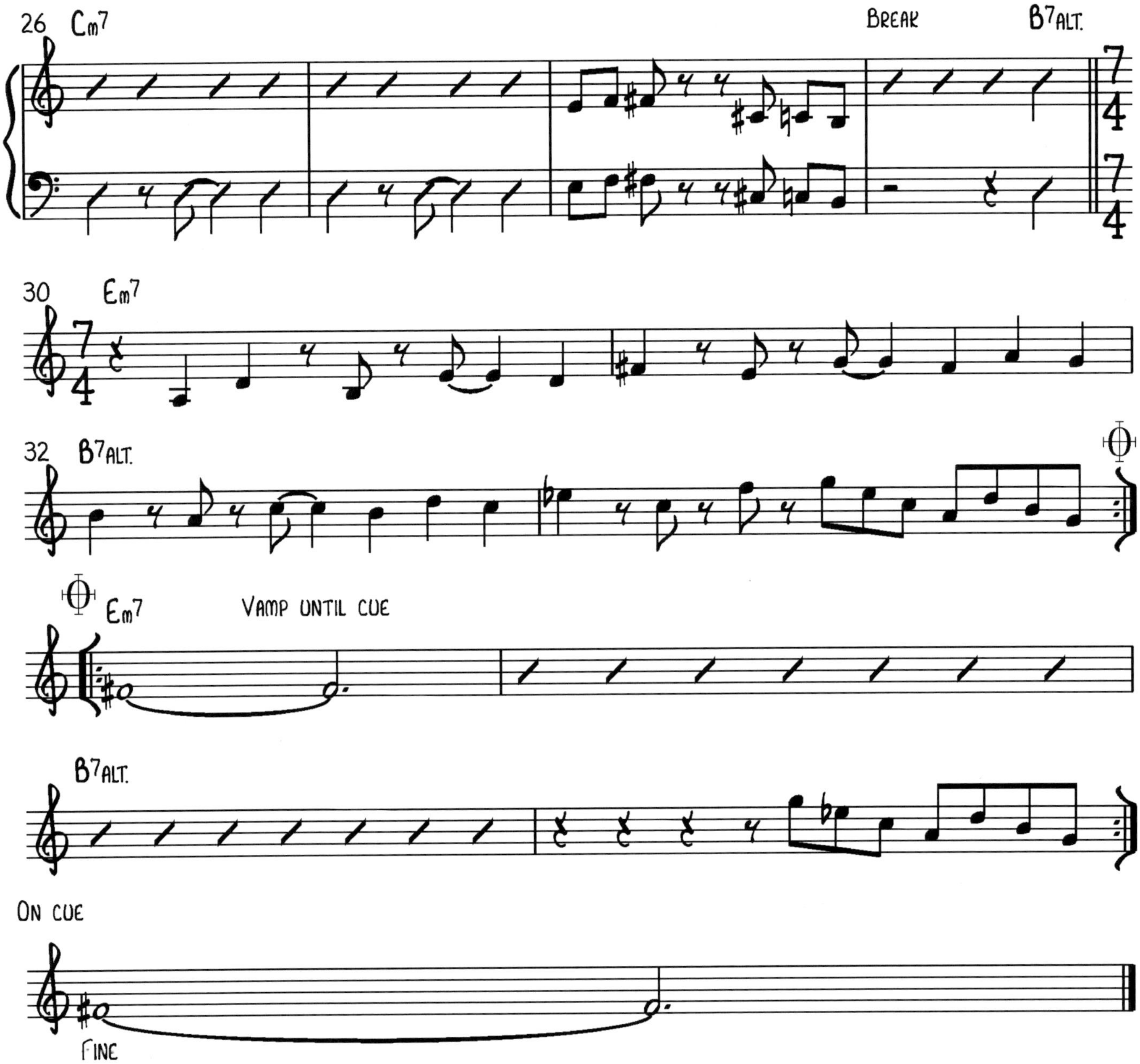
26
Cm7
BREAK
B7ALT.
30
Em7
32
B7ALT.
Em7
VAMP UNTIL CUE
B7ALT.
ON CUE
FINE

HEAD IN: PLAY A1 TO A4, REPEAT A1 AND A2
SOLOS: A1 OPEN, CUE TO B OPEN, CUE C AS INTERLUDE
HEAD OUT: A1 TO A4 ONLY

DAVE ALLEN

PULSION

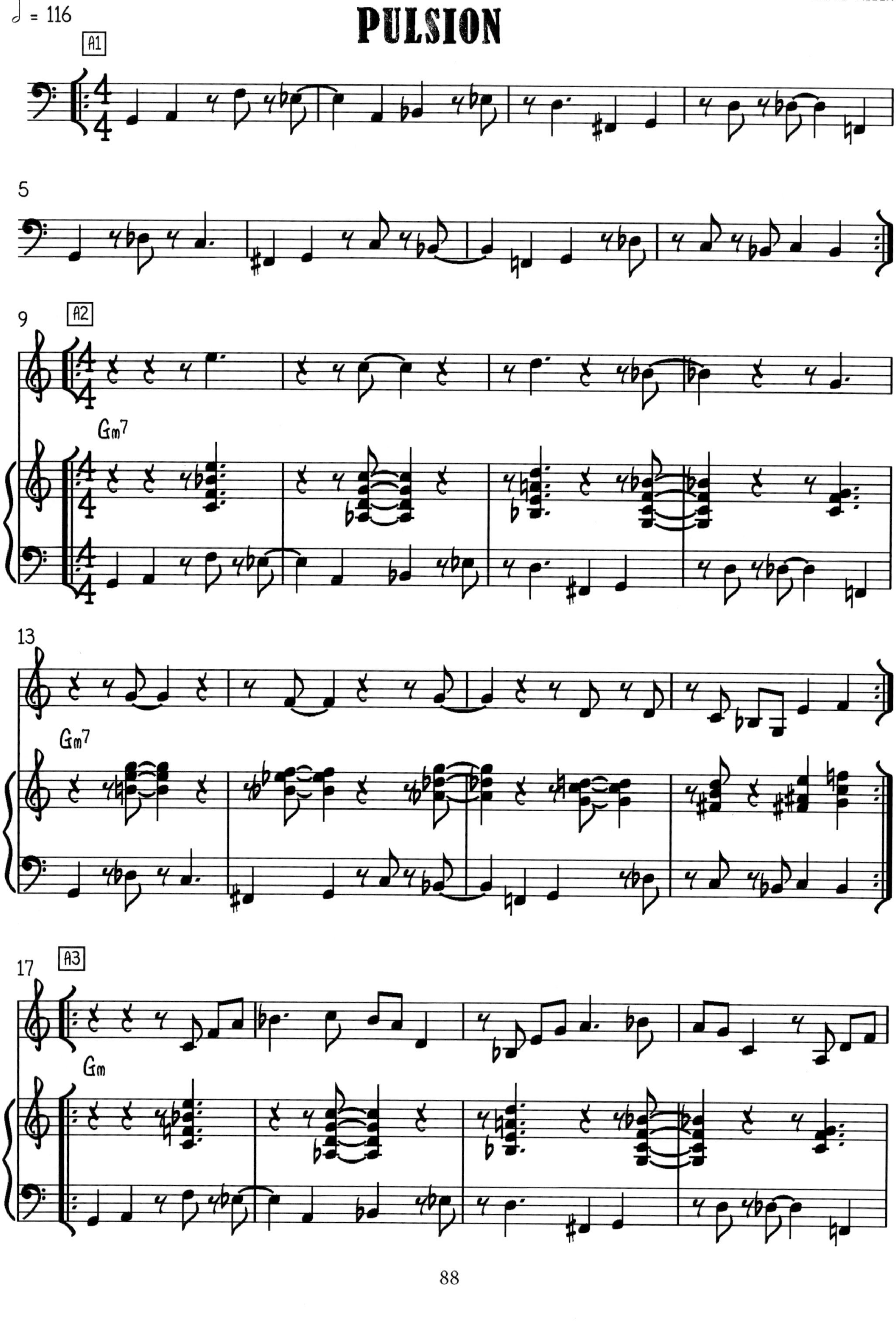

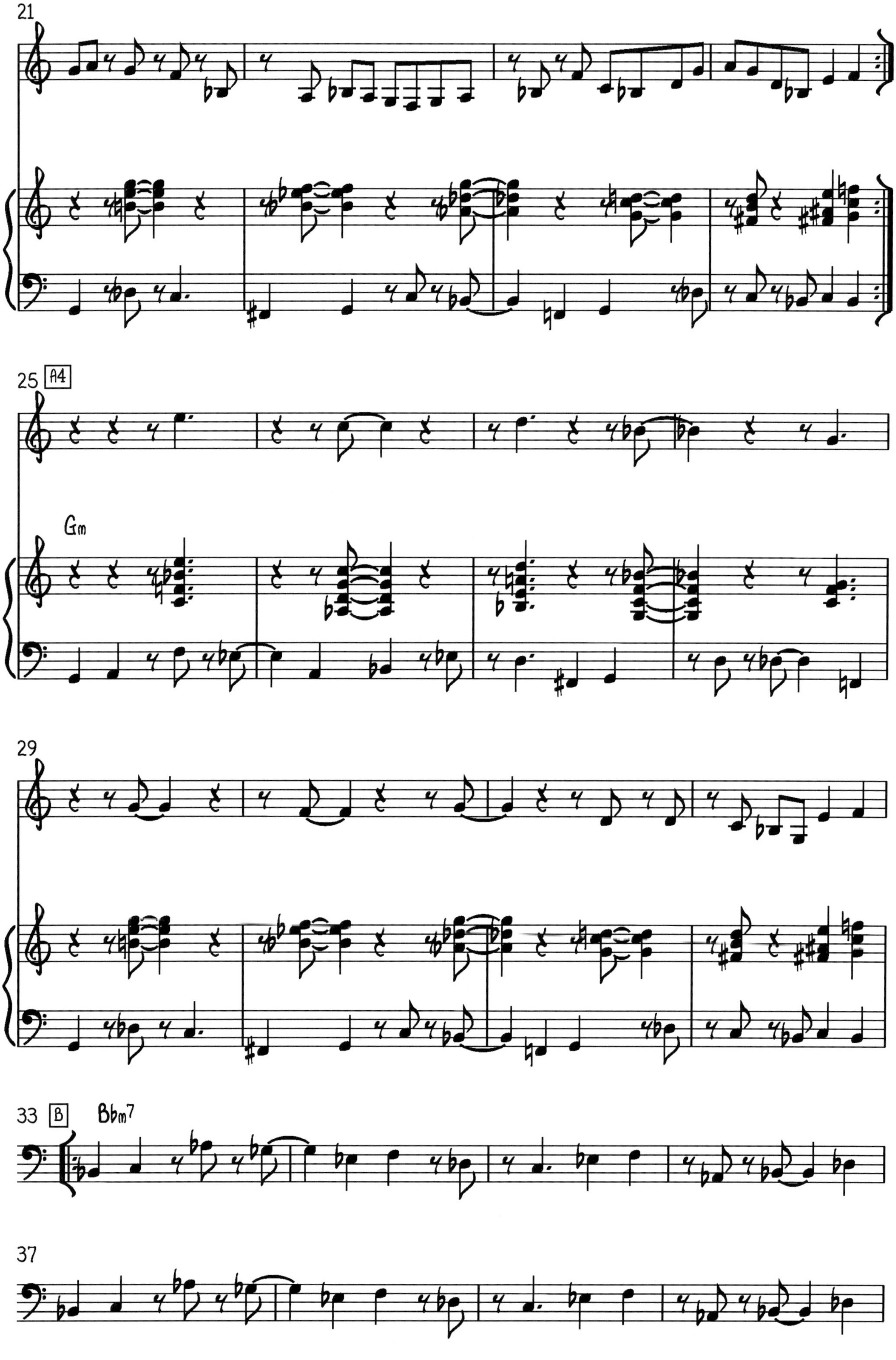
21
25
A4
Gm
29
33
B
Bbm7
37

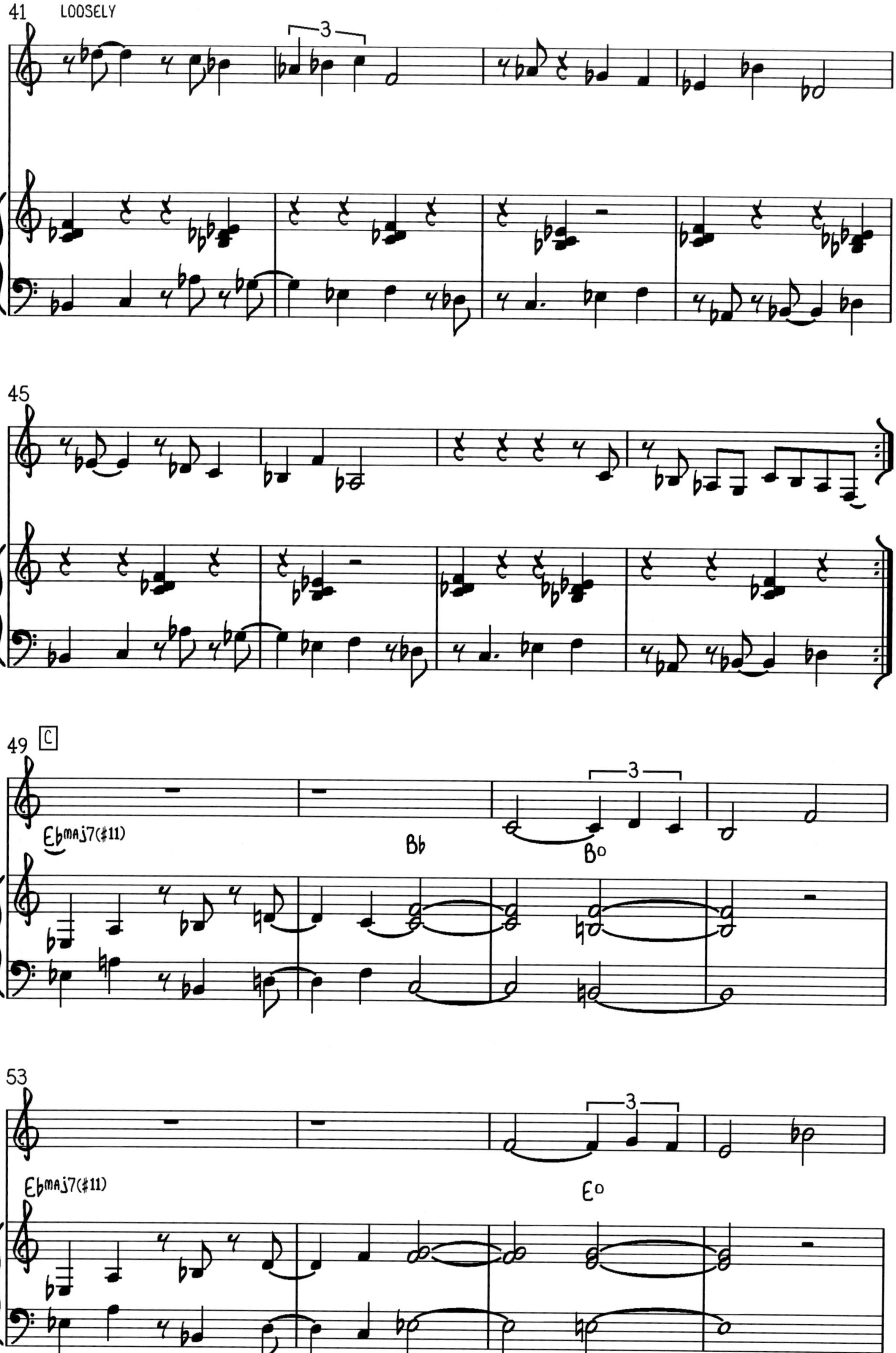
41
LOOSELY
3
45
49
C
3
E♭maj7(♯11)
B♭
B°
53
3
E♭maj7(♯11)
E°

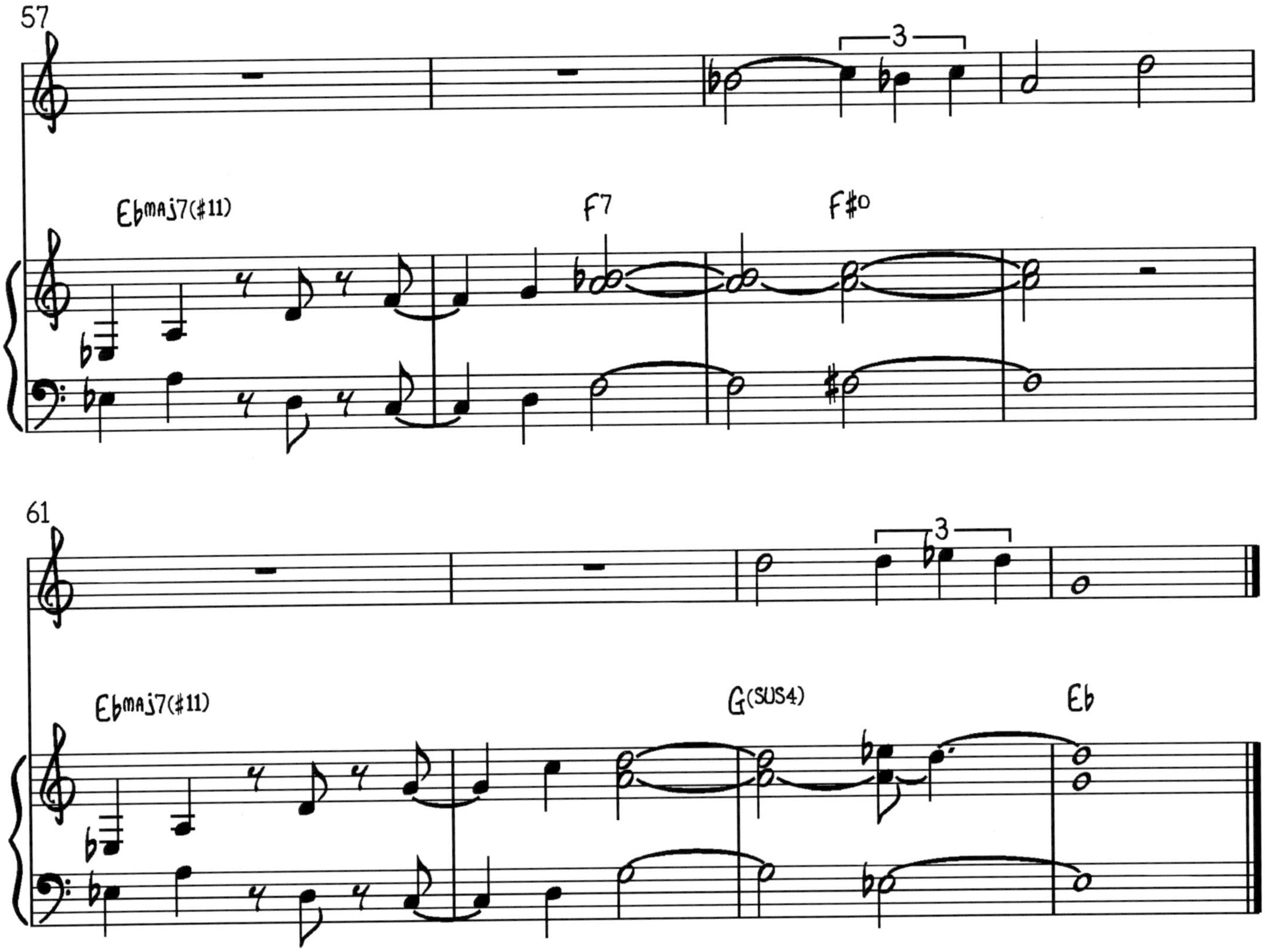

Instructions for "Slipping Glimpser"

Head In: A / A / B / Interlude / A

Melody for B2 is a 5-note loop and a 7-note loop played simultaneously. Both loops begin after an 8th-note rest not included in loop. Play this for 4 cycles (8 measures), then play B3.

Solos: B open, cue Interlude, solo on first two A sections. Last soloist cues Interlude and the head out is played from the top.

Head out: A / A / B / Interlude / Coda

The Coda also uses two looped melodies which can be played, improvised over, or faded to end. The entire band can improvise freely as there is no written part for the rhythm section except for beginning on F minor tonality.

SLIPPING GLIMPSER

♩=180 Intro

Dave Allen

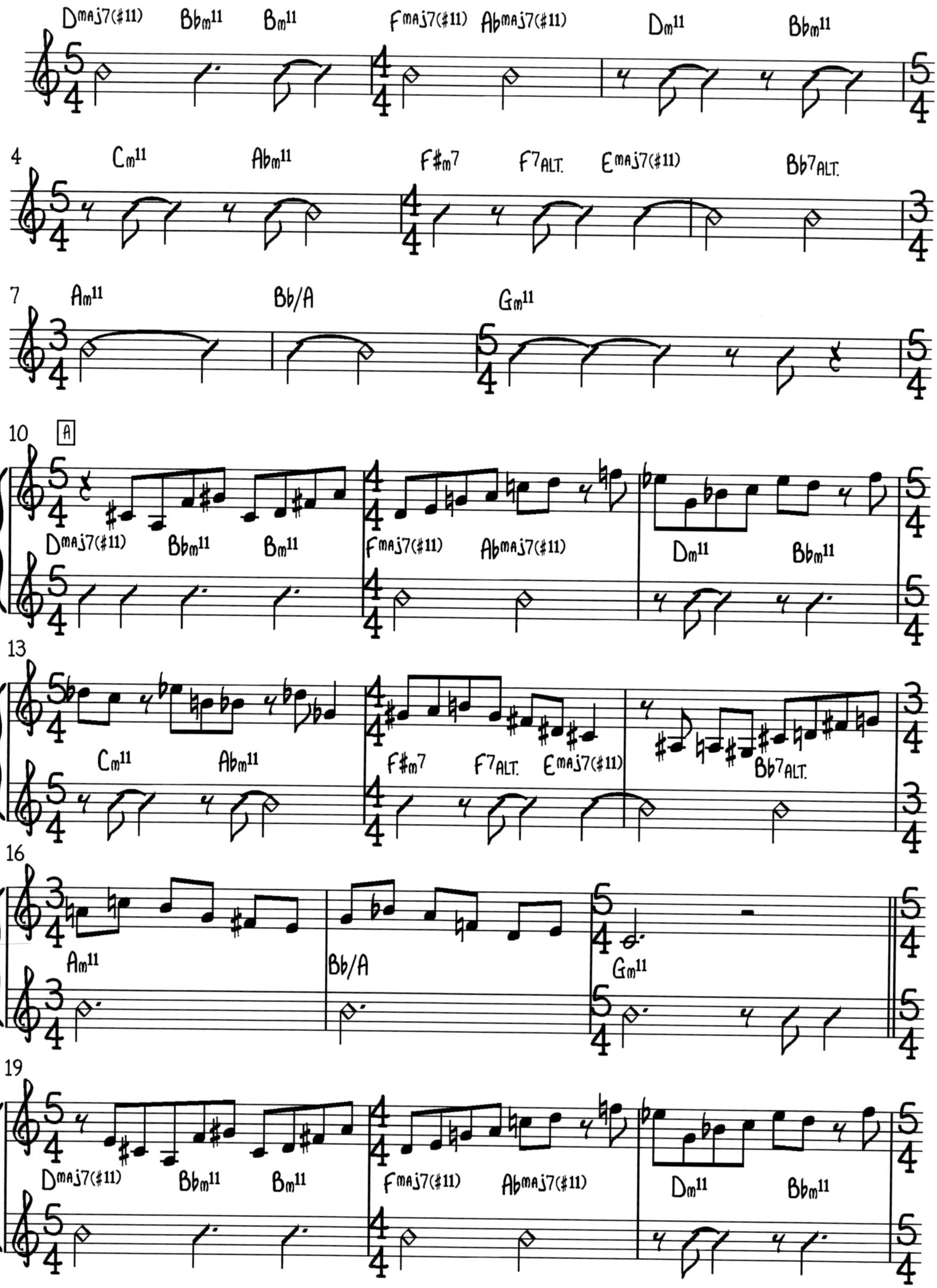

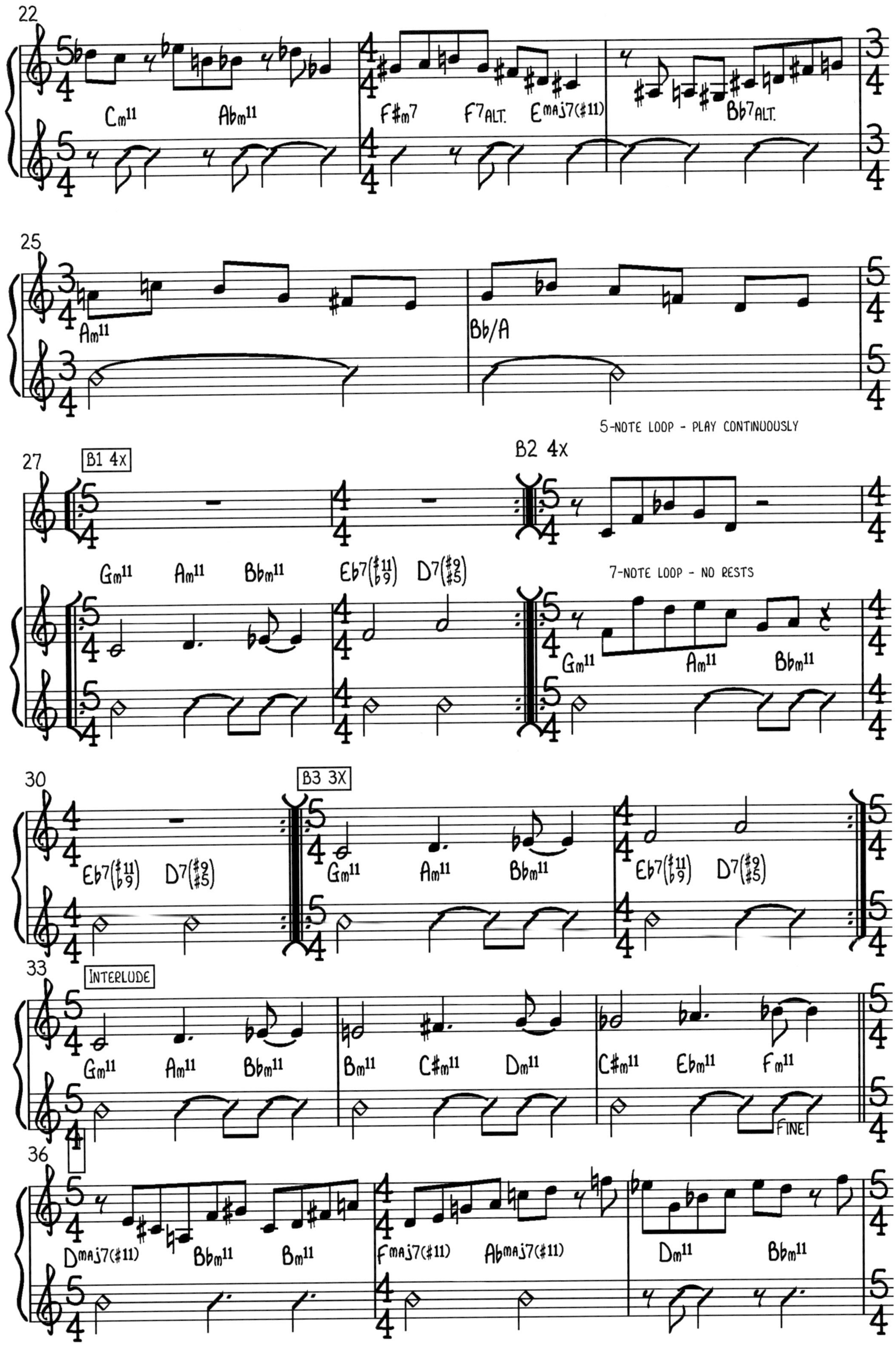
22
Cm11
Abm11
F#m7
F7ALT.
Emaj7(#11)
Bb7ALT.
25
Am11
Bb/A
5-NOTE LOOP - PLAY CONTINUOUSLY
27
B1 4X
B2 4X
Gm11
Am11
Bbm11
7-NOTE LOOP - NO RESTS
30
B3 3X
Gm11
Am11
Bbm11
33
INTERLUDE
Gm11
Am11
Bbm11
Bm11
C#m11
Dm11
C#m11
Ebm11
Fm11
FINE
36
Dmaj7(#11)
Bbm11
Bm11
Fmaj7(#11)
Abmaj7(#11)
Dm11
Bbm11

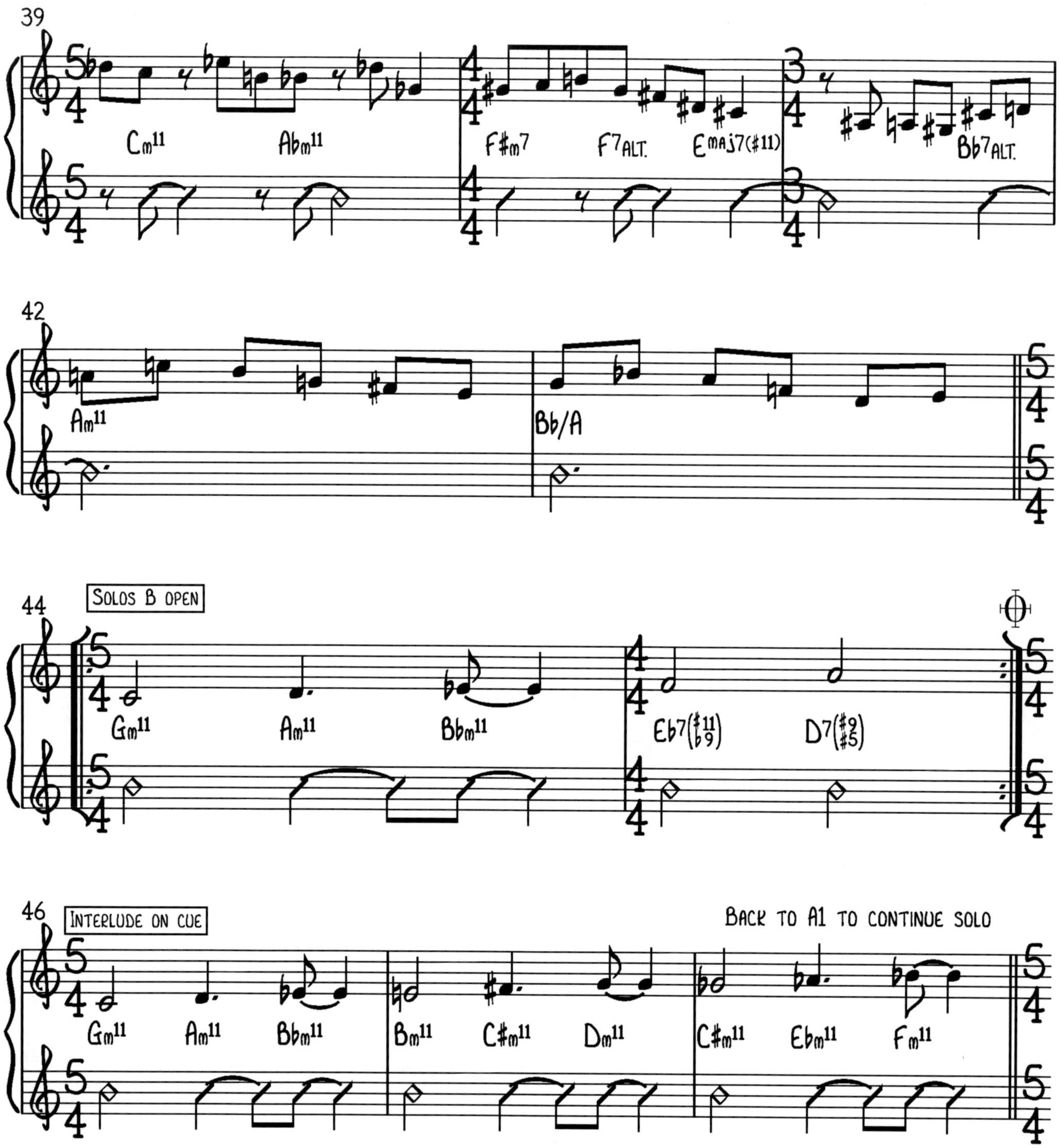
39
Cm11
Abm11
F#m7
F7ALT.
Emaj7(#11)
Bb7ALT.
42
Am11
Bb/A
44
SOLOS B OPEN
Gm11
Am11
Bbm11
Eb7(#11 b9)
D7(#9 #5)
46
INTERLUDE ON CUE
BACK TO A1 TO CONTINUE SOLO
Gm11
Am11
Bbm11
Bm11
C#m11
Dm11
C#m11
Ebm11
Fm11

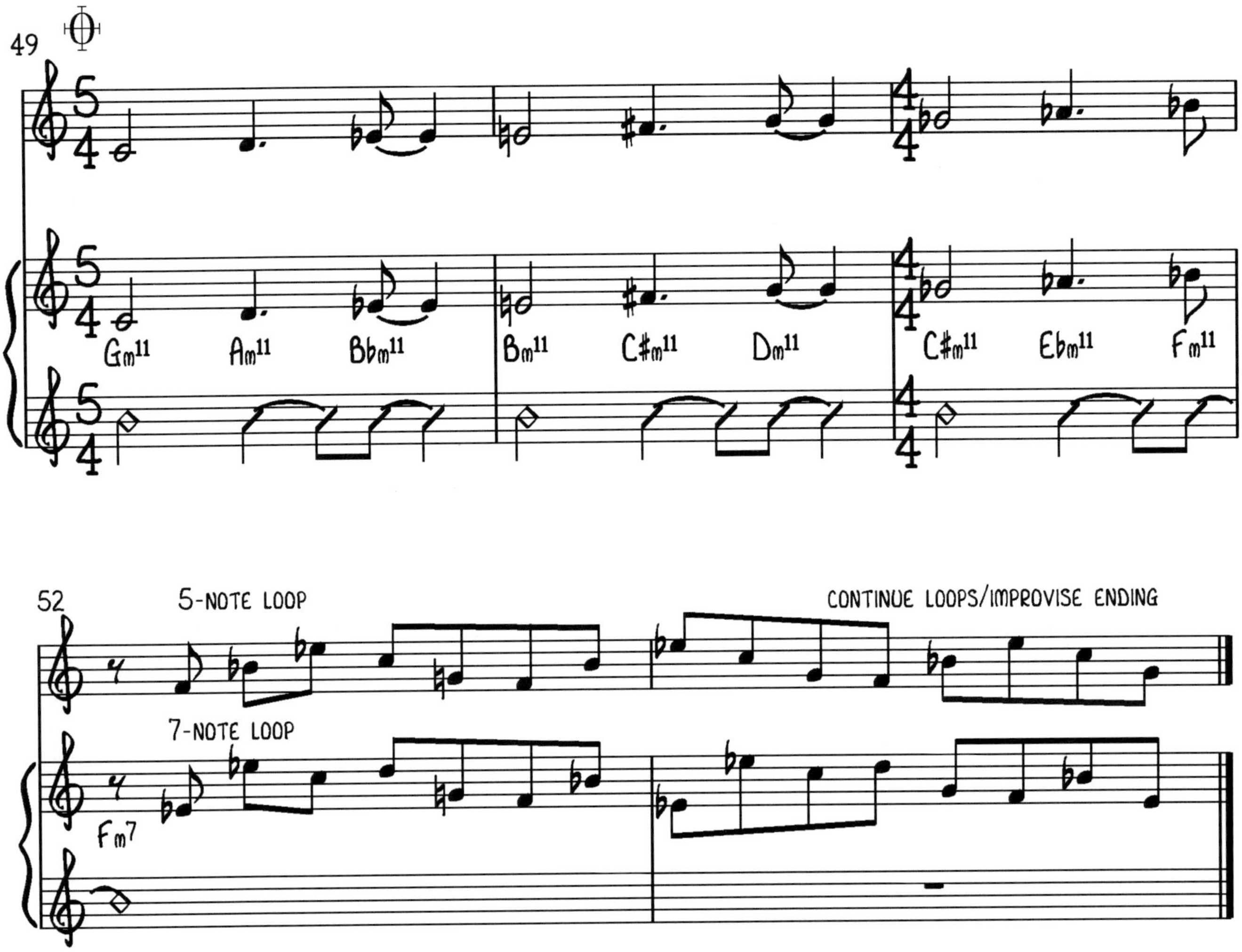
49
Gm11
Am11
Bbm11
Bm11
C#m11
Dm11
C#m11
Ebm11
Fm11
52
5-NOTE LOOP
CONTINUE LOOPS/IMPROVISE ENDING
7-NOTE LOOP
Fm7

DAVE ALLEN

GUITARIST / COMPOSER / EDUCATOR

Born in Philadelphia, Dave Allen began performing and composing at the age of 15. After discovering the music of John Coltrane, Pat Metheny, and Keith Jarrett, he moved to New York City to attend the Manhattan School of Music where he studied with Jack Wilkins and John Abercrombie. Over the next twenty-five years Allen performed with many of the most respected musicians in jazz today, including Jeff Ballard, Joey Baron, Dave Binney, Seamus Blake, Ravi Coltrane, Marcus Gilmore, Drew Gress, David Liebman, Donny McCaslin, Tyshawn Sorey, Mark Turner, Dan Weiss, Miguel Zenon, and many others.

Allen has toured with his own projects and as a sideman throughout the U.S., Europe, and Asia. He has released three critically acclaimed recordings, the most recent being *"The Sky Above Her",* and has been written about in the *New York Times, Downbeat Magazine* and *Jazz Times Magazine. All About Jazz* writes: "Allen has found a true voice, his effortless technique downplays the apparent complexity, paradoxically creating a cool surface sheen that has a white heat glowing beneath it...music that seduces both the body and mind, again and again."

As a composer, Allen is known for his challenging but lyrical music, which features multi-metered, rhythmic layering, as well as intricate chromatic-based harmonies. As an educator, Allen specializes in exploring modern rhythmic and harmonic vocabulary in both improvisation and composition. Allen has been a faculty member of the New York Jazz Academy and The Bahcesahir University graduate program. He has also taught at New York University, Temple University, and is currently a senior lecturer at The University of the Arts in Philadelphia.